You Could Look It Up

By the same author:

Big-Time Baseball

Where Have You Gone, Joe DiMaggio?

Bo: Pitching and Wooing

Voices of Sport

Now Wait a Minute, Casey

The Record Breakers

The Incredible Mets

Joe Namath's Sportin' Life

Reprieve from Hell

Ten Great Moments in Sports

Reggie Jackson: The Three Million Dollar Man

Ron Guidry: Louisiana Lightning

You Could Look It Up
The Life of Casey Stengel

Maury Allen

Times
BOOKS

Second printing, October 1979

Published by TIMES BOOKS, a division of Quadrangle/The New York Times Book Co., Inc. Three Park Avenue, New York, N.Y. 10016

Published simultaneously in Canada by Fitzhenry & Whiteside, Ltd., Toronto.

Copyright © 1979 by Maury Allen

Library of Congress Cataloging in Publication Data

Allen, Maury, 1932–
    You could look it up.

    Includes index.
    1. Stengel, Casey. 2. Baseball Managers--United States--Bibliography.
    3. New York (City). Baseball club (American League) I. Stengel, Casey.
    II. Title.
GV865.S8A63 1979   796.357'092'4 [B]   79-51424
ISBN 0-8129-0830-9

Manufactured in the United States of America

FOR SHEL
Brotherly love is the joy of a grand slam home run.

Acknowledgments

TO GIVE BIRTH to a work of this kind, the midwives must all make their contributions. Firstly, the progenitor, agent Julian Bach, who created this idea and helped it sail through some rough seas. Secondly, Senior Editor of Times Books, Roger Jellinek and his assistant, Bob Weil, who smoothly, calmly, and patiently brought it from fruition to completion.

Then there were the contributions of all my sportswriting colleagues on the *Post,* the *Times,* and the *News,* past and present; and the authors, Harry Paxton for his brilliant *Casey at the Bat: The Story of My Life in Baseball* (Random House, Inc.), Joseph Durso for his fairly amazin' *Casey: The Life and Legend of Charles Dillon Stengel* (Prentice-Hall, Inc.); and E.P. Dutton and Doubleday and Co., Inc., for the right to quote from past works of my own, *Now Wait a Minute, Casey* and *Where Have You Gone, Joe DiMaggio?* There were also the newspaper librarians at the *Kansas City Star,* the *Toledo Blade,* and the *Los Angeles Times.*

How can one adequately thank the kind and aged old-timers, such as Rube Marquard, Burleigh Grimes, Runt Marr, George Kelly, Babe Herman, and so many of the younger fellows, Al Lopez, Johnny Cooney, Tommy Holmes, Max West, and the kids, Rod Kanehl, Ed Kranepool, Ron Swoboda, Richie Ashburn, Whitey Ford, and too many others to list, for their patience in recalling their days with Casey?

The doors to some of these long-lost names were opened for me by Casey's "foreign secretary," June Bowlin, a Hall of Famer to be sure, and Edna Stengel's brother, John Lawson. Much thanks to them.

And lastly, no book of mine can ever be written without the

understanding, love, and compassion of my own team, my splendid wife, Janet, and Jennifer and Teddy, super fans and super kids.

Maury Allen
Dobbs Ferry, New York

Contents

You Could Look It Up

He who is of a calm and happy nature will hardly feel the pressure of age, but to him who is of an opposite disposition youth and age are equally a burden.

PLATO

1. My God,
We've Hired a Clown

EVERY DAY AMERICAN C-54 cargo planes were haul-
ing four thousand tons of coal and food through the air
corridors to Berlin. President Harry S. Truman was "giving 'em hell" from the back of his campaign train. On the
Upper West Side of Manhattan at Morningside Heights,
General Dwight D. Eisenhower was being installed as
president of Columbia University. A newspaper poll listed
the five most virile Americans as Earl Warren, Clark
Gable, Victor Mature, singer Jack Smith, and Lou Boudreau.

The poll was released October 11, 1948. Boudreau, the
player-manager of the Cleveland Indians, was the handsome, dark-eyed, wavy-haired thirty-one-year-old who
was that afternoon scheduled to bat fourth and play shortstop for the Indians in the sixth game of the World Series
at Braves Field, against Boston. The Indians were ahead,
3–2.

A week earlier on October 4, Boudreau had smacked
two home runs and knocked in five runs as the Cleveland
Indians defeated the Boston Red Sox 8–3 in the American
League's first pennant play-off after a furious race. The
Indians and Red Sox had battled for the last three weeks
of the season with the New York Yankees for the flag. The
Yankees, despite the heroic efforts of Joe DiMaggio, who
played brilliantly with an aching heel, were finally elimi-
nated two days before the season ended.

DiMaggio, in Boston for the World Series, slipped out
of his hotel room early on the morning of October 11 and
drove to Wellesley, Massachusetts. There he stood up as

best man in the wedding of his younger brother, Dom, the center fielder for the Red Sox, to Miss Emily Alberta Frederick, at the St. Paul's Roman Catholic Church. DiMaggio returned to Boston after the wedding. He watched as pitchers Bob Lemon and Gene Bearden combined to beat the Boston Braves in the final game for the championship. He returned to his Boston hotel for dinner, and a call from one of the Yankee co-owners, Dan Topping.

"We've picked our manager," Topping said. "We'd like you to be there at the announcement tomorrow at noon at '21'."

"Certainly."

Most New York sportswriters took the late train from Boston to New York. Yankee publicity man Red Patterson began calling reporters in the early evening, alerting them to a "major announcement" the next afternoon at "21".

The next day, Columbus Day, 75,000 marchers and 167 bands were passing before the Fifth Avenue reviewing stand and in front of more than a million people. It was a sunny, crisp early fall afternoon. The blare of distant bugles from the bands seeped through the entrance of New York's posh "21" Club at 21 West Fifty-second Street. A cab pulled up. "Good day, Mr. DiMaggio," the doorman said, as he opened the door and the glass reflected the small, highly polished, ornamental figures of black jockeys. The Yankee party, including George Weiss, Topping, Del Webb, and Oakland owner Brick Laws arrived soon after with the guest of honor, the new manager of the Yankees.

Upstairs, a battery of microphones had been placed upon a lectern. The New York press, including some of the giants of American sports journalism, was there in force: Grantland Rice of the *Sun,* Dan Parker of the *Mirror,* Tom Meany, a well-known sports author, John Drebinger of the *Times,* Red Smith of the *Tribune,* Jimmy Powers of the *News,* Jimmy Cannon of the *Post,* and Frankie Graham of the *Journal.*

Topping bent slightly into the microphones and began, "I am happy to make the announcement," he said, looking like a man with a severe case of indigestion, "that Casey Stengel has been appointed manager of the New York Yankees."

Holding a press release in his hand but never reading from it, Topping extolled Stengel's talents, citing his long playing career, especially in New York with the Brooklyn Dodgers and the New York Giants and his many years as a baseball manager. He emphasized his 1948 minor-league championship at Oakland. He then discussed his personality. "We all know Casey is a very likable fellow," said Topping.

Stengel was motioned to the microphones. The reporters began to applaud. It was obvious there was already great warmth between these hard-boiled writers and the new manager.

"Some of us had known him for more than a quarter of a century," says Drebinger, the *Times* baseball writer for more than forty years. "If you didn't like Casey Stengel you didn't like anybody."

By 1948 the New York Yankees had won fifteen pennants. From the time they had obtained Babe Ruth from Boston in 1920, they had been the most glamorous team in sports. Ruth, already a favorite character for the Yankee fans, became a national hero after his record of sixty homers in 1927. When he signed a contract calling for $80,000, an outrageous sum in 1928, he was told the President of the United States didn't even make that kind of money. "Sure I make more," the Babe said, "I had a better year than he did."

In 1925, a huge, soft-spoken New Yorker by the name of Lou Gehrig joined the team and played 2,130 consecutive games before being forced to retire as a result of a rare disease known as amiotrophic lateral sclerosis, a debilitating muscle ailment that had begun sapping his strength in 1938 and took his life in 1941. When Gehrig fielded a routine ground ball and flipped to pitcher Johnny Murphy for the out one early spring day in 1939, his teammates patted his back and applauded him vigorously for the play. "I knew then I was hurting the club," Gehrig said. He asked manager Joe McCarthy to replace him.

Ruth and Gehrig had been the most devastating tandem of hitters the game had ever seen. And when Ruth left the Yankees in 1935, Joe DiMaggio, the marvelous rookie from San Francisco, arrived the following year. The Yankees won four more straight pennants. They finished third in 1940 and then won three more in 1941, 1942, and 1943. They returned to their former glory after the war with a pennant and a dramatic World Series triumph over Brooklyn in 1947.

At a victory party celebrating the triumph, general manager Larry MacPhail, part owner with Dan Topping and Del Webb, got roaring drunk. He battled his two partners and soon after the partnership was dissolved. MacPhail was out. MacPhail's appointee as manager, Bucky Harris, did not survive the next season. The Yankees had finished an exciting third, had drawn 2,373,901 fans for their all-time high, but they were not in the World Series. Harris was fired.

"Harris had been a popular manager," says Smith, now the Pulitzer Prize-winning sports columnist of the *Times*. "I think the writers were angry at the way he was dumped. The Yankees had had a pretty good season. A lot of the sportswriters would probably have chopped them up in print if it was anybody but Casey."

Casey Stengel had been a popular figure on the New York sports scene for more than thirty-five years. He had been a better-than-average player with the Brooklyn Dodgers, a successful part-time player with the Giants, an entertaining talker, a comic, a clown, a guy who thought winning was important but having fun while winning even more important.

"It was the clown image that dominated his personality and was on everyone's mind at the selection press conference," says Smith. "I remember George Weiss telling me how strongly Del Webb was against the move because of that clown image. The Yankees were serious business."

Weiss apparently won Webb over late Sunday afternoon when they discussed the selection. Weiss had listed Stengel's virtues in his soft-spoken but firm manner. He talked about how Stengel was a successful teacher of baseball, how he worked well with young players—and the Yankees were an aging club in 1948—how he would mollify the press, and how he would please the fans.

"He's a clown," Webb shouted. "I don't want a clown managing the New York Yankees."

"I've been in this game a long time," Weiss said. "I never knew a man who could talk baseball all night the way Casey can. He is a dedicated baseball man. You can ask him anything about any move he makes in a game and he'll always have an answer. Casey never makes a move without knowing why he does it. He isn't a clown. He's a great baseball man."

Webb was moved. He told Weiss he would accept his man, Stengel, if Dan Topping, his partner, agreed. Topping, who had turned over the running of the club completely to Weiss, would not get in the way of this major decision. So the decision was agreed upon and Stengel was the choice.

Casey Stengel slipped close to the microphones. He wore a gray plaid suit with huge lapels, a heavily starched white shirt, and deeply shined black shoes. He had luminous blue eyes and his expression changed often, an amazing countenance control Joe Garagiola would years later describe as "Casey Stengel's change of face." He appeared smaller than his advertised height of five feet ten inches ("Do old ballplayers shrink?" one sportswriter asked a friend) and his thinning gray hair seemed tinted with a strange mixture of orange juice. He opened his mouth and his voice sounded as if he had just swallowed a ten-pound bag of crushed gravel.

"I want first of all to thank Mr. Bob Topping for this opportunity," he began, his tone heavy and his face unsmiling. The press began to titter at the gaffe, recognizing that accuracy in names was not Stengel's long suit as he publicly rewarded Topping's playboy brother Bob instead of Dan for the job.

Stengel seemed not to notice the cause of the ripples of laughter. After a pregnant pause for the rewinding of some camera equipment and tape recorders, he plunged straight ahead like the proverbial bull in the china shop.

"This is a big job fellows," Stengel said, "and I barely have had time to study it. In fact I scarcely know where I am at."

At fifty-eight years and seventy-four days of age, Stengel had spent his entire adult life in the business of baseball. Almost always a man of extreme confidence, arrogant, brash, pushy, ill-tempered at times, funny so often, irreverent, sarcastic, never still, Stengel, on that October afternoon, was humble, reserved, frightened.

"These were the serious Yankees he was being called on to manage," says Red Smith. "When guys fired questions at him about the team he said, 'I never had big players like this.' "

Yet the reaction of the press to the Yankee decision to hire Stengel was unanimous. They all praised it, the clown image notwithstanding.

In the *Times*, under a head proclaiming: STENGEL SIGNS AS YANKEE MANAGER WITH 2-YEAR CONTRACT FOR UNDISCLOSED SUM, John Drebinger wrote, "Meet the new manager of the Yankees, Charles Dillon (Casey) Stengel, one-time hard-hitting outfielder, manager of both major- and minor-league clubs, sage, wit, and gifted raconteur, as glib with the wisecrack as the late Jimmy Walker."

Sports editor Leonard Cohen of the *Post* wrote, "Stengel has settled down—or should have—to the business of acting his age. The Yankees insist they have not hired a clown and I'm inclined to believe them." Cohen, stressing the local angle, reported that Casey felt that he had never really left the big city. "Once you played in Brooklyn," Casey told Cohen, "you are always identified with the borough. People who don't know me would stop me on a street in California and say, 'Hey, aren't you from Brooklyn?' "

The Yankees had counted on this press reaction. Weiss, a clever man who detested the press ("You can buy any of them with a steak"), knew Casey would serve as a buffer between himself and the snoopy newspapermen. He also knew that Stengel was a first-rate manager, probably the hardest working manager around at the time, anxious to try new plays and new players, innovative, dedicated, and possessing a remarkable memory bank for information on players. No other manager ever recalled such trivia about so many players that would be useful in a pinch. "I had this player in Brooklyn," Casey once said, "and you could ask him for a match and find out what bar he was in the night before. After we traded him to another club I always went up to him before the game with a cigarette and asked for a match. If he pulled out a match from some bar, I knew he had been out late and I could pitch him fastballs."

It was this incredible store of information that sold Weiss on Stengel. He also liked the fact that Casey understood the business end of the game. Casey had run the Worcester club in the Eastern League in 1925 as president as well as being manager and right fielder. He had also owned a piece of the Boston Braves when he managed there.

"George and Casey got along real well," says Hazel Weiss, George's widow. "They had been in a lot of business deals together."

Fresh out of Yale in 1925, Weiss operated the New Haven club in the Eastern League. He was a dour, humorless man with a lust for a buck and a good deal. Weiss trusted Casey and they dined together frequently when their teams played against each other. The warmth between Stengel and Weiss astounded most observers who saw Stengel as a jovial fellow and Weiss as a recluse. Sportswriter Jimmy Cannon had publicly scorned Weiss by calling him Lonesome George, but perhaps the most fitting description came from Weiss' beloved Hazel. After he had been forcibly retired by the Yankees in 1960, he leaped back into baseball in 1961 as president of the Mets. Hazel Weiss was thrilled at the end of George's forced retirement.

"I married him for better or worse," she said, "but not for lunch."

"Every time I was underemployed," Stengel once said in explaining the relationship, "George would hire me." Weiss had hired Casey for the Yankee farm club at Kansas City in 1945 and now was hiring him again. He would hire him once more with the New York Mets.

Stengel would be forever grateful and never stopped thanking Weiss publicly. "We fought over some things," Casey once said, "but he never stopped paying me. If your checks don't bounce, why wouldn't you like the man?"

Weiss and Stengel met the afternoon after the "21" press conference in the team offices at 745 Fifth Avenue. They studied the personnel of the Yankees.

"We gotta go slow, George, I gotta wait until spring training to find out who I can fire," Stengel said.

The Yankees were a team in disarray after the 1948 season. They had lost the pennant by only a couple of games but were seriously aging. First-baseman George McQuinn retired. Outfielder Tommy Henrich would probably be brought in to play first base. "The only quality players still at their peak," wrote Milton Gross in the *Post*, "are Tommy Henrich and Phil Rizzuto." Rizzuto, the ebullient shortstop, was the key to the defense and an important lead-off batter. Aging players included second-baseman George Stirnweiss, third-baseman Billy Johnson, and catcher Gus Niarhos. There was hope for a young infielder named Jerry Coleman, a medical school student named Bobby Brown, and a tremendous minor-league hitter named Gene Woodling. Woodling and Hank Bauer, a man whose face was described as "looking like a clenched fist" would compete for one of the open outfield spots in 1949. An outfielder and catcher named Yogi Berra would work under coach Bill Dickey on his catching and thank Dickey by saying, "He learned me all his experiences." Vic Raschi, Allie Reynolds, Ed Lopat, and relief pitcher Joe Page would anchor Stengel's 1949 pitching staff.

The key man on the team, of course, was the great DiMaggio, the Yankee Clipper, Joltin' Joe, the embodiment of the Yankee tradition of style and success for a dozen years. On November 25, 1948, DiMaggio turned thirty-four, an advanced age for a ballplayer. He was coming off a marvelous season with a .320 average, 155 runs batted in, and 39 home runs. But he was suffering from a heel injury, a bad back, and sore knees. The wear and tear of a dozen years of exceptional play was taking its toll. No man played harder. "I once asked him," said his friend, Edward Bennett Williams, the famed attorney, "how can you play so hard all the time?" DiMaggio told Williams, "There is always some kid who may be seeing me for the first or last time. I owe him my best."

DiMaggio had come to the Yankees in 1936. He hit .323 as a rookie with 125 runs batted in and 29 homers. He had batted as high as .381 in 1939, and in 1941 he became the most famous athlete in America during the excitement of his fifty-six-game consecutive hitting streak, an achievement unlikely to be equaled. He had married an actress named Dorothy Arnold, had fathered a son named Joe Jr., served three years in the army during World War II, and emerged from service an even bigger national hero. His excellence on the field, his reserved personality, his dedication to the Yankees, his grace under pressure made him a formidable American figure.

He was also a man of tremendous pride and dignity and many people were afraid he and Stengel would not hit it off. There were suggestions he coveted the managerial job for himself. He denied it. "You know me, boys," he told reporters, "all I want to do is play ball."

DiMaggio carried the burden of leadership of the team with him at all times. His close friend, restaurateur Toots Shor once tried to console him after a tough Yankee loss. "It wasn't your fault, Joe, you had four hits." Said Di-Maggio, "We lost. Every time we lose it's my fault." Di-Maggio would eat dinner after nearly every Yankee win in Shor's. The boisterous Shor would show Joe off by screaming to a politician like Mayor William O'Dwyer of New York or an actor like Jackie Gleason or another athlete like football star Sid Luckman, "Hey, you crumb bum, come over here and say hello to the Clipper."

"When the Yankees lost," Shor once said, "he wouldn't come in. He would come to the door of the joint, send in the doorman, and call me out. Then we would walk up and down Fifth Avenue together not saying a word, just letting him cool off, until he could go home and sleep."

DiMaggio's importance on the team was such that most players treated him deferentially. The clubhouse man,

Pete Sheehy, who has been around the Yankees more than half a century, did not.

"I remember one time I made Joe really laugh," says Sheehy. "He had this big red welt on his backside. The players had gone on the field and DiMag stood near a long mirror and examined the mark. 'Hey, Pete, take a look at this.' I walked over and saw the red mark. 'Yeah, Joe, there's a mark there all right. It's from all those guys kissing your ass.'"

Stengel, who had never managed a great star at Brooklyn or Boston, had to deal first with DiMaggio and his influence on his teammates before he could address himself to the rest of the team. No manager can succeed if the star players on a team openly or subtly oppose him. From the moment he arrived as Yankee manager in 1931, Joe McCarthy never had a moment of peace with Babe Ruth. Not until Ruth was sent away in 1935 did the Yankee players shift their loyalties from the big player to the manager. Would DiMaggio and Stengel be Ruth and McCarthy all over again? DiMaggio said he had no managerial ambitions and was more worried about his impending heel operation than he was with feuding with the new manager.

"I'll tell you this," says Phil Rizzuto, "I think Stengel was as much in awe of Joe DiMaggio in 1948 as any player on the team."

Casey Stengel's reputation in New York had preceded him. He was immediately identifiable to fans, press, and the general public. Even people who knew nothing of baseball knew Casey Stengel's name. He was a character. For Yankee fans the question was, "Could he adjust to the image of the Yankees?" One man wrote a bitter, scathing letter to the Yankee front office. "How could you hire this guy?" asked Ronald James, a Manhattan engineer. "He just isn't a Yankee." Other fans, generally those who liked his wacky style, complimented the club on the move. One cab driver, upon seeing him after the "21" press conference said to him, "Hey, you're Casey Stengel, aintcha? I just heard aboutcha on the radio. Well, I wanna wish you luck even though I'm a Dodger fan."

"Yeah," said Stengel, "I used to be one myself."

The people in the front office, who never challenged Weiss publicly, were severely questioning his move privately.

"The general consensus," says Lee MacPhail, who was in the Yankee farm department and is now president of the American League, "was that Stengel simply didn't fit in with the Yankees, that image of dignity, class, refinement. Everybody knew Casey Stengel, he talked a lot, he was loud and he drank publicly. When we heard it, there were a lot of people around the Yankees who said in one way or another, 'My God, we've hired a clown.' "

The crowning of the clown was over and Stengel, wearing a brown felt hat with a feather and a light topcoat against the early fall chill, walked back to the Yankee offices. He paused in front of the Yankee logo at their offices and later that night told Edna in the hotel, "I'm scared. It's an awful big job." She held his hand, patted him softly on the brow, and said, "You are a big man. You can do it. I love you."

Stengel flew home to Glendale, California, a couple of days later with a briefcase filled with rosters of all the Yankee clubs, major and minors, scouting reports on all the players, and medical reports on those players who might be recovering from injuries at spring training.

Yankee players across the country read the news with disbelief.

"I think a lot of guys looked at him as an interim manager," says Ed Lopat, an important Yankee pitcher from 1948 through 1955. "We all knew about him. When you thought about Casey Stengel taking over, all you could do was smile."

"I knew him when I was a sixteen-year-old kid trying out for the Dodgers," says Phil Rizzuto. "I was at one of those things where all the scouts look at you. I came up to hit and the pitcher hit me in the back. Casey came running out of the dugout screaming, 'You're too small. Go home and get a shoebox.' I guess that's the first thing I thought about when we hired him."

George Weiss, leaving nothing to chance, had hired Jim

Turner, who had been a pitcher for Stengel in Boston, as the Yankee pitching coach.

"Weiss called me from New York late in 1948," says Turner. "He told me he was thinking of making some changes. He left it vague. He didn't say if he wanted me to coach or manage. He just told me to stay available and to keep it a secret."

"With guys like Turner and Bill Dickey and Frank Crosetti around," says Lopat, "Weiss was ready with a successor if Casey failed."

The sun had just broken through the darkness on the first morning of spring training at St. Petersburg, Florida, in 1949. There were no thoughts of failing. There were only thoughts of this new beginning for Stengel and the Yankees. Clubhouse man Pete Sheehy, who slept in a back storage room of the clubhouse, was just working his way out of bed when he heard a knocking on the front door. The players weren't due for another three hours. He moved cautiously to the door, pulling on his pants and tightening his belt as he walked. He opened it slowly to see the face of Casey Stengel staring back at him.

"I couldn't sleep," said Stengel.

Sheehy showed Stengel the manager's office. Casey hung up his suit jacket, pulled off his trousers, and sat in his underwear. The clubhouse man brought a cup of coffee and Casey lit up a cigarette. Sheehy started back out of the room, turned, and asked, "Is there anything else I can get you, skipper?" Stengel got up, walked to where his new Yankee uniform, number 37, hung on a hanger, rubbed his fingers down the famous pinstripes, and said, "Nope, I got everything now."

Stengel sat at his office desk. Stripped now to his undershirt and shorts, he studied the Yankee roster, smoked a pack of Camel's in the next ninety minutes, met with his trainer, Gus Mauch, greeted the coaches on their arrival at 9:30, put on his uniform, and walked out into the main area of the clubhouse.

"You fellows know the league better than me," he began. "Just play ball and we'll be all right. I don't want

to make too many rules because you don't like 'em and I
don't, either. We'll have workouts scheduled in the morning and afternoon, twice a day so we can commence getting ready for the season, which is a busy one. Talk to the
coaches if you have any questions since they are all very
bright men and will help you with your work if you let
them."

"It was a pretty straightforward talk," remembers Rizzuto. "He didn't put on any act. No Stengelese that day."

"Casey always had this gift for digression," says Red
Smith. "I have this theory. I think he polished the gift with
the Yankees because he always had crowds of writers
around him."

The Yankees took the field the first spring training day
and Stengel admitted great concern about DiMaggio. The
Big Guy was still not recovered from winter surgery on his
right heel.

"That might be a break for you," Grantland Rice told
Stengel. "You're a lucky guy. If you had DiMaggio, everybody would expect you to win."

The Yankees began getting into shape for the season.
DiMaggio, who always set his own pace, worked out
alone. He had talked to Stengel early about his aching
heel and Stengel had said, "Just tell me when you're
ready." In spite of the earlier surgery, the heel had become more and more painful. The Yankees broke camp,
started a barnstorming tour with the Dodgers through
Texas, and were shocked to wake up one morning to find
DiMaggio gone. With the swelling, discoloration, and pain
increasing in the heel as the result of a spur, DiMaggio had
visited a Dallas surgeon. He recommended an additional
operation and suggested DiMaggio return to Johns Hop-
kins Hospital in Baltimore where he had undergone earlier surgery on the same heel.

"It was a shock to wake up and find DiMag gone," says
Jerry Coleman. "It took the heart out of the ball club and
made everybody grouchy. We played the Dodgers that
day and Jackie Robinson stole four bases against us. It was
the first time I had seen Stengel really furious. He walked
through the clubhouse after the game and you could hear

a pin drop. No matter that it was an exhibition. We didn't like to lose and we certainly didn't like to lose to Brooklyn. As we began undressing he suddenly said, 'Look in your lockers. See if he got your jockstraps, too.' Then he walked out."

Stengel put Cliff Mapes in center field Opening Day in Washington. He moved Henrich permanently to first base and put Berra behind the plate. Then he sat back and waited for the Yankees to play like Yankees.

The Yankees stayed near the top in the early days of the race. Most of the stories about the Yankees concerned the return of DiMaggio. No date had been set after the heel surgery and some of the players thought he might never play again.

"Casey seemed to be feeling his way along," says Tommy Henrich. "He'd check with Doc [trainer Gus Mauch], find out who could play, make out the lineup card, and sit back and watch. He was lively on the bench, cheering and yelling, but he wouldn't get on the players very much. He knew we were all putting out, doing our best. One day we lost a game to Washington. We were on the train later to Cleveland. We had a couple of beers and were playing Twenty Questions. Casey walked by and listened for a second and then said, 'I got a question. Which of you guys ain't gonna be here next year?' You see, Casey Stengel was all baseball."

In early June the Yankees had pulled ahead of the Red Sox by seven games. Left-hander Eddie Lopat was pitching against Philadelphia and was leading 14–1.

"The guys were all giggling on the bench. Casey suddenly started screaming about a cutoff play we had blown a week before, really yelling loud, carrying on in the midst of this win. I turned to the Chief [pitcher Allie Reynolds] and said, 'Hey, you think the old man has lost his mind?' Finally the game was over and we won big. I walked up to Casey and asked him why he was so angry on a day we won so easily. He winked at me and said, 'I learned that from McGraw. If you bawl them out while they're losing, they may punch you in the nose. Do it while they're winning and they'll listen.' "

The Yankees were moving closer to a vital series against the Red Sox on June 28. Stengel sat down at breakfast one morning with Jim Turner and said, "I wish we had the Big Guy up there."

DiMaggio had been working out lightly for a couple of weeks. On June 27, one day before the Boston series, the Yankees were scheduled to play an exhibition for sandlot baseball at the Polo Grounds against the Giants. DiMaggio came to Stengel before the game.

"I'd like to try it," he said.

"Great," said Stengel. "I'll let you play a couple of innings then pull you out."

For several weeks DiMaggio had awakened each morning, stepped gingerly off the bed onto the floor, and felt stabbing pain in his heel. On this morning the pain had subsided. He would try it on the ball field. He dressed quickly, put in a special cushion for the heel area, and took some fly balls. His name was in the starting lineup, batting in his accustomed fourth spot. The sportswriters spotted DiMaggio's name on the card. They asked Stengel how long he would play.

"I don't know if he will play two innings or ten," he said. "All I know is he is splendid in his line of work and we need him in there."

DiMaggio played the entire game. He failed to hit in four at bats but swung easily. He caught three fly balls and ran without pain. The Yankees left on a late train for Boston. DiMaggio stayed back. The next morning he awoke without pain, walked around his Manhattan apartment, and called his friend, ticket broker George Solitaire. "Drive me to the airport," he said. "I'm going to Boston."

After missing the first sixty-five games of the season, he started the first game of the Boston series, had a single and a home run, hit two home runs in the second game and another in the third game as the Red Sox were shocked that a man could perform such feats after being out of action all season.

Stengel was overwhelmed by DiMaggio's incredible performance. Their relationship would cool in time, but after that series, Stengel said, "He's the best I've ever had."

Years later he was asked to evaluate DiMaggio as a player. "Now wait a minute for crissakes, you're going into too big a man. Maybe he woulda been an astronaut if he wanted. He could hit some balls off the moon and see if they'd carry. There were a lot of great ones and Ruth could pitch, too, but this fella is the best I had.

"About DiMaggio," he continued with all systems go, "you don't have to falsify anything. He started in with a bang and never stopped. Of course when he played for me he was handicapped, but you wouldna knowed it if you didn't see him limping in the cabs and in the clubhouse.

"The best thing he had—and I'll give you a tip—was his head," said Casey, without coming up for air. "He saw some of the faults of the pitcher and he would hit the ball, and he didn't hit it just on Sunday, neither."

There were rumors of friction between DiMaggio and Stengel, especially in 1950 and 1951 because Casey benched DiMag once, dropped him from the fourth spot, and played him one game at first base.

"What do you mean, did I get along with him? I played him, didn't I? They said I didn't like him, but every time I saw him, my wife, Edna, would say hello to him and poke me and I would say hello. You don't have to say hello a lot if a man can play flawless like DiMaggio."

After the three-game sweep in Fenway in late June, the Yankees thought they had seen the last of the Red Sox in the 1949 pennant race. It had barely started. On the Fourth of July, the traditional marking point for a baseball pennant race, the Red Sox were twelve games out of first place. They were in fifth place in the eight-team American League. Cleveland, in second, trailed the Yankees by five and a half games.

Suddenly the Red Sox got hot. Ted Williams was hitting home runs at a pace that would give him his most productive year ever, 43 homers and 159 RBIs. Johnny Pesky, Vern Stephens, Bobby Doerr, and Dom DiMaggio, the other big hitters on Tom Yawkey's highly paid team known as the Millionaires, were ablaze with the fervor of the best pennant race in forty-one years. The Red Sox were 24–8 in August and closed to within two games.

In the National League, the Brooklyn Dodgers and the St. Louis Cardinals were neck and neck in the same kind of race. The country was going wild with the excitement of these two marvelous pennant chases.

The Yankee player injuries, which were to total seventy-one at season's end, were forcing Stengel into juggling players daily.

"I would go to him each day and say, 'Your left fielder can't play today,' " says trainer Mauch. "He would just say, 'Thank you, doctor,' and show no emotion."

Now it was September and the Red Sox kept coming on. On September 18 the lead was still only two games. Then the Yankees suffered a blow. DiMaggio was hospitalized with a virus. "We'll have to do it without the Big Guy," Stengel told the players.

On September 26 the Red Sox beat the Yankees 7–6 at Fenway Park. On a disputed squeeze play, DiMaggio's sub, Cliff Mapes, attacked umpire Bill Grieve and was thrown out of the game. Bullpen catcher Ralph Houk and Stengel, raging at the umpire's feet with caps flying, language salty, and faces afire, were also excused. They were fined one hundred dollars each. The Red Sox had gained first place by a game.

On September 30, the Red Sox beat Washington and the Yankees lost to Dick Fowler of the Philadelphia A's. Boston led by one game with two games in the season to go: two against the Yankees, two in Yankee Stadium, two games that only meant the pennant.

"We're not so bad off," said coach Bill Dickey, trying to console the Bronx Bombers after the Philadelphia defeat. "Yesterday we had to win three. Now we only have to win two games to win it."

Saturday, October 1, 1949, was a gray, gloomy day in New York. The clouds billowed over the stadium. Stengel arrived early by cab, as was his custom. This time he found more than a dozen players lounging near their lockers. They couldn't sleep.

"It was quiet," says Ed Lopat. "We knew what we had to do. We didn't have a meeting. Casey just went about his business, same as normal."

Some few days earlier DiMaggio, whose ailment had now been diagnosed as pneumonia, was released from the hospital. He was terribly weak. A day had been scheduled for him that Saturday and in his condition he asked the Yankees to change it. It was too late for that. He came to home plate on Joe DiMaggio Day and received two cars, a motorboat, three hundred quarts of ice cream, a huge Wisconsin cheese, and assorted gifts. He moved to the microphones.

"I want to thank my fans, my friends, my manager, Casey Stengel, my teammates, the gamest, fightingest bunch of guys that ever lived." His voice was rising now and he said, "And I want to thank the Good Lord for making me a Yankee."

There were 69,551 fans in the stadium and their applause was deafening. DiMaggio stared at the ground. When it was over he walked off the field with his mother, his eyes filled with tears, walked to the bench, and told Stengel, "I'd like to try it."

The Red Sox got four quick runs off Allie Reynolds. A victory would give them the pennant. Catcher Birdie Tebbetts of Boston yelled over to the Yankee dugout, "You guys can ask me for a loan from my World Series share."

The Yankees, with DiMaggio leading off with a double to right, got two runs in the fourth. They got two more in the fifth, and, with left-hander Joe Page throwing smoke, the game stay tied until the eighth inning. Then Johnny Lindell hit his sixth homer of the year and his first in sixty-two days, and the Yankees won 5–4.

The pennant race was tied. One game to go. Winner take all.

On Sunday, October 2, 1949, Stengel seemed completely at ease before the biggest game of his life.

"There had been so many injuries," says Ed Lopat. "We all knew now he was a marvelous manager. One game couldn't change that. Win or lose, by then, Casey Stengel had become the manager of the New York Yankees."

The Red Sox failed to get a man on off Vic Raschi in the first inning. Phil Rizzuto led off for the Yankees and hit a line drive toward the left-field corner. Ted Williams, trying to get between the baseball and the wall, allowed the ball to slice past him for a triple. Tommy Henrich bounced out to Bobby Doerr at second base and the Yankees led 1–0. It stayed that way for seven breathless innings.

The Yankees crashed through for four runs in the bottom of the eighth inning to break the game open. The Red Sox got a couple of men on in the top of the ninth and Bobby Doerr flied deep to center. A healthy DiMaggio would have caught it easily. But now, weakened by the pneumonia, spent from a grueling season, weighted down with worry, DiMaggio could not catch up with the ball. It went for a double and two runs scored. DiMaggio was jogging in from center field.

"I can't make it," he told Stengel, who replaced him with Cliff Mapes. Al Zarilla flied out, Billy Goodman singled, and Birdie Tebbets, the squeaky-voiced, loquacious catcher, fouled out to Henrich. It was over with a 5–3 Yankee victory.

The Yankees had won the most dramatic pennant race in league history. The players raced off the field and the fans raced on. Some thirty minutes later, with thousands still milling on the field, the huge scoreboard brought tidings that the Dodgers had beaten the Phillies and won the National League pennant.

Another Subway Series.

Before all that, Stengel, drenched in champagne, hugged George Weiss, shook hands with Dan Topping and Del Webb, did a soft shoe for reporters, and announced, "I never coulda done it without my players."

Now that it was over, now that Stengel had a pennant win at age fifty-nine for the first time, now that all the injuries hardly mattered, John Drebinger could write in the *Times*, "Perhaps it was destined from the very beginning that Casey Stengel and his amazing Yankees were to win the 1949 American League pennant."

If fate had any part in the pennant, it was natural that fate would put Stengel's first pennant winner against his first team, the Brooklyn Dodgers, in his first World Series.

The Dodgers had become the National League's best team simply because they cornered the market on the best young players, black and white. A team with Duke Snider, Gil Hodges, Pee Wee Reese, Carl Furillo, and Preacher Roe, also had the great Negro players, Jackie Robinson, who broke the color line two years earlier in 1947, big right-hander Don Newcombe, and catcher Roy Campanella.

The Dodgers had never won a World Series despite pennants in 1916 (Casey Stengel was a player on that team), 1920, 1941, and 1947. Now was their best chance with their best team and the Yankees decimated by injuries and a brutal pennant race. The Dodgers were slight favorites as the Series opened in Yankee Stadium on October 5.

More than 66,000 fans came to the game, many of them riding the subways from Brooklyn for a nickel to root for the Dodgers, their beloved Bums.

For Dodger fans, it was not to be. Allie Reynolds shut out Brooklyn 1–0 in the first game. After Preacher Roe shut the Yankees out 1–0 in the second game, Stengel's Yankees won the next three games. The Yankees took a 10–1 lead in the final game at Ebbets Field, Joe Page relieved a tired Raschi, and the Yankees held on for a 10–6 win. DiMaggio, in a weakened condition, played all five games but managed only two hits for a .111 average.

Rookie Yankee manager Casey Stengel was a world champion.

A few days later, back home in Glendale, Casey Stengel sat in a rocking chair in his wood-paneled den, looked across the room at an old neighbor and baseball pal named Babe Herman, pursed his lips, shook his head, and said, "Babe, I won one. I won one."

"You sure did, Casey," Herman said.

Casey Stengel leaned back in his rocking chair, looked sweetly at a picture of himself nearby in the uniform of the 1912 Brooklyn Dodgers, and smiled a happy smile. No man was more entitled.

2. The K.C. Kid

LOUIS STENGEL was born on August 23, 1860, some four months after the Republicans nominated Abraham Lincoln for the presidency, some seven months before Lincoln was inaugurated, and some eight months before the outbreak of hostilities after the firing on Fort Sumter, on April 12, 1861. His father, Charles Stengel, had come to the United States with his parents, two brothers, and three sisters from Augsburg, Germany, in 1851 when he was thirteen. The family settled in Utica, New York, with relatives. The family name was originally spelled "Schtengal." In 1855 the family moved west and settled on a small farm near Rock Island, Illinois. At age twenty-one, Charles Stengel married Katherine Kniphals of Rock Island. Louis was born the next year. Late in 1864, with the Civil War still raging, Charles fell ill of tuberculosis, lingered for four days, and died. Katherine Kniphals Stengel tended the farm alone, cared for her young son, and soon was befriended by a widower by the name of Charles Wolff. He had one small daughter. After a courtship lasting more than three years, they were wed.

Louis was a husky lad with a long thin face, light blue eyes, and large ears. He attended a one-room schoolhouse in Rock Island, walking some eight miles back and forth to school each day, and quitting to work on his stepfather's farm in 1875. When he was twenty-six, he met and married Jennie Jordan, a handsome blond girl with delicate features, a shy smile, and fine upbringing.

Jennie Jordan had been born in Davenport, Iowa, across the Mississippi River from Rock Island, in 1861. Her uncle

23

Lovely Jennie Stengel, Casey's mother, in a family photo taken shortly after her marriage to Louis E. Stengel in 1886.

was Judge John F. Dillon, her mother's brother, who had served on the Iowa Supreme Court and the United States District Court, and had served as counsel for the Union Pacific Railroad. Her father, John Jordan, was a prosperous merchant and investor in railroads. The Jordans frowned upon the marriage of their only daughter to a farmer, and they did what they could to discourage the match. But Jennie was persistent. With farming such a tenuous profession, Louis Stengel promised his in-laws he would look for another business. He soon read of a job in the insurance trade in Kansas City, Missouri, with Joseph Stiebel and Sons. He applied by mail, was hired, and soon moved his new bride to Kansas City.

Kansas City was bustling by then. Explored by the Spanish in the 1500s and then by Lewis and Clark in 1804, the town was part of the territory of Missouri that had been admitted into the Union in 1821 as the twenty-fourth state. The Transcontinental Railroad, built at the time of the Civil War, brought trade, prosperity, and culture and created a major urban link be-

Young Charles Stengel, aged three, in his first official photo, beautiful blue eyes, curly blond hair and caught, for once, with his mouth closed. Jennie couldn't keep him in curls and a dress much longer.

tween the established East and the emerging West. With the railroad came a flood of settlers who pushed Kansas City's population to over 100,000.

Their first child, Louise, was born at the end of that first year of marriage in 1886. A year later a son named Grant was born, and, on July 30, 1890, a sweltering summer day in Kansas City, Jennie Jordan Stengel was delivered of a son by a midwife, shortly before midnight. He had a shock of curly, blond hair like his mother and his father's features, and was an extremely active baby. He was named Charles (for his paternal grandfather) Dillon (for his maternal grandmother) Stengel.

"I think the thing I remember about him most," sister Louise said in a *Kansas City Star* interview years later, "was that he almost never cried. He was a very active baby, talked early, and was a good eater."

Young Charles talked fast. He stumbled over words and soon was speaking in that questioning, ungrammatical, rapid-fire way that would later become celebrated as Stengelese.

Jennie allowed young Charles' curls to grow extremely long, trailing almost to his waist, and dressed him in a girl's dress almost until he was five years old. When young Charles was seven, the family visited with Grandfather Jordan in Davenport. The boy followed his grandfather everywhere and copied all his moves, even going so far as to imitate his grandfather chewing tobacco. He also noticed that his grandfather had short hair while he, Charles, still had flowing blond curls.

"I'd like to get my hair cut like you," Charles said.

Grandfather Jordan gave the boy fifteen cents, told him to walk down the street to a place with a colored pole outside, go in and tell the barber he had been sent for a haircut, and get the curls cut off.

"When I came back," Casey recalled years later, "and my mother and my aunt and my grandmother saw me, they took and grabbed me and slapped me for getting those curls cut off. They said, 'Who told you you could get your hair cut?' And I said, 'My grandfather.' They sure did jump on him."

In tears, Jennie Stengel raced to the barbershop, barged in where few women ever went, collected the curls off the floor, and kept them for years in an envelope.

Young Charles was a rambunctious child, quick to wrestle with his brother Grant, quick to argue over the dinner table with Louise, always playing hide-and-seek with his parents when they prepared to leave the house for a family outing.

In wintertime there would be sledding and sliding down the big hills near the Stengel home with dozens of screeching children, boys and girls, falling in waves down the snowy inclines. Young Charles had another favorite winter pastime, snowballing. That consisted of hiding behind a street pole until a wagon came by with a man dressed in a high hat. He would fire at the hat and if he knocked it off, more than likely the man would angrily jump out and give chase. It helped Charles develop running speed that would come in handy later on.

Louis was soon given a new job by the insurance company. They had purchased some street sprinkling machines and he would ride the machines, pulled by old, tired horses, downtown shouting, "Five cents a spray, five cents a spray." Young Charles would often accompany him on his rounds, getting to know all the side streets of Kansas City and learning how to shout, "Five cents a spray."

In good weeks Louis Stengel would bring home some twenty dollars. The income was supplemented with sales from a small farm maintained behind the house at 1129 Agnes Avenue where the Stengels lived. Louis had a cow and he sold milk to some of his neighbors. One day he told Grant he would give him a nickel if he could fill a pail from old Fawn and deliver it. Grant subcontracted part of the job out to Charles for a penny. He was supposed to keep the flies off Grant with a switch. As he watched the bucket fill slowly, he got an idea. If some water was poured into the bucket it would be filled quicker. More buckets, more nickels for Grant, more pennies for Charles. This charade went well until a neighbor complained, "Your milk is too thin, Louis." Louis investigated and discovered his sons had hustled him. He was angry enough to smack them but amused enough at the ingenuity to excuse them. "Don't do it again," he said.

Money was scarce and though the Stengels had enough to eat, there never was an overabundance of food. Jennie had to learn how to stretch food and Charles and Grant learned how to pick up a snack or a sandwich out of the house. They had a dog called Sport. They taught him to do some tricks, and when performing out of the neighborhood, he would earn a sandwich or a nickel for the show.

The family moved constantly, always looking for bargains such as one month's free rent as an inducement for a move. When they moved to Brooklyn Avenue, near the site of the Kansas City baseball park, Casey and his father would often coop pigeons on their roof, putting out some bread crumbs hoping to end the day with more pigeons in their coops than they had started with.

With money being short, young Charles would pick up employment where he could to help out. His first job was as a pump-turner for the organ at the St. Mark's Episcopal

Church in Kansas City. He earned twenty-five cents a day for the job, but it didn't thrill him, and when the family moved, he dropped out of church and never was a church-going man after that.

He also held a job at the W.F. Grant Company, manu-facturer of medicines. His job was to put medicine in smaller jars, cork the jars, glue, and label them. Once five cases were filled he would get a dollar.

Kansas City was a fast-growing town in Stengel's youth and Charles often worked as a water boy on construction sites. He was paid three dollars a week for carrying buck-ets of water. "I thought," Stengel said later, "that was a fine way of strengthening my arms."

He also worked as a delivery boy for a flower company, bicycling after school and during vacations to weddings and parties around town.

None of these jobs satisfied his most serious craving. While he was still in high school, Stengel found out he could get paid anywhere from one to three dollars for playing baseball. Once he made that discovery, no other job would ever hold him.

Charles had developed a strong physique, with a thick chest, well-muscled arms, and long legs. He also had two floppy ears, inherited from his father and cause for some grief. Neighborhood boys would call them "sails" and shout, "Goin' sailing, Charlie?" and howl with laughter. Stengel would often have to attack a loudmouthed kid, wrestle him to the ground, and punch his face until he shouted, "I give up."

Kansas City was a rough town with the roaring days of the pioneers not in the too distant past. Stengel's first hero was Jesse James, and "cowboys and Indians" was more of a true-life adventure tale than a game for Stengel and his friends. The cattlemen still met in Kansas City and on Saturday nights would get to tearing up some of the downtown saloons. Fighting in the streets was as common as a dusty day and "likkered-up" cowpokes would often start brawling in sight of everyone.

The sons of these cowpokes and rough characters were classmates of Stengel's. Fights would break out for the slightest insult and a kid who couldn't handle himself in a brawl would be in serious trouble.

Soon Charles was following brother Grant into town baseball games, playing with fourteen- and fifteen-year-olds when he was barely past twelve. Grant was a better ballplayer and thought seriously about professional baseball until his heel was severed when he was pushed off a surrey during some horseplay. Years later, after people had noticed the name of Stengel in big-league box scores, they would assume it was Grant. "I see your brother is in the major leagues and doing good," Kansas City people would say. "That's myself that is in the major leagues," Stengel would answer. Grant never played much baseball after the injury. He tried many jobs until he settled on one as a Kansas City cab driver, a popular figure along Independence Avenue and Kansas City streets. He later married, had no children, and was a widower for many years. Louise stayed home and never married, living with the elder Stengels and caring for them until their death about nine months apart in 1937.

At the turn of the century, baseball was easily the most popular sport in America. Nap Lajoie, Ed Delahanty, and Honus Wagner were the popular baseball heroes of the time. Kansas City had a team in the Western Association and baseball interest increased tremendously with the establishment of the American League to battle the domination of the National League in 1901. Louis Stengel played some ball, encouraged his sons to play, and was not above a wager on a game. He also was a good cardplayer who would turn more and more to that leisure activity as the sprinkling business deteriorated when motor-driven cars replaced horses on the cobblestone streets. Louis retired in 1915.

Young Charles had started at the Woodland Grade School in 1896. He was in second grade there when he was taught to write. He picked up his pencil with his left hand and began his letters. His teacher scolded him, pulled him by his ears and deposited him in a closet for the sin of writing left-handed. His writing would always be labored, with large, childish letters guided by the wrong hand for him, the right hand. Typical of his character, he would see this outrageous practice as a plus.

"I was naturally left-handed," he said years later, "and in baseball that helps you out to have a well-developed right hand as well. That's the hand I used to catch the ball and if you look it up you would see I caught a lot of 'em."

On January 27, 1906, Charles Stengel entered Central High School. Among the famous graduates of Central are basketball coach Phog Allen and actor William Powell.

"They had a lot of acting classes at Central High and Bill Powell was in all of them," Stengel once said. "He did this Shakespeare real good and had a big voice. He was a tall, thin fellow and they dressed him up in women's clothing for some plays because it wasn't ladylike to do them parts. He wasn't no sissy though, you can be sure of that. One time when we were playing basketball we both went up for a ball. He came down with the ball and I came down with a cracked tooth from his sharp elbows."

Stengel had played enough baseball with his brother Grant to realize he was a pretty good player. When March came and Central High posted a sign reminding those interested in baseball to report to the field March 20 for tryouts, Stengel showed up. He easily made the team and played second and third base, and pitched for three seasons. "I always looked around every year to see what the opposition looked like. If there was no second baseman I became a second baseman," said Stengel. "If there was no third baseman, I became a third baseman. If there was no pitcher I became a pitcher. It didn't matter none that I was left-handed. Nobody seemed to notice or care if you could hit."

Stengel also played on the basketball team for three years at Central High.

"He didn't have much finesse," says Ernie Mehl, the retired sports editor of the *Kansas City Star,* "he was mostly all arms and legs and always moving. Basketball in those days was just an excuse for knocking somebody down in short pants and high socks."

During Stengel's time at Central there was only one season with a football team. He was a fullback and the team captain in 1908, but the sport was immediately discontinued after a player was kicked in the head during a game.

Stengel's basketball team won the city championship in 1909. Stengel's performance in a game against St. Joseph's High is well remembered by a chipper eighty-eight-year-old lady named Fern Carper Zwilling. She was a sophomore that year at St. Joseph's and later married a ballplayer named Dutch Zwilling, a lifelong pal of Casey's.

"Oh, he was a monkey on the basketball court," says Fern Zwilling. "He kept looking at the stands every time he put a basket in. He was built nicely, with wavy blond hair. After the game he came over and said, 'Hi, I'm Charlie Stengel.' I remember that because we all knew him as Dutch Stengel, but I guess he thought that was too rough for our sweet young ears."

Stengel, like all youngsters of German ancestry of the time, was called Dutch. All his classmates, teammates, and friends addressed him as Dutch.

Dutch chatted for a while after the game with young Miss Carper and then said, "Let's go out for an ice-cream after I dress. You don't have to be afraid, my sister Louise is here."

"We were all thrilled that the star wanted to take us out. We were just sophomores and he was a senior," says Mrs. Zwilling. "Then he brought Louise over, introduced her, and we all went out."

Louise Stengel, blond and starting to grow chubby, was a constant companion of her brother's. Four years after that basketball game, Fern Carper, now married to Dutch Zwilling, was standing in a hotel lobby in St. Louis. Casey walked in. He was playing for the Brooklyn Dodgers. "He knew Dutch from ball and took one look at me and said, 'That's the girl from St. Joe's. I bought her ice cream.' Dutch and I were good friends with Casey after that. I remember when he was managing Toledo and Dutch was managing Kansas City in the same league. I used to wait outside the gate for Dutch and Louise would be waiting outside for Casey."

Casey's best schoolboy friend was Harold Lederman,

whose father owned a cigar store in Kansas City and who later became a successful jeweler. Casey would always introduce Lederman to sportswriters by saying, "This is my Jewish friend from Kansas City and he can sell you a ring cheap."

Another pal from his Kansas City days was Runt Marr, who went on to become a successful baseball scout and discovered a great pitcher for the Cardinals named Bob Gibson.

"We used to hang around the Grand Billiard Parlor, me and Dutch and talk about those ballplayers and shoot a little pool and drink a little beer," says Marr. "Dutch did good in everything he tried."

Casey's athletic ability was already proven and one year while he was in high school he showed another skill. He danced better than anybody in school.

"They had this dance contest in town with the winner getting five silver dollars," says Marr. "Me and Casey— only we called him Dutch then—entered with these two girls. You had to dance every night for fifty days. I gave up along about the twentieth day or so, my feet beginning to hurt so bad I almost cried. But Dutch—he just kept dancin' away till he won himself that money. I couldn't dance like Dutch, but I done other things real good. People ask me my reasons for longevity. I just tell them good whiskey and bad women. Did I tell you I married five times? Loved them all. Sadie was my first wife, we had one boy, he's sixty-four years old now, lives with his mother. Then I had Agnes, Inez, and Juanita. Married Sarah just last month. I think I'm gonna keep her for a while."

Stengel's dancing probably helped get his feet in shape for the years of standing on hard baseball fields. It was something he always loved, dancing at every Yankee victory party for years.

"Outside of baseball," said Edna Stengel, "I think Casey loved dancing most."

Even though he was a tough, confident youth, who would fight at the drop of an insult, real or imagined, he was also acquiring some of the graces that would identify him as a ninteenth-century gentleman all his life. In his senior year in high school he asked to call on a girl a few blocks away. He dressed up for the occasion and then realized he didn't have a good pair of shoes. He simply borrowed Grant's. They were too small and he had to sit in the girl's house in pain and left early. He rushed home, took off the shoes, and heaved them into a closet. Grant spotted them a few days later.

"Mom, Mom, has Charlie been wearing my shoes?" Grant asked.

"No, I don't think that boy could wear those shoes with those big feet of his," said Mrs. Stengel. "How could he put them on?"

Grant soon confronted his younger brother. They argued heatedly and Grant smacked Charlie in the kisser and started moving away.

"I couldn't catch him," laughed Stengel later, "because I couldn't perambulate as fast as he could."

In 1909 Stengel pitched Central High to the state baseball title. He pitched fifteen innings and won 7–6. The headline in the *Kansas City Star* read, "KC'S STENGEL PITCHES CENTRAL TO TITLE." It was this headline that had much to do with establishing his name in the form that came to be used by everyone, Casey Stengel.

The local professional team, the Kansas City Blues, had scouts at the high school championship. They liked what they saw in the youngster and soon discovered he was seriously interested in baseball. They were ready to approach KC's Stengel and change his life in a most drastic way.

The trail would lead away from Kansas City to points east and west, but Stengel would never forget his roots, never lose the warmth he felt for his hometown and the people he knew in Kansas City, so many of them showing up as his guests for the World Series and so many of them doing favors for him.

"I remember once he was in some financial trouble and his friend Harold Lederman loaned him some money," says Ernie Mehl. "He never stopped talking about it."

The Stengel family links to Kansas City are slim now.

The hot shot 1909 Missouri State Champions, Central High, with pitcher-second baseman-third baseman "Dutch" Stengel, back row, left. Notice the tiny glove on Dutch's right hand.

Louise never married. Grant never had any children. Casey and Edna never had any children. There are no Stengel heirs in the city.

In fact there is only one Stengel in the Kansas City phone book, Joseph Stengel, a maintenance man for J.C. Penney.

"We are distantly related," he says. "My family is from Illinois and my mother has a family tree with his name in it. Anytime a boy gets born around here they call him Casey."

Joseph Stengel said he never met Casey Stengel, but he did have one request.

"Say, there is one thing you might help me out with," he said. "I heard Casey never had any children and he left a lot of money. Do you think they might be looking for any distant relatives to help out with that will now?"

3. May Be Too Damn Aggressive

SOME FEW BOYS IN KANSAS CITY in 1910 dreamed of growing up to be William Howard Taft, the President of the United States. Most dreamed of being Ty Cobb or Honus Wagner. Cobb had come out of rural Georgia to win three straight American League batting titles, with a .377 average for the Detroit Tigers in 1909. He was a fiery competitor, already painted as a villain by the sporting press, unfriendly with his teammates, loud, profane, and humorless. Wagner, on the other hand, was an affable Dutchman from Carnegie, Pennsylvania, gregarious, well-liked by teammates and the press, and a marvelous hitter with four straight batting titles. He was a bandy-legged shortstop with enormous fielding range and a strong arm.

"He was a Dutchman," says Runt Marr, "—my real name is Clifton and I think you are only one of four or five people in the whole world who know that—and he was Casey's hero."

Baseball had an enormous hold on the popular imagination in 1910. It was an American institution, a part of the fabric of life, a link between father and son. For any boy, playing baseball was simply the patriotic thing to do.

"We'd sit around," says Marr, "and argue about the relative merits of all the great players. We had these little picture cards, see, the ones that came in the cigarette packages, and we'd study their faces and their batting stances and the way they wore their caps and the way they buttoned their uniforms and we'd copy them. We all knew baseball was a tough life, but we knew Dutch Stengel could make it. He was tough as a boot."

On the night of March 14, 1910, Dutch Stengel, Runt
Marr, and a half a dozen of their cronies sat around the
Grand Billiard Parlor in downtown Kansas City. Instead
of playing pool, they leaned against a table and talked
about Dutch's impending adventure. One of their own
was on his way to play professional baseball.

"That made Dutch a king with us," says Marr. "I remember how he sat there and said, 'When I get to the big
league, I'm goin' right up to Cobb and Wagner and all
them fellas and just say I'm anxious to show you what I can
do.' See, Dutch was never afraid of none of those big
fellas. He knew he was pretty good. We all wanted to play
baseball in the big league. Only thing is, Dutch got to go
and the rest of us didn't."

The next morning, March 15, 1910, a windy, snowy day
in Kansas City, Charles "Dutch" Stengel stood on the
platform of the Union Pacific Railroad waiting for the 8:15
local north to Excelsior Springs, Missouri, the spring training grounds for the Kansas City Blues professional baseball team. He was nineteen years old, a chesty one hundred seventy-five pounds, with long, loose arms, a thin
waist, and thick thighs. His face was angular and his jaw
seemed to protrude from the bottom. His ears, long and
fleshy, were the most noticeable part of his appearance.
He wore a long, plaid, cloth coat and a peaked cap on his
head. He carried a small cardboard suitcase bought for
him by his father and a brown bag of lunch with a chicken
sandwich and a piece of blueberry pie baked by his
mother. His brother Grant had come to the station with
his mother to see Charles off.

"Now just listen to what they tell you before you go to
arguing," Grant said.

"I wanna play in the big league, don't I? Why would you
argue with anybody if you ain't made the team yet?"

"Now boys," said Mrs. Stengel. "Let's not get into that.
Charlie will do his best. We know that."

"Board," bellowed a conductor, "all aboard . . . eight-
fifteen local . . . Liberty . . . Excelsior Springs . . . Elmira
. . . Nettleton . . ."

Dutch Stengel jumped on the train as it began to move slowly out of the station. He peered out of the coach window, waved at his mother and brother, and shouted, "Don't worry none. I'll be good."

The Blues were an independently run baseball team. They signed their own young players, trained them, sent them to other clubs in lower leagues for seasoning, brought them back for experience, and hopefully sold them to big-league teams. Unlike today, these minor-league clubs were not owned by any major-league organization. Their operations were sanctioned by professional baseball and some players were loaned from the big-league clubs to the minor-league clubs for seasoning. In that case, they would still be owned by the big club. Professional baseball was divided into categories according to level of skill in the leagues. The major-league clubs gave the ratings. Kansas City was an AAA club, considered one notch below a major-league team. The ratings went from AAA through AA, A, B, C, and D, the lowest professional classification.

With only high school and some amateur experience in Kansas City area games behind him, Dutch Stengel could not be expected to make the Kansas City club. He would be farmed to a lower classification as soon as they got a line on him.

Stengel had pitched, played the infield, and played the outfield at Central High. Now he would have to choose his position as manager Danny Shay broke his squad up into groups. Stengel decided he would try out first as a pitcher. After he had worked out for a week with the Blues, he sat on the bench for the first exhibition game of the spring. Smokey Joe Wood, a Kansas City hero and already in his third year of professional ball at age twenty, was the starting pitcher for the Boston Red Sox against the Blues. Stengel had written his parents a letter from the training camp earlier in the week. "We're going against Boston and Smokey Joe Wood. I hope to get in for an inning but I'm not sure. They never tell you here how you're doing and why should they because they don't have to pay you until the season starts next month." His parents, sister, brother, and more than two dozen classmates from Central High came to the old Kansas City park on Brooklyn Avenue for the game.

"Hey, kid," Shay screamed at him, "get the water bucket and bring it out for the regulars."

When Stengel was spotted walking across the field carrying the water bucket, some of his classmates let out a howl. "There's Dutch, there's Dutch," said Runt Marr. "Yeah, yeah, I see," said another classmate. "He's making the field wet with the water. Hey, water boy. Hey, Dutch, you make a good water boy."

Stengel was humiliated but kept his eyes on the ground. His classmates simply were jealous. They wanted to be on that field, dressed in that uniform of the professional Blues, water bucket or not.

The next afternoon Stengel started an exhibition game against a semiprofessional team from Kansas City, the Baby Blues, a club supported with funds from the KC Blues. He was hit hard. Four days later the club went by train to Omaha, Nebraska, for two exhibition games there. Stengel started again. He was hit hard again. "I'm really an outfielder," he told manager Shay after that game. Said Shay, "I can see that." Stengel would always have a similar retort for unsuccessful players. "I seen what they done," he would say, more anxious to try other green players because, "they ain't failed yet."

Soon Shay was hitting Stengel fly balls in the outfield but dismayed at his chances of becoming an outfielder. "You're built like a horse, with that big rear end of yours," Shay said. "No wonder you can't catch a fly ball." Shay was also fond of calling Stengel "billiard ball head" because, said the manager, "Your head is as hard as an ivory billiard ball."

Baseball players in 1910, major and minor leaguers, were not coddled. The managers were tough, hard-nosed men for the most part, anxious to win so that they could move up the managerial ladder. They had little patience for inexperienced kids. They were sometimes bitter at the failure of their own careers and used the younger players as foils for this frustration. Jobs were scarce, competition

was keen, and kids who couldn't take some vicious needling would not survive. A man needed a tough skin to
withstand the verbal abuse from the manager and from
the veteran players.

Though the general attitude of players was to ignore
youngsters, there were cases of individual players, for
reasons of common decency, kindness, or compassion,
who helped and advised younger men. An outfielder
named Spike Shannon, who had played for the Browns
and the Giants from 1904 through 1908, was finishing up
his baseball career at age thirty-two with the Blues. Another veteran named Pat Flaherty joined with Shannon
in helping young Stengel. Flaherty, an ex-pitcher, would
hit huge fungoes over Stengel's head in the outfield
while Shannon would sit on a bench and advise him how
to go back.

"Flaherty would hit the ball over my head, and I was
supposed to run back as far as I could," Stengel recalled,
"and see if I could get to it. I'd miss the ball sixty feet, fifty
feet, forty feet, right or left, forward or back. But after
about ten days I was getting within five or ten feet of some
of them."

Flaherty, who had been pitching professionally since
1899 at Louisville and would later that season go back to
the majors with the Phillies, taught Stengel a lesson in 1910
he would never forget.

"Flaherty took a big windup and pitched to me," Stengel said, "and when the ball came back to him he pitched
it again real quick. I wasn't ready. I was looking down at
the plate and getting my feet set. And he unloaded with
one and hit me in the stomach and knocked me flat. And
he said, 'I just wanted to give you a tip. Never take your
eye off the baseball.' And that's still the most important
thing you could teach a ballplayer to this day. A manager
that had nerve enough to do it, if he could rig up a machine that would ring a bell every time somebody wasn't
watching the ball, everybody would be guilty at one time
or another.

"A man that I wanted to teach quick I'd tell him, 'watch
the baseball, whether you're on the ball field or on the

bench.' So he watches the pitcher, watches the ball go to the plate, watches it go back. He sees all the plays at all the bases—whether the fielder tagged the man, where he threw the ball after, whether he put his foot on the bag or didn't put his foot on the bag. So therefore he becomes bright. He sees how the other players hold the ball, how they make the different plays. He knows how many times they throw bad."

Stengel was soon dispatched by manager Shay to the Blues' Class D club at Kankakee, Illinois. Before the season opened, he practiced vigorously in his new outfield position. He felt confident he could hit, but he was uncertain—since he hadn't played much outfield—if he could catch a fly ball. He soon impressed his Kankakee teammates with his dedication. A likable fellow, a storyteller, and a guy willing to buy a beer for a teammate, Stengel soon found fast friends on the Kankakee club. Two of his pals were Willard Scheetz and Bill McTigue, two nineteen-year-old cousins from Nashville. Stengel got Scheetz to hit fungoes over his head and got the cousin to relay the ball back to the batter. Since it was a long throw in from the outfield, Stengel used the time to practice sliding, another skill he was deficient in. He would put his glove down on the grass, practice sliding into it on his right side, get up, chase the next batted ball, throw it in, drop the glove again, and practice sliding into it on his left side. One of Stengel's teammates, second-baseman Joe Gilligan, noticing his erratic behavior, said, "Stengel is one fellow who won't be here next year."

"Why?" asked Bill McTigue, "is he going to the big leagues?"

"No," said Gilligan, looking across the field at an insane asylum, "he's going in there."

Stengel and Gilligan had a tough time getting along, the pugnacious, wisecracking Dutchman from Kansas City and a loud, abrasive, fast-talking Irishman from New York. One day Stengel accidently stepped on Gilligan's foot chasing a fly ball. Angry words were exchanged. Later they met in the office of the team treasurer, a local mortician. "You smart aleck," Gilligan said, "why don't you watch where you're going? I yelled for the ball all the way."

Said Stengel, "Is that so? All right, duck nose, I'll listen to you."

Gilligan, insulted, cracked Stengel across the face, knocking him backward and depositing him in one of the mortician's open coffins.

Stengel seemed to have a thing about noses. Years later, in a classic photo taken by Frank Worth, Stengel would measure up his nose against Billy Martin and Ernie Lombardi. It would be Lombardi by a schnozz.

Baseball in 1910 was no game for gentlemen. It was hard and hectic, the travel unpleasant on rickety railroad trains, the field conditions poor, the status among townspeople negative. Fights were common in the clubhouse and on the field among teammates and opponents. The game was peopled mostly by uneducated farm boys and kids from rural areas. It was a true test of survival. Stengel's salary was $135 a month at Kankakee and that didn't provide for gracious living.

Stengel lived in a boarding house for four dollars a week with meals provided. As a bonus for good play the club presented meal tickets to the players good for redemption at a local diner. A game-winning homer would be worth a steak dinner and a shutout would be redeemed at the diner for pork chops.

"Sometimes," Stengel said years later, "I used to save these chits for when I was real hungry. When I left Kankakee I still had a couple of those unredeemed chits in my pocket. I was in a hotel in Chicago after I managed in the big league and I saw this guy from the diner. He ran the place and I went up to him and said, 'I still got two of your chits' and he looked at me and pulled out two bucks and bought them back."

Stengel met a pretty, dark-haired high school senior at Kankakee named Matilda Benson. Her father owned a clothing store in town. Stengel came a-calling a couple of nights and they sat on the Benson front porch and looked at the stars.

"It was going real well," says Runt Marr, "until Dutch

had this o for 4 day and forgot to show up when he was invited for dinner. The girl had dressed up and all and Dutch was just back in his room all night thinking about how he had missed those curve balls."

On July 18, 1910, the Class D Northern Association folded. The Kankakee franchise was finished. The club was broke and Stengel was still owed a half month's salary. He didn't get the $67.50, so he took his Kankakee uniform instead. In 1956, while he was managing the Yankees, he was given a birthday party in Kansas City. His thank-you address, a little longer and more convoluted than Lincoln at Gettysburg, recounted his experiences in baseball for forty-five years. The highlight of the talk was his reference to his time in Kankakee . . . "and the money they owed me was not what put them out of business, but I didn't get it and I'm not going to write it off as a bad debt in case the league starts up again and I can put a claim in for it and why wouldn't ya even though some of my teammates are dead at the present time and you could look it up."

The wire services reported the remarks and the people of Kankakee were stung. A local banker decided to pay the debt for the town. A check for $483.05—$67.50 plus interest since 1910—was presented to Stengel in a home-plate ceremony at Comiskey Park in Chicago. Casey turned the check over to the Kankakee Little League.

Dutch Stengel, the Kansas City Kid, had done right well as the Kankakee Kid. He batted .251 in 59 games, hit 3 homers with the dead ball of the time, batted in 22 runs, and stole 16 bases—despite his large rear end—for fifth place in the league. Stengel also was listed as pitching 4 innings, the first and last time he ever pitched in professional ball.

"I mighta been able to make it as a pitcher," he said years later, "except for one thing. I had a rather awkward motion and every time I brought my left arm forward I hit myself in the ear."

The Kansas City club, which owned Stengel's contract, assigned him to Shelbyville, Kentucky, in the Blue Grass League, a Class C club. The last surviving member of the Shelbyville Blues of 1910 died in 1978. His name was Isador

J. Sanders. He was eighty-nine years old when he died at
the St. Mathew's Nursing Home in Shelbyville.

"His room was filled with mementos of his playing days
with Casey Stengel," says his son, Albert Sanders. "I think
Casey was a most important influence on his life. Casey
sent him a warm birthday telegram one year and sent him
an autographed Mets cap when he was eighty. My father
always told me you could hear yelling for the team from
Casey no matter what the score was. He never gave up.
My father said Casey Stengel was blessed with unique
lungs."

At twenty years of age, Stengel had already begun to
develop two of the trademarks that would remain with
him as calling cards of his personality all of his life. He
could yell at a game for the entire length of a contest and
then talk endlessly about it afterward. He could also remember minute details and minute figures in his life half
a century later. When Sanders was eighty and received
his Mets cap, Stengel penned a small note with it. "Don't
wear this tilted to the left side of your head like you used
to do when we played," Stengel wrote. It had been sixty
years since Stengel had seen Sanders in a cap but he still
recalled the odd way the Kentucky man wore his.

Late in August of 1910, the Shelbyville franchise folded.
The club was quickly purchased by a plumber in nearby
Maysville, Kentucky, and moved there. The franchise
went out of business while the team was playing a road
game in Lexington.

Stengel batted .269 in sixty-nine games in Shelbyville
and Maysville. His fielding improved each day with hard
work. His running speed was above average and the sliding practice had begun paying off as he soon developed
into an excellent, aggressive base runner and slider with
an uncanny ability for twisting his body away from a tag,
a skill some major-league baseball players never learn.
Veteran major leaguers often slide feet first into a tag
rather than attempt to evade the tag. Casey Stengel, at
twenty, was already learning his lessons well, stressing the
small things, developing his appreciation of baseball's fundamentals.

First known professional box score. Dutch Stengel, playing center field and batting second for Class D Shelbyville, Kentucky Blues, had a single in four trips and was thrown out stealing. The game was played July 28, 1910 and the box score was presented to Stengel sixty years later. *(Courtesy of R.G. Potter.)*

There were a half-dozen games left in the Kansas City season when Stengel's season ended at Maysville. He was instructed to report to the Kansas City club. He got into three separate games as pinch hitter and got a single in his second time at bat.

When the Kansas City season ended, Stengel considered his future. He still was uncertain about his prospects as a professional baseball player, though he knew he had progressed in that one year with four different clubs. He needed a job for the winter unless he entered school. His father, ever the pragmatist, warned Charlie, "You'd better have something to do if the baseball doesn't work out." Billy Brammage, a friend of Stengel's from the local baseball scene, mentioned that he was entering Western Dental College in Kansas City. The tuition fee was fifty dollars. All applicants were accepted on the presentation of the fee. Stengel took a trolley downtown, presented the school registrar with fifty dollars, and entered dental school.

"Why don't you become an orthodontist?" one of his professors asked the young student. "Everybody will have to pay to have their kids' teeth fixed. They won't always pay for their own—they'll owe for dental bills. But if you become an orthodonist, which is new now, you'll get more money and you'll get rich because everybody will pay for his son or his daughter."

Applying the same lust for life he showed as a ballplayer, Stengel worked hard and played hard in dental school. He read all his assignments and paid attention to all his instructors. He also managed to keep his classmates laughing. He once put a cigar in the mouth of one of the corpses the class was working on. Another time he covered himself with a sheet, lay down on an empty slab, rose slowly as his classmates howled, and scared some of his friends half to death.

"We had all these courses in anatomy at the college," Stengel once said, "and we'd get to cuttin' up and this one time we had a stiff and I managed to cut off his thumb and put it in my pocket. Then I walked home and saw my friend Harold Lederman. We're talkin' and then I had to

Our hero is now a serious dental student at Western Dental College in Kansas City. Stengel, seated second row extreme left, kept his classmates in stitches. Notice the lone female dental student in the graduating class of 1912. Stengel made the photo but not the graduation.

The senior year photo at Western Dental College. The elegant youngster could easily have carried off the title of Doctor Stengel, DDS, had he chosen that route instead of baseball.

go and I put my hand in my pocket, felt that loose thumb, put it in my hand, and shook hands good-bye with Harold. Only I left the thumb in Harold's hand."

Stengel was an average student in the two winters he attended dental school. His class picture shows the face of a serious young man, decked out in splendid suit and tie, looking for all the world like a successful young professional man. Legend has it that Stengel failed to return to dental school in 1912 after attending in 1910 and 1911 because no left-handed dental equipment was available. He told this writer years later that was not the whole truth. "I didn't go back because I had a different job I liked better," he said. His different job was playing center field for the Brooklyn Dodgers.

Early in 1911 Stengel received a letter from the Kansas City Blues advising him that he had been assigned to Aurora, Illinois, in the Wisconsin-Illinois League, a Class C league. It was a definite sign the Blues thought he was a major-league prospect. Stengel accepted their letter with no false modesty. He immediately wrote to Al Tebeau, the owner of the Aurora team that he wanted $200 a month to play for them in 1911. They wrote back that their best offer was $150 a month, a fifteen-dollar-a-month raise over his 1910 salary. Stengel fumed. Then he wrote back, "I'll take $175 month or I'm going back to school." Tebeau, knowing he might be able to sell Stengel for a goodly sum, didn't want to lose him. He agreed to pay the outrageous salary of $175 a month.

"I don't think it was always the money," says Runt Marr. "I think Casey enjoyed arguing with these owners and getting his own way."

Stengel reported to Aurora on March 7, 1911. He now felt comfortable as a professional, made friends easily with his new teammates, and started off well as a hitter. He began to apply much of the information he had gathered as a rookie the previous year. He studied pitchers. He learned their patterns. He watched where the outfielders played him and tried to hit away from them. He noticed when infielders were playing in and drove the ball by them. He knew when they were playing back. He bunted. He had become, at twenty-one years of age, a very smart baseball player. He studied, he learned, he prospered.

One day Tebeau, who had a gambling establishment, a saloon, and a brothel in Aurora, watched Stengel play cards with his teammates on a train. Stengel enjoyed the fraternity of the games more than the gambling. He had been a big loser in a poker game with his teammates.

The next day Tebeau sat next to him on the bench and said, "You look to me like you can go to the big leagues. But if you want to be a big leaguer, you'd better quit playing cards. If you don't, you'll be broke every payday. I know, that's my bread and butter, this gambling business. And you sure can't play cards."

Stengel took the hint. He never played poker again. In fact, years later, he explained his success in baseball by saying, "I don't play cards, I don't play golf, and I don't go to the picture show. All that is left is baseball."

A scout for the Brooklyn Dodgers named Larry Sutton was scanning the minor-league averages one day. He saw that an unknown kid named C. Stengel was leading the league. He was in Chicago, so he took a train over to nearby Aurora for a look at the kid. Sutton watched Stengel play for several days, jotting down small notes on a pad he carried in his breast pocket. "Good hands, good power, runs exceptionally well, nice glove, left-handed line drive hitter. Good throwing arm. May be too damn aggressive, bad temper," he wrote.

Stengel had argued with an umpire named Arnie Arundel. Stengel had been called out on strikes with Sutton in the stands observing him. The discussion became very heated. Arundel was hoping Stengel would disappear from view as he bent over to dust the plate with his broom. Stengel wound up and smacked the umpire in the ass with the bat to the utter delight of the crowd. It cost Stengel a two-day suspension and a twenty-five-dollar fine.

Stengel batted .352 with Aurora, led the league, stole fifty bases, led the league in hits with 148, and had blond hair. The blond hair was almost as important as the hits. Sutton had a superstition. He liked light-haired players because he believed they held up better in the summer heat. Sutton recommended the Brooklyn Dodgers draft Stengel from the Aurora club for the sum of $1500.

Stengel returned to dental school after the 1911 season ended, spent some time with the boys in the Grand Billiard Parlor, entertained his pals with stories about professional baseball, and awaited his 1912 contract. The Dodgers had assigned him to their Montgomery, Alabama, team, a Class A club, and offered him $150 a month.

"I made more than that in a small league," he told Marr. "I won't take it. I'm goin' back to school."

When Sutton convinced him he would get a chance with the Dodgers at the end of the 1912 season, Stengel accepted the deal. He reported to the Montgomery club. He knew his chance would come at the end of the year.

Stengel started quickly in the tougher league. He was hitting well, fielding well, and running fast. Sometimes too fast. Like so many young players before him and so many after him, his aggressiveness on the field was hurting him. There was more to think about than just hitting and running and catching the ball. He had to think about the other players, about what else was happening on a field, what the score was, what the situation called for. Several times, showing his speed, he would slide into a base with a beautiful fadeaway performance only to get up, dust himself off, and realize the inning was over because he had neglected the fact that the batter had swung and hit a line drive and he had been doubled off base. "He's a dandy ballplayer," one scout said of Stengel, "except for one thing, it's from his shoulders down." Quick to jump on a young player's mistake, the fans and the opposing players began calling Stengel "rock," short for rockhead and asking him from the stands, "Were you born in Rock Island?" Manager Johnn Dobbs of the Montgomery club said, after Stengel had been doubled up on a play, "That boy is concrete."

"See, the thing you gotta remember about professional ball in those days," says Runt Marr, "was that everybody was mean, the managers, your teammates, the opposing players, and especially the crowds. Some of them came to the park just to give you hell."

Through it all Stengel prospered. His play improved, his mistakes grew less frequent. He was gaining confidence in his play, confidence in his person, certain he could make the big leagues if he was given the chance. Like most ambitious youngsters in and out of baseball, he became a brain-picker. He would seek out veteran players, ask them about conditions in the big leagues, seek helpful advice, store it and record it in that incredible brain of his, always able to bring the information forth when necessary to help him maximize his physical talents.

Stengel had become friendly with a thirty-six-year-old infielder named Norman Arthur (The Tabasco Kid) Elberfeld. Kid Elberfeld had played in the majors from 1898 to 1911. In 1912 he had been released by the Washington Senators and signed as a free agent with Montgomery. He would return to the majors again in 1914 for a short while as a teammate on the Dodgers of Casey Stengel. Elberfeld was a generous man with his time and his wisdom. Like Stengel, he enjoyed talking baseball for hours at a time.

The grizzled old veteran and the blond-haired youngster, recently turned twenty-two, sat together on trains, roomed together in hotels, dined together in restaurants, shared thoughts on the bench and in the hotel lobbies. Elberfeld, using a short bottle-shaped bat, was a whiz at placing the ball between the fielders. He and Stengel often worked plays where Stengel would start to steal a base and Elberfeld would smack the ball through the vacated infield spot, second base, shortstop, or third base.

They had become good friends and now, as almost always happens in baseball, one or the other would move on. This time it was Stengel moving up and the older man staying back. Elberfeld, who had enjoyed his stay in the big leagues, was not resentful as so many older players were in the bitterness of their baseball middle-age. On September 15, 1912, after Stengel had been notified he was to report to Brooklyn for the final three weeks of the Dodger season, Elberfeld organized a small farewell party for the departing friend. He ordered that Stengel buy two jugs of wine for $6.00, buy a new suit ("You gotta dress like a big leaguer before they believe you are one," Elberfeld said) for $22.00, and a new suitcase for $17.50. The players partied until the wine emptied. Then, singing lustily, they walked with Stengel to the train station.

"Keep your ears open and your mouth shut up there," said Elberfeld.

It was wonderful advice for most players going to the big leagues. For Charles Dillon Stengel it just wouldn't work. His mouth was as much a part of his game as his bat, ball, and glove.

4. King of the Grumblers

THE OVERNIGHT TRAIN rattled north from Alabama. Young Charlie Stengel was filled with anticipation. He was so excited and so high from the wine he consumed with his teammates, he never entered the dining car. He slept most of the trip, arrived in New York in the early afternoon of the next day, and took a cab to the Palace Hotel on Forty-seventh Street and Broadway in Manhattan. There his uncle, Charlie Jordan, Jennie's brother, who was in New York on business, awaited him. "I was so hungry," Stengel said years later, "I commenced gettin' sick. My uncle asked me how I was and I said, 'I gotta eat before I talk' and he bought me a steak."

There were three major-league baseball teams in New York. The struggling New York Highlanders (later to be the Yankees) were finishing last that September under manager Harry S. Wolverton. Their 1912 record would be 50–102, worst in team history, and Wolverton would soon be replaced by Chicago's famed Peerless Leader, Frank Chance. The lordly New York Giants, under the leadership of Little Napoleon, John McGraw, and playing in a magnificent stadium at Coogan's Bluff, along the Hudson in fashionable Harlem, called the Polo Grounds (important polo games were played there when baseball wasn't), were driving for their fourth pennant under McGraw. Ty Cobb was hitting over .400 for the Tigers for the second straight season (he had batted .420 in 1911 and would finish at .410 in 1912) and third-baseman Heinie Zimmerman of the Cubs would bat .372.

A former Princeton president, Woodrow Wilson, now

the governor of New Jersey, was the Democratic standard-bearer in the presidential campaign after winning the nomination through the efforts of William Jennings Bryan, a bitter foe of the political power of New York's machine politicians of Tammany Hall. Wilson's chances were improved through a split in the Republican party among the Progressives, led by former President Theodore Roosevelt, and the loyal Republicans, led by President William Howard Taft.

With the country's attention focused on this heated political skirmish, Charles Dillon Stengel set out by elevated train and trolley car to Washington Park in the New York City borough of Brooklyn. The Dodgers had won the National League pennant in 1900 but for a dozen years had been a floundering second-division club, embarrassed with their failures while their neighbors to the north in Manhattan piled success upon success. Bitterness between the two New York National League clubs was deep; on-field fights among the players of both teams and among the fans of both teams in the stands were common occurrences. The Dodgers were a bad ball club, but hopes were high that things would improve in 1913 in their new park, now under construction in Flatbush, called Ebbets Field, named after the team owner, Charles Ebbets. Young Stengel was reporting that afternoon to a broken-down field at Washington Park.

Stengel left the hotel at 8 o'clock in the morning. He took the Broadway elevated to the south end of Manhattan. There he switched to the trolley car, crossed over the Brooklyn Bridge, switched to another trolley at the Brooklyn terminus, and rolled on to the Borough Park section of the old borough. Brooklyn had been first settled by the Dutch near Gowanus Bay in 1636, had grown into a large city by 1700, had prospered as a port independently of the other areas of New York through the eighteenth and nineteenth centuries, and had been incorporated as part of New York's boroughs in 1898, a move many residents always viewed with regret. Manhattan had dominated the rest of New York City, and the baseball team, the Brooklyn Dodgers, as poorly as they played, were dearly beloved as the borough's own, independent of New York, the snobbish Giants, the colorless Highlanders, and the rest of the major-league teams.

A bad ball club is often a brawling ball club. The Dodgers of 1912 were typical: poor on the field, raucous in their conduct, hard-drinking, and foulmouthed. These were a bunch of tough guys with a minimum of talent and a maximum of fight. They were young Stengel's first big-league team and he would mesh marvelously with them.

"I got to the office at Washington Park that first day," Stengel recalled years later, "and I commenced walking in. I was shocked. It was so run down I couldn't believe it. They didn't expect me in the office, didn't believe I had really been told to report from Montgomery, and didn't know'd if they wanted me. I was afraid they'd send me home. Someone told me where the clubhouse was. I walked in, took a nail, and hung up my jacket."

The Dodgers were a seventh-place club. They needed revamping. Manager Bill Dahlen, a former shortstop who had played on Brooklyn's only pennant winner in 1900, wanted a quick look at the new twenty-two-year-old outfielder. It was another rebuilding year for Brooklyn, a euphemism for a lousy team, then as now. There was some talent on the club, a slugging first baseman named Jake Daubert, a fine receiver named Otto Miller, a brilliant left-handed pitcher named Nap Rucker, and a soft-spoken outfielder from Hamilton, Missouri, named Zachariah Davis (Buck) Wheat, who would have thirteen seasons over .300 in nineteen big-league years and would earn a spot in the Baseball Hall of Fame.

Stengel had been the first player to arrive in the clubhouse. Soon the others began drifting in. He tried to make conversation with a couple of players, as he had always promised Runt Marr and his pals he would, but they ignored him. All he got was a grumble. The Dodgers were not an especially friendly lot to outsiders. Nobody was more of an outsider than a kid joining the team for the final few weeks of the season with as good a chance to be back in the bushes in 1913 as in Ebbets Field. They made sure not to make friends until they were certain the newcomer could play, could help the team, or would buy a beer. A crap game soon started among some of the players. Stengel threw a five-dollar bill on the cold wooden floor. He was in the game. Manager Dahlen, a chesty square-jawed New Yorker from the small town of Nelliston, had been alerted by the office upon his arrival that the new outfielder, Stengel, was in the clubhouse. He spotted the rookie on his knees with the dice in his hand. "What the hell did you come here to do?" he bellowed. Stengel looked up and sheepishly replied, "To play ball." Dahlen, shaking his head at the nerve of this young punk, screamed, "Then get the hell out on the field. We didn't bring you here to be a crapshooter." Stengel walked toward the nail where his clothes hung, picked up his thin outfielder's glove, smiled at Dahlen, and said, "No, I didn't think you did." Dahlen shouted, "Get some swings. You're in center field."

Dutch Stengel walked out into the early afternoon sun. Nap Rucker, a marvelous left-handed curve ball pitcher, was loosening up throwing batting practice. Stengel could not force his way into the routine. The regular players had an order for hitting and there was no space in that pregame schedule for a rookie. That would continue for several days. One day Stengel arrived at batting practice carrying printed cards. He slipped one to team leader Jake Daubert. The card read: HI. MY NAME IS CHARLES DILLON "DUTCH" STENGEL AND I WOULD LIKE TO TAKE BATTING PRACTICE. The card broke the ice. Daubert showed it to the other players, there were laughs all around and soon Stengel was one of the boys.

But on that first day, September 17, 1912, without batting practice, fresh off an overnight train, with very little sleep and a still-nervous stomach, Stengel was in the Dodger lineup. Soon to be known as Casey from his hometown of KC (Stengel could never quite decide which of his Dodger teammates started calling him that), he would play fourteen years in the major leagues, collect 1,219 hits, smack sixty homers with a dead ball (not to be confused with the sixty homers Babe Ruth hit in 1927 with a lively ball), and record a creditable .284 average.

"I had a lot of good days in the big league and a lot of bad ones," Casey once said, "but none that I remember better than the first one."

The opposing pitcher for the Pittsburgh Pirates that day was a husky right-hander from Olathe, Kansas, named Claude Hendrix. He had a blazing fastball and won twenty-three games in 1912.

"I was what you would call an anxious hitter," said Stengel. "The first good one I saw I liked to hit. So that's what I commenced doing."

The first pitch he saw in the big leagues he liked, so he commenced hitting a single into left center field. Today, umpires usually call a halt to the proceedings and capture the baseball for a rookie when he records that event.

"I rounded the base all lit up, you know, with that first hit," Casey recalled. "The first baseman was Dots Miller, a tall skinny guy which died of the TB when he was a young fella, and I said, 'Hi, my name's Stengel and I just come up' and he didn't say nothin' but spit tobacco juice and just missed my new shoes. Some of them fellas in the big league weren't real friendly then."

Stengel followed his first hit with a single past third, a ground single to center, and a line drive to right. With the Dodgers winning 7–4 in the eighth and Stengel at the plate for the fifth time, Fred Clarke, the Pittsburgh manager, removed Hendrix and brought in a hard-throwing left-hander named Rube Robinson. "Let's see what you can do now, you big busher," yelled Clarke. Undaunted, Stengel defeated the move by switching his stance at the plate to that of a right-handed hitter.

"I never hit right-handed," Casey said. "I wanted to see the look on Clarke's face. He was shocked, which is to say amazed at me being a switch-hitter that day, which I wasn't and which I wasn't advertised to be. By now, they didn't know me, they let me have four balls and now I had four hits and a walk on my first day. I figured the big league was easy and the writers figured I was Ty Cobb."

In 1964, at an old-timer's game at Shea Stadium, Zach Wheat remembered something else from Casey's first day.

"I was in left field and Stengel was in center. He could run and played a shallow center field. Then Honus Wagner came up. He used to hit those sizzling line drives with spin. The ball would start low over the infield and rise. That was the dead ball, remember, and he would have hit many homers with the lively ball. As it was, he was cracking some walls," Wheat said.

The veteran whistled over to the rookie, trying to motion him deeper in center for Wagner. He waved again and Stengel shook his head and moved in another step.

"He was a stubborn Dutchman and didn't like to be told anything. I figured if Wagner caught one he could never catch it. Sure enough, he hits one of those sizzlers. Casey runs like hell, but it's way over his head, just like I figured. Casey finally gets the ball off the wall, Wagner has a triple, and Casey looks over at me, grins, takes off his cap, and makes a deep bow. I had to laugh. We became good friends. Tell you the truth, there never was a day around Casey I didn't laugh."

In the one-cent *New York Times* of September 18, 1912, the lead story concerned a police scandal, the selling of a captaincy for $15,000. The *Times* reported a light turnout in the Democratic primary and over a two paragraph story on the front page this remarkable headline: GUNS TO FIGHT AIRCRAFT—WONDERFUL WEAPONS TO BE USED ON NEW BRITISH SHIPS.

On the only page of sports an unsigned article began, "Pittsburgh's winning spurt, twelve victories, was halted on the threshold of the thirteenth at Washington Park yesterday when the Superbas [soon to be the Dodgers] and the Pirates clashed in the final battle of the year. The meeting was not half as sweet to the four thousand Brooklyn fans as the work of Stengel, a new outfielder who was purchased from the Montgomery club of the Southern League. Stengel reported yesterday morning and was promptly put to work. Both the batting order and the lineup being subjected to shifts for the newcomer. His debut proved a grand success. He went to the plate five times and on each of his first four trips landed on Hendrix and Ferry for a clean hit. On his last time he faced Smith and drew a pass giving him a perfect average."

Stengel started against the Cubs after the Pittsburgh series. On a play at second base he slid hard into fiery little second-baseman Johnny Evers. Franklin P. Adams in the *Times* had made the Chicago infield famous in a poem that gloried their ability at making double plays. Adams had written "Tinkers to Evers to Chance, the saddest of possible words," for Giant fans, as shortstop Joe Tinker would pick up a Giant ground ball, flip to second-baseman Evers, who would relay to Frank Chance at first (he would be the Peerless Leader of the Yankees in 1913) for a double play. Evers leaped off the bag, just escaping Stengel's spikes and screamed at the newcomer, "You'll get a ball in the face if you slide that way, busher." Stengel leaped up, moved close to Evers, and screamed, "That's the way I slid in the bushes and that's the way I'll slide here. Take a good look at me because I'll be here a long time."

Stengel had quickly shown the Cubs he could not be intimidated. Ballplayers with more talent than Stengel's had often been run out of the game by intimidation, threats of violence, attacks on their manhood. A baseball player in 1912 had to quickly assert his toughness or be brushed back endlessly by pitchers, cut by infielders, or ridiculed by opposing players. It was a verbal war. Stengel would never lose a fight of that kind in his life.

After the Chicago series, there was a series with the Phillies and then Stengel's first meeting with the hated Giants. Casey got his first look at a rawboned left-hander by the name of Rube Marquard.

"I guess you'd have to say he was a real good player and a funny man," Marquard recalls. "I went over to the Brooklyn club later and he kept everybody laughing on the bench with his carrying on and the faces he made at the umpires."

Marquard, ninety years old, still remembers how he pitched to the young left-handed hitting Dodger rookie.

"In those days you handled the young fellows all the same way. You threw a pitch at their heads to see if they could take it. You didn't try to hit anybody, but you had to lean them off the plate. I had this roundhouse curve. I threw the first pitch at his head and then threw the round-house. I don't recall him hurting me in any game," Marquard says.

"He was a good hitter, what you would call a tough out," Marquard says. "After he had been around awhile, you had to make good pitches to get him."

Stengel must have learned something from his opening game incident with Honus Wagner because Marquard says, "He played center field deeper than most. He was leaning on the fence in Brooklyn. Nobody hit it over his head unless they hit it out of the park."

Speaking from his Pikesville, Maryland, home, Marquard, sounding a lot like Casey Stengel, said, "I gotta quit now. I'm hard of talking."

The 1912 season ended, Stengel went home a hero to his gang in Kansas City at the Grand Billiard Parlor, decided not to finish dental school, and waited to read the final averages in the *Star*. He had batted .316 in seventeen games.

In 1913 he established himself as the regular Dodger center fielder and would play there until 1914 when new manager Wilbert Robinson converted him into a right fielder because Stengel threw left-handed and Robinson felt he could throw quicker from the corner than a right-hander could.

As he gained confidence and security as a big-leaguer, his conduct became more suspect. It was one brawl after another, one hassle with umpires, one fight with the front office. Stengel was an angry young man, if one of the funniest. One time he and some teammates battled some wisecracking fans in Coney Island. Stengel was called into the office of team president Charles Ebbets for a reprimand.

"What kind of hoodlums do we have on this club, anyway?" asked Ebbets.

"We only had four beers," protested Stengel, as he held up four fingers to make the point.

"Yeah," said manager Robinson, "you only had four beers, but they were as big as pails."

A clubhouse clique, led by Stengel with pitchers Jeff

Dutch Stengel, soon to be known as Casey, in official team photo of 1913 Brooklyn Dodgers in opening season at Ebbets Field. Casey is at center and pal Zack Wheat is to the right next row.

Pfeffer and Leon Cadore, and assorted Dodgers, plotted aggravation for Robinson, smart-alecked umpires, and generally raised hell in the next few years with the Dodgers. They complained to Ebbets about low salaries, poor conditions in the new Dodger clubhouse at Ebbets Field, lousy food on the trains, and bugs in their hotel rooms. Grumble, grumble, grumble. Soon they were labeled the Grumblers and Casey Stengel was known as the King of the Grumblers. It didn't matter so much what Stengel did, it mattered that he was noticed.

Stengel had another good year in 1914 with a .316 average, slumped to his major-league low of .237 in 1915, mainly due to some mysterious ailments, and came back up to .279 in 1916 as the Dodgers won their first pennant since 1900 and their last until 1920, by which time Stengel would be gone from Ebbets Field. Dodger fans would have to wait after that one until 1941 for another pennant.

Boston beat Brooklyn four games to one in the 1916 Series. Stengel started four of the five games and batted .364 with four singles. He sat out the second game of the Series (he was starting to be platooned, playing against right-handers only) when a big Boston left-hander named Babe Ruth pitched fourteen innings and won 2–1.

Years later Stengel talked of his first Series against the Red Sox. "Ruth threw hard and had great control," remembered Casey. "He was the best in the league then in everything, pitching, hitting, hitting home runs, and making money. As for myself I didn't get to face him since I was a left-handed batter and he being a left-handed pitcher and it becoming fairly well known that I had trouble with left-handed pitchers."

Stengel batted .257 in 150 games in 1917 as the United States entered World War I. Stengel, single and twenty-seven years old, believed he might soon be drafted. If he was to play baseball in 1918 he wanted more money. He always wanted more money. Stengel had held out every season he had been a Dodger. Stengel was paid $5,400 in 1917 and after batting only .257 was sent a contract calling for a pay cut of $1,300 for the 1918 season. He was outraged. From his Kansas City home he wrote Charles Eb-

Casey Stengel of the 1917 Brooklyn Dodgers. He was a leader of the Grumblers, a group of hell-raising, beer-drinking Brooklyn players.

bets a letter. "Dear Charlie," he began. "I received the contract but know it wasn't mine when I saw the figures. You must have sent me Red Monahan's [the batboy] by mistake." Several days later he received a new contract from the Dodgers without any note. This contract called for a $1,700 pay cut. He asked Ebbets if it would be all right if he signed the one calling for a $1,300 pay cut. He did and was traded to Pittsburgh on January 9, 1918, for infielder Chuck Ward, a future Hall of Famer, spitball pitcher Burleigh Grimes, and pitcher Al Mannix along with second-baseman George Cutshaw and $20,000. Ebbets was simply fed up with fighting over salary with the King of the Grumblers.

"I knowed I shouldn't have been such a smart aleck," Stengel told Runt Marr.

Grimes would later succeed Stengel as manager of the Dodgers in 1937.

"I remember facing Casey Stengel a lot," says Grimes, a vigorous gentleman of eighty-seven, as he sits in a rocking chair at Cooperstown, New York, during a visit from his Holcombe, Wisconsin, home. "He stood at the plate with a closed stance and that big butt of his in your face."

Grimes' memory of Casey at the bat is as sharp today as it was sixty years ago.

"He was what I called a long swinger," says Grimes. "His bat came from way behind his ear to way out front. He always stood with his right foot closer than his left to the plate, sort of looking over his right shoulder at the pitcher. He would move his feet around in the box a lot. If he moved that front right foot up he was trying to get you to pitch inside so he could pull the ball. If he moved back, he was looking for an outside pitch he could slap to left field. A real smart fellow, that Stengel."

Grimes was a pretty smart fellow himself and he knew the best way to get a hitter like Stengel off stride was to throw him a change-up and foul up his stance.

"He couldn't hit a change-up," says Grimes. "I'd throw him one floater after another and he'd be way out in front. He'd pop up and you'd hear him all the way back to the bench saying, 'Why did you swing at that bad ball, Casey, why did you swing at that?' He was some comic out there."

Grimes was a rambunctious sort of fellow himself, but has mellowed with the years.

"At my age any day you get up you consider a good day," he says. "No use fussing about it. As for Casey Stengel, a funny fellow, all the time. He had a good attitude and a lot of fun. That's why you're writing about him, ain't it?"

Casey Stengel left Brooklyn with a heavy heart. He had spent more than five seasons there, loved by the fans, and loving them. It would always be sweet memories for him, his zaniness well remembered by old fans who cheered the announcement of his return as the team's manager in 1934. They would recall his hustling play on the field and his antics off the field. But on June 6, 1918, Ebbets Field would see a performance by Casey Stengel that would forever enshrine him as one of baseball's greats comics, kooks, flakes, entertainers, screwballs, eccentrics, whatever the popular term of the day might be.

The Pirates were playing their opening series of 1918 in Brooklyn. Casey Stengel was in right field for Pittsburgh and batting fifth. When the public-address announcer walked in front of the stands with his megaphone and announced Stengel's name, it was greeted with loud boos, hisses, and derisive noises of every description. Dodger players were cheered in Brooklyn, no matter what they did. Ex-Dodgers were booed unmercifully upon their return as some sort of traitors, though, of course, they had nothing to do with their exits from Flatbush. Fans increased the booing as Stengel went to right field, now remembering his failures at bat, his poor season in 1917, his vigorous contract battles, and any of a hundred imagined excuses for venting their spleen.

Stengel stood in right field in the bottom of the first inning talking to his old buddy Leon Cadore, who was in the Dodger bullpen. All of a sudden a bird crashed into the brick wall against the bullpen. Years later Stengel told this writer what happened next.

"The bird was stunned," he said. "He commenced shaking himself a little to see if his head was still on. Cadore reached over and picked him up. Cadore had those big fingers for pitching and doing card tricks and coin tricks, hiding a nickel and making a quarter come out of his hand, things like that. He picked the bird up, gave it to me, and I put it under my hat."

Not quite sure what he intended to do with the bird, Stengel just let it sit there. The bird, still stunned by the crash, sat quietly. Soon the inning ended and Stengel jogged into the Pittsburgh dugout. He was the first hitter up in the second inning. He grabbed three bats from the bat rack, began pumping them menacingly, and walked to the plate. The crowd was booing him fiercely now.

"The bird commenced wiggling and I had to get rid of it," Stengel said.

He dropped the three bats and grabbed his eye as if something were in it. Umpire Cy Rigler dutifully called time and Stengel stepped back from the plate, bent over, and lifted his cap to the crowd.

Out flew the injured sparrow, now fully recovered from the crash, as the crowd oohed and aahed and broke into laughter as the bird flew off into the aviary Hall of Fame.

Dodger manager Wilbert Robinson, a flake himself (he was once hit by a grapefruit thrown from a plane flown by famed aviatrix Ruth Law, spreading seeds all over his chubby body) was unconcerned about Stengel's antics. He knew Casey was zany, unpredictable, and impossible to be angry at.

"Well, there's no use getting excited about it all," said Robinson. "He's got birds in his garret, that's all."

Rube Marquard, Casey's former teammate, had shut the Pirates out 1–0 that day with Stengel going hitless in two at bats against the great left-hander. The *New York Times* dutifully reported the score and the ease with which Marquard had dealt with the Pirates and then said, "The contest was sort of a family reunion for it gave Brooklyn fans an opportunity to greet two of their erstwhile favorites, George Cutshaw and the ever nonchalant Casey Stengel, who grounded out and fanned against Marquard before being removed from the game."

There was no mention of the bird-in-the-hat in the *Times* story, but soon the players in the league were passing the news around the grapevine, "Did you hear what Casey did now?"

So Casey Stengel came to be remembered as the man who let a bird fly out of his hat, as much as for anything else he achieved or said or did in more than sixty-five years in baseball. There were several composite photos made later to re-create the incident and a painting of Casey and his flying bird hangs on the wall of his Glendale home.

"We thought it so typical of Casey Stengel we had it repeated at an old-timer's day game," said longtime Dodger publicist Red Patterson. "We had Casey at Dodger Stadium, got a sparrow, whirled it around a few minutes by its tail, and put it under his hat. Casey was sent up to home plate, took a deep bow, lifted his cap, and bent over. The damn bird fell to the ground with a big plop. It wasn't dead, but the whirling had made the bird dizzy and put him to sleep."

For several days there were more stories about Casey and the bird than about the play of the Dodgers and the Pirates. As he would for half a century, Casey had been able to gain center stage with one short act.

Stengel was not terribly happy in Pittsburgh. After night life in New York, he found the town dull. He was unhappy that owner Barney Dreyfuss refused to consider a raise. Without his fellow grumblers, he did most of his grumbling to himself. He continued to argue with umpires and was thrown out of a Pittsburgh game in the Polo Grounds. He was so angry he pulled his uniform shirt off his back and carried it to the center-field clubhouse over his shoulder. He was fined $50.00 for disrobing on the field. The telegram announcing the fine was pinned to his uniform shirt the next day as he took the field. He figured that would be worth a laugh. It was. It was also worth a two-hundred-dollar fine. Angry with the umpires, unhappy with the Pirates, and annoyed at a world seemingly unappreciative of his comedy, Stengel drowned his sorrows with friends in an old favorite Brooklyn bar. Like thousands of young men before him and thousands more after him, Stengel joined the navy to get away from the world. It also excused him from paying the two-hundred-dollar fine because not even the National League would be cruel enough to chase a sailor for that dough.

Stengel's brother Grant, excused from service because of his bad heel, was quick to needle his twenty-seven-year-old younger brother when informed he had joined the navy and beat the fine.

"That's real smart," Grant wrote him. "Because to keep from paying the two-hundred-dollar fine you gave up a salary of four thousand dollars a year. Now you can live on navy pay of fifteen dollars a month."

As a trainee in bell-bottom trousers, open middie blouse, and a long, flowing navy tie, Stengel was assigned to the Brooklyn navy yard. Ships were outfitted there for the journey to Europe with men and supplies. They also came back from Europe, many after being hit by torpedoes, for repairs. Stengel finished a four-week training course in naval conduct and procedures and was soon assigned to the base as a painter. It was well known among the officers that they had the famed Dodger and now Pittsburgh outfielder Casey Stengel in their midst. As often happens in the military service, an officer, running the base baseball team, asked the major leaguer to serve on it as a player and a manager.

"You do this," the officer said, "and you won't have to paint ships anymore."

"It ain't that I don't like paintin' your ships," Stengel told the lieutenant commander, "it's just that baseball is more my line of work and every man should do his own line of work if we are to win the war, got it?"

Then he winked at the officer. They clearly understood each other, and he was moved into a new, more comfortable barracks with the other athletes on the base.

"We specialized in playing those shipwreck teams," Stengel said. "Players who had been at sea for three or four months were still seasick. As soon as the ships came in, I jumped on board, got to the athletic officer, and scheduled those games at Prospect Park. I believe you could have a good record that way."

One day, while playing against one of those "ship-wrecked" teams, Stengel saw a boy on a bicycle watching the practice before the game. Stengel had $50 in his pocket and didn't want to play with it since he was afraid it would blow away as he slid. He didn't want to leave it in his pants in the locker since that wasn't safe. Just before the game started, he took the money out of his uniform pants and handed it to the kid. "Here, son, hold this for me until the game is over. I'll give you a nickel."

The game began. Stengel got a hit and ran to second base on a grounder. He slid hard, got up, dusted himself off, checked the pitcher, and looked over behind the diamond. In the distance, as far as he could see, he spotted the small, moving figure of a boy on a bike. "He was still holding my money," Stengel recalled.

The New York Times reported, "The astute police have been requested by Casey Stengel, onetime outfielder with the Brooklyn and Pittsburgh National League baseball teams, but now a toiler in a shipyard, to find the boy and the $50 which disappeared simultaneously yesterday from that part of Prospect Park where Mr. Stengel was practicing baseball. Boy and money were missing when the practice hour ended, and although Mr. Stengel has made all the traditional motions of informing the police, his expectation of ever glimpsing his cash again is exceedingly small."

"I can still see that little kid riding away on his bike with my fifty," Casey said years later.

On November 11, 1918, the war ended and Stengel was soon mustered out. He returned to Kansas City, anxious to get back to baseball, after playing in only thirty-nine games for the Pirates and hitting .246. He had learned in the navy that baseball was a damn fine life, especially for a man like himself, twenty-eight, getting better looking as he grew older, more sophisticated, a ladies' man who enjoyed the gay bachelor life, a marvelous dancer, raconteur, devotee of vaudeville and theater, a lover of life, a man with a bright future.

He returned to the Pirates in 1919 and started another

lifelong friendship, this time with a young, handsome banjo-playing first baseman by the name of Charlie Grimm.

Jolly Cholly Grimm retired from baseball in 1975 and lives in Scottsdale, Arizona. At eighty-one, his mind is clear, his eyes are sharp, and his voice is strong.

"Wow," he says, "when you talk about Casey Stengel, you talk about a guy who could stay up all night, drink you under the table, and talk more baseball than any man in history."

Grimm, a young, struggling first baseman in 1919, remembered Casey's hitting style as he tried to develop his own.

"Casey was a real good hitter," he says. "He would punch the ball anywhere it was pitched. He wasn't what you would call a power hitter but who was? In those days we were hitting a lump of coal and it wouldn't go very far."

On August 31, 1919, the Pirates decided they had had enough of Stengel's complaints about money. They traded him to Philadelphia. He immediately fired off a wire to William Baker, the Philadelphia owner. THERE'S NOT ENOUGH MONEY HERE. STOP. WILL NEED MORE TO GO OVER THERE. STENGEL. Soon a telegram came to Stengel at the Schenley Hotel in Pittsburgh where he was living. THERE'S NOT MUCH MONEY HERE, EITHER. BAKER.

Stengel fumed. He decided to go home and forget about the Phillies. He could always return to dental school. He went to the railroad station and fired off another telegram. IF THERE ISN'T ENOUGH MONEY IN PHILADELPHIA I'LL BE IN KANSAS CITY, MISSOURI. Then he boarded the next train west.

He rounded up some friends in Kansas City and organized a semipro team that barnstormed through Kansas, Oklahoma, Texas, and on into California. He made several thousand dollars on the tour but returned to the Phillies for the same $5,300 salary he was stuck with. He batted .293 in 120 games in 1920, a memorable baseball year because the former pitcher Babe Ruth played his first season as a Yankee and hit 54 home runs. The Golden Age of baseball was about to begin.

As a part-time player, Stengel was hitting .280 for the Phillies on July 26 when he was suddenly traded to the New York Giants. He was on a rubbing table with a bad back when Philadelphia manager Wild Bill Donovan said, "We've traded you to McGraw." Casey leaped off the table, jumped a foot in the air, and let out a howl. "I thought you had a bad back, dammit," said Donovan. "I don't anymore," said Stengel.

Casey Stengel was going back to New York, back to the night life and the dancing he enjoyed so much, back to the bright lights of Broadway, back to a contending team with a chance at the pennant, and back to a team led by the man many already considered the best manager in baseball, the Little Napoleon, John McGraw. No serious baseball player—and Casey was that even though his antics sometimes obscured his interests—could fail to profit from playing with McGraw.

Casey Stengel was slowing down when he reported to McGraw, thirty-one years old, losing some speed in the outfield, his arm growing weaker, his bat not as quick as it once had been, his ability to adjust to the curves of good left-handed pitching almost nil. He was hired by McGraw, who saw perfect potential in the veteran outfielder. John McGraw would use Casey Stengel sparingly, playing him against certain pitching, spotting him here and there, maximizing his declining abilities. The word had not yet come into popular use but the idea was as old as the game. John McGraw would "platoon" Stengel and neither Casey Stengel, nor John McGraw, nor any player who ever played for either of them again, would fail to understand "platooning."

5. Mr. Stengel
and Mr. McGraw

THE COUNTRY had come out of the world war and now, in the summer of 1921, every aspect of American life seemed to be flourishing. The arts and sciences were filled with bright young men. The new movie business was bursting with energy. President Warren G. Harding, a former newspaper reporter and Ohio governor, was a popular President.

In baseball Ty Cobb was being challenged as the premier hitter in the American League by teammate Harry Heilmann, who would beat Cobb out for the batting title with a .394 mark, while Cobb batted .389. The following year Cobb would hit .401 at age thirty-five and lose the batting title again to George Sisler's .420. In the National League, Rogers Hornsby would hit .397 for the league lead. These high averages were taken for granted by baseball fans. Their attention was turned away from averages to home runs. One man, George Herman Ruth, a flamboyant twenty-six-year-old from Baltimore, was hitting homers at a record pace. He had hit 54 in his first year as a Yankee and now, in 1921, he was hitting them even more frequently. The Babe would collect 59 homers to break his own record that year and lead the Yankees to their first American League pennant ever.

The Babe commanded enormous newspaper attention with his hitting and his all-pervasive personality. New York had until then been a team with one great club, the Giants, and two also-rans, the Yankees and the Brooklyn Dodgers. Now the Babe and his team were stealing the town away from the Giants. The man who served as the manager and general manager of the Giants, John J. McGraw, the feisty forty-eight-year-old from Truxton, New York, didn't like all this one damn bit. To make it worse, the Giants and Yankees shared the Polo Grounds, and McGraw did everything he could to remind them they were second-class citizens, tenants, in his ball park on the Hudson. The fans couldn't care less whose park it was. They were rushing in record numbers to see the Babe.

McGraw had been a scrappy third baseman, as well known in Baltimore, where he broke into the National League in 1891, for his tough tags as for his line drive hitting. He was a small man, some five feet seven and less than one hundred and fifty pounds in his playing days. He had fought his managers, his teammates, the opposition. He had fought umpires, the fans, and the sporting press. His nature was unsmiling, combative, and nasty. He looked at baseball as a life-or-death struggle in which only the tough survived. He was damn tough. He managed at Baltimore and then shifted over to the Giants in July of 1902, a couple of years after his Baltimore club had entered the new American League. He would bring his feisty personality and his abrasive manner to the older league.

As a manager McGraw was a tyrannical disciplinarian. He expected nothing less than complete obedience from all his players, entertaining no second-guessing from them, the fans, or the press.

"You did it his way," says Hall of Famer George (Highpockets) Kelly, who was with him ten years, "or he got you out of there real quick."

McGraw was an innovator, a gambler in a game, a manager willing to defy tradition and standard practice. He managed with extreme confidence, never fearing the wrath of his employers. They simply feared him. He studied every aspect of the game and every player in it. He picked up small things and used them freely.

"We were trailing the Pirates 3-0 in a game against Pittsburgh," Kelly says, "and we got the bases loaded and I was up. The count was 3-0 and I was sure I'd have the

John McGraw, Stengel's manager after he was traded to the New York Giants in 1921. McGraw was one of his earliest heros.

take sign. I looked over at Mr. McGraw and saw the hit sign. I almost swallowed my gum. Babe Adams, a real good one, was throwing for the Pirates. I did what Mr. McGraw said. I hit."

What he hit was a huge drive over the left-field roof, a grand slam homer and another win for McGraw's Giants.

"When I asked him about it later he said he knew Adams would give me a fastball down the middle, the automatic you know, and the rest of the time he was curving me and I couldn't hit his curve," Kelly says.

Since he called so many pitches in a game and allowed the players more time to concentrate on the act of hitting the ball while he concentrated on the thinking, players prospered under McGraw. The Giants had won six pennants when Casey Stengel joined them in 1921.

McGraw had watched Stengel closely for nine years as an opponent. He knew of his reputation as a character, a hell-raiser, a comic, a guy who could enliven a team in its darkest days with some of his antics. McGraw also understood that Stengel was a student of the game, as he himself was, that he was dedicated, that he worked hard, hustled, and was ambitious about his career. McGraw always did his homework when he reached out for a new player by asking trusted friends what they thought of the man. McGraw had played for ten years with Wilbert Robinson. They had been close friends as players and later when McGraw managed the Giants he hired his pal as a coach. They had engaged in a bitter argument resulting in McGraw's firing of Robinson, who wound up as his managerial opponent in Brooklyn, but they had always respected each other. McGraw asked Robinson about Stengel and Robinson replied, "He's a little batty but he gives everything he's got on a ball field."

McGraw saw the growing strength of the Yankees, the attention paid to Babe Ruth, and the shift in the loyalty of the fans to the Yankees. The Giants had to win in 1921 after finishing second three times in a row or risk further erosion of their strength in the city. McGraw saw in Stengel an experienced veteran player, a man who could play when necessary, a ballplayer who would not question his judgment and could help some of his younger players. It would be the kind of move Casey Stengel would make himself as a Yankee manager with such players as Enos Slaughter, Johnny Mize, and Johnny Sain thirty years later.

Casey Stengel hadn't been born old. It just always seemed that way. Even in July of 1921, shortly before he turned thirty-one, most Giants fans wondered why McGraw picked him up. Through the first four months of the 1921 season Stengel had played in only twenty-four games for the Phillies. He would play in only eighteen more for the Giants, since he was actually nursing a bad back. He finished the season with a .284 average, being spotted here and there by McGraw, being used as a pinch hitter, playing once or twice a week to rest a more important man.

When he wasn't playing, he sat next to McGraw on the bench, studied his moves, asked questions, learned the thinking of his new manager, filed away the experience, discussed it often with teammates George Kelly, Frank Frisch, and Irish Meusel. McGraw, who could be mean, brusque, and testy with his players, could be surprisingly warm and patient when a player humbly asked for the dispensing of baseball wisdom. McGraw dispensed much of it to Stengel, who, while not losing any of his public countenance as a comic, was privately considering the possibilities of remaining in the game he loved when he couldn't play anymore.

Maneuvering his players, shifting their positions, gambling on unconventional plays, McGraw, by his will and his brains, pushed the Giants past the league-leading Pittsburgh Pirates in mid-September and won the pennant going away. The Yankees won their first pennant, and the first all-New York World Series opened at the Polo Grounds on October 5, 1921, the first under Commissioner Kenesaw Mountain Landis. It shaped up as a match of competing managerial geniuses, McGraw and his Yankee counterpart, Miller Huggins. It was also the last of the nine-game World Series format. The Yankees won the first two games, lost the next two, and won the fifth for a

3–2 lead. Babe Ruth wrenched his knee in that game, also suffered from an infected arm, and could only pinch-hit in the final three games, all won by the Giants. Stengel sat on the bench for all eight games but received a full share —a tribute to the respect his teammates had for him—and showed the check for $5,265.00 to his father, saying, "I made more money sitting with the Giants than I ever made standing with anybody else."

Stengel was nearly thirty-two years old as the 1922 season began. He had lost most of his running speed. His arm was weak. He had trouble hitting left-handed pitching. What the hell did McGraw need him for anyway? To platoon him.

Stengel, a left-handed hitter, was platooned most of the year with Bill Cunningham, a stocky right-handed hitter. In 84 games, having McGraw pick his spots, Stengel batted .368, a career high while Cunningham batted .328 in 85 games. The Giants won their second straight pennant easily, by seven games, over the Cincinnati Reds.

Stengel had started as a center fielder in Brooklyn. He had been converted into a right fielder by Wilbert Robinson in 1914, and now under McGraw, he was to play a new outfield position, sun fielder. Each baseball park has a different sun field, making the art of catching a fly ball on a clear, sunny day, a treacherous act. Stengel, applying all his tricks, had learned to tilt the peak of his cap lower and bend sideways to shade the sun as he caught a ball. McGraw, in his attention to infinite detail, had noticed Casey's skill. "You're a good sun fielder and that may be the best thing you can do for me," McGraw said. More than thirty-five years later Stengel would berate himself, when Yankee left-fielder Norm Siebern, a bad sun fielder, blew a fly during the World Series in the Yankee Stadium sun field, by saying, "I shoulda know'd better than to play a blind sun fielder out there."

Stengel started two games in the Series against the Yankees in 1922, had two singles in five at bats, and was humiliated when McGraw sent Cunningham in as a pinch runner in the second inning of the second Series game, a demeaning act Stengel would repeat as a manager when he sent Dale Long up to pinch-hit for Clete Boyer in the second inning of the first World Series game in 1960.

"I was so damn mad when McGraw done that," Stengel said years later, "I couldn't see straight."

George Kelly was a .328 hitter for the Giants that year, a marvelous fielder, and a close friend of Stengel's. He is eighty-five years old, lives in Milbrae, California, and remembers the good relationship Stengel had with McGraw, despite being platooned.

"See, you have to remember we were all tickled to death playing ball in those days," Kelly says. "Casey didn't like being platooned, but he didn't fight it. Whatever McGraw said, that was the way it was."

Kelly said Casey Stengel, Frankie Frisch, and Irish Meusel, outfielder and brother of Yankee Bob Meusel, were always together.

"They all spent a lot of time talking baseball in saloons, but they were ready to go the next day. McGraw saw to it that you attended to business," says Kelly.

When the 1922 Series ended, Stengel, Kelly, and a dozen other players including Waite Hoyt, Herb Pennock, and Joe Bush of the Yankees, and Amos Strunk of the White Sox, went on a barnstorming tour of the Far East. A photo of Stengel, Kelly, and a Japanese official, taken in Tokyo, hangs in Kelly's den.

"Nobody knows who that little Japanese guy in the middle is," says Kelly. "I haven't told this story for years. We played against college teams mostly. Before we got there, the fans had rioted at one of these college games. Dozens of them poured on the field and a lot of people were hurt. Three or four were killed and the government stepped in. They ordered total silence in the ball park except for one person appointed as official rooter for each team. They would get up, cheer after each play, and sit down. Casey went through a pantomime of cheering with the guy each time he stood up. That little Japanese guy in the middle of the picture between Casey and me, that's our official rooter."

One of the brightest, warmest, most delightful men around baseball then was a handsome right-handed pitcher for the Yankees named Waite Hoyt. He was on the barnstorming trip. He had known Casey Stengel a long time.

"I was a high school kid in Brooklyn," says Hoyt, as he approaches his eightieth birthday. "I went over to pitch batting practice at Ebbets Field in 1915. Casey took one look at me, a big, hard-throwing, wild kid and said, 'I'm not going to hit against him.' George Cutshaw, a Dodger infielder, had batted against me in semipro games. He told Casey I had good control. Casey said, 'I'm crazy, but I'm not that crazy.' Then he jumped in, took a couple of swings, and jumped out. 'I ain't worrying about his speed. I just don't like facing pitchers with uniforms made by their mothers.' I was wearing an amateur uniform and it was a little baggy. Casey always kidded me about my uniform."

Hoyt was to meet Stengel's Giants in the 1922 Series.

"I was a successful pitcher with the Yankees now and I had made an advertisement for Lifebuoy Soap. It was on the billboards all over. I'm starting to pitch and all of a sudden somebody throws a bar of Lifebuoy at me on the mound. I pick it up, figure it's Stengel, and aim for him. I just missed McGraw. That quiets things down. A little while later I hear a voice saying 'My Daddy uses Lifebuoy, my Daddy uses Lifebuoy.' I looked over and saw it was Casey. All you could do was laugh."

Hoyt says the trip to the Far East was organized by Herb Hunter, an old player, who picked Stengel as a last minute fill-in.

"Hunter was sort of a dandy and always wore a posy in his lapel," Hoyt says. "Casey didn't have much clothing with him as we all boarded the *Empress of Canada,* out of Vancouver. This was an elegant trip on an elegant ship. Casey was wearing a sporty cap on his head. Hunter kept staring at the thing. He thought it wasn't dressy enough. As we were leaving and Casey wasn't looking at him, Hunter grabbed that cap off Casey's head and threw it out of a porthole."

Several days later a formal dance was held in the ballroom. The *Empress of Canada* was a British ship and formal dances were splendid occasions.

"There was an elevator you had to take from the top deck down to the ballroom," recalls Hoyt. "George Kelly stood by this elevator and in a very British accent yells, 'I say there, Mr. Stengel, old chap, are you coming up the lift?' Just then Casey appears in the elevator shaft wearing a tweed suit, a British monocle in his eye, and carrying a cane. Everyone was in hysterics except the British. They didn't think it was funny at all."

The ship sailed on and reached Japan. The team played some twenty games in the Orient and gathered together for a farewell banquet with officials of the American Embassy and the American business community.

"We had this newspaper man, Buck O'Neill, with us on the trip, a real pain in the ass," says Hoyt. "He was writing about what we thought about Japanese customs all the time instead of writing about the ball games. At the farewell banquet he makes a speech about what a wonderful country Japan was, how marvelous their wrestlers and baseball players were, how Japan was improving as a culture, while the United States wasn't. We knew the reporters there would make a big deal of this and everybody would be annoyed back home. Then Casey got up."

As always, the great linguist from Kansas City was turned on by the crowd and immediately began a forty-five minute speech that kept his audience howling. He told stories about his early days as a schoolboy in Kansas City, about playing for the Brooklyn Dodgers, about experiences with McGraw. He had one final act.

"He began reciting a poem called 'Outhouse on the Farm,' " says Hoyt. "It was so hilarious people were literally falling off their chairs with laughter. I can't remember hearing anything as funny with those incredible rhymes and descriptions of what happens in this outhouse on the farm. Casey saved the day. Everybody had forgotten what O'Neill had said and everybody left the banquet laughing."

Casey Stengel returned home to Kansas City with a new addition for the Stengel family. He brought a chow dog home by the name of Ah Ming. Casey's father used to take Ah Ming downtown by streetcar and when people asked, "What is that, mister?" Louis Stengel would say, "That's a baby lion."

In the spring of 1923, knowing his playing days were nearing an end, Stengel's ears perked up and his face brightened when McGraw came to him and said, "I'm taking an interest in you. Would you like to be a coach on this club in later days?" McGraw had recognized Stengel's dedication to the game. He understood that under that rubbery face and floppy ears lay a great baseball brain. McGraw was also a terribly vain man who was anxious to anoint players with his wisdom. He was childless, and in some deep, psychological way, he wanted his wisdom and his words passed on to succeeding baseball generations. In effect, he chose a thirty-two-year-old bachelor named Casey Stengel, single-minded about baseball, to be his conduit to the future. McGraw was too crusty to be fatherly and Stengel was already too old to be considered anyone's "boy," but the rapport was there all the same. Stengel would always consider himself McGraw's player in later years, often invoking the name of his Giants manager as one does of any teacher or master. It would be an experience that in so many ways would be repeated many years later when Casey Stengel, manager of the New York Yankees, aged and crusty now, would develop an incredible closeness with an aggressive, hard-driving pugnacious character, much like the young McGraw, the young Cobb, and the young Stengel, named Billy Martin. So when McGraw chose Stengel from among his veterans to lead a second team that spring, it was with much forethought.

Stengel responded that he would indeed like to coach (how quietly is a career born) and was soon leading the Giants B squad in spring training camp at San Antonio, Texas. The Giants would win again in 1923, Stengel would bat .339 in seventy-five games as a platooned player with Bill Cunningham, and the World Series against the Yankees was scheduled to open October 10.

It would be the first World Series in the new Yankee Stadium across the river from the Polo Grounds in the

Bronx. Stengel, who had injured his heel when he leaped against the fence in Chicago and landed on a concrete base, was not expected to see much action. Hoyt was the starting pitcher in the first game and McGraw, always wily, surprised Stengel and his entire club, by playing the veteran left-handed hitting outfielder against the fireballing Yankee. McGraw took one look at the short right-field wall and wanted left-handed hitters in the lineup in Yankee Stadium.

As it turned out, Hoyt didn't have good stuff and was replaced by veteran Joe Bush in the third inning. Stengel was up against Bush in the top of the ninth with the score tied at 4–4. Bush threw a change-up and Stengel smashed it on a line into left center field.

"I didn't think it was hit too hard," recalls veteran sportswriter Fred Lieb, still active as a journalist at ninety-one. "It looked to me like a routine single."

Stengel had an uncanny ability to slice balls along the line in left, so left fielder Bob Meusel was pulled over near the foul line. Center-fielder Whitey Witt was pulled over toward right center, anticipating that Stengel might try and pull a ball to right for a home run over the short wall. The ball had enough to get through the spread outfielders and crashed on a couple of bounces against the bleachers some four hundred fifty feet from home plate. Witt finally overtook the ball and fired it to Meusel in deep left field. Meusel, with the best arm on the club, fired a strike to shortstop Everett Scott, stationed in short left behind the infield grass for the relay. Stengel had run hard around first, charged past second, and, sizing up the possibility, raced around third at full speed.

"You could hear him yelling, 'Go, Casey, go, go, Casey, go' above the noise of the crowd," says Jumpin' Joe Dugan, the Yankee third baseman that day and now a regular visitor to the Fenway Park press box in Boston. "It was the damndest thing."

So Casey went, around and around, until the shoe, padded to soften the impact of his sore heel, began to give out, forcing him to stumble the last twenty feet, sliding hard with the game-winning run, completely spent.

Damon Runyon, who would go on to create many immortal Broadway characters, was a sportswriter who wrote that day, "This is the way old Casey Stengel ran yesterday afternoon running his home run home to a Giant victory by the score of 5 to 4 in the first game of the World Series of 1923. This is the way old Casey Stengel ran running his home run home when two were out in the ninth inning and the score was tied, and the ball still bounding inside the Yankee yard.

"This is the way—

"His mouth wide open.

"His warped old legs bending beneath him at every stride. His arms flying back and forth like those of a man swimming with a crawl stroke.

"His flanks heaving, his breath whistling, his head far back, Yankee infielders, passed by old Casey Stengel as he was running his home run home, say Casey was muttering to himself, adjuring himself to greater speed as a jockey mutters to his horse in a race, saying, 'Go on, Casey, go on.'

"The warped old legs, twisted and bent by many a year of baseball campaigning, just barely held out under Casey until he reached the plate, running his home run home.

"Then they collapsed."

Stengel was the toast of the town. The Runyon column had made him a big hero, almost as big as the Babe in a completely different way. At thirty-three years of age, with tired legs and floppy ears, old Casey Stengel showed there was still some life in the old guy and every old guy reveled in it.

Two days later he faced Sad Sam Jones in a scoreless game. The Yankee bench began riding him unmercifully, deriding him for his theatrics before, during, and after his home run, making fun of his ears, needling him about his advancing years, driving him to white heat with anger. Jones threw another change-up—that was the book on Stengel—and he pulled it hard over the wall in right for a homer in the seventh inning to win a 1–0 game for the Giants. He went into his home run trot and as he neared third, making out as if a fly were at the end of his nose, he began flicking it with his thumb at the Yankee bench. Everybody got the message, including Judge Landis, the new, stern commissioner of baseball. He fined Stengel $50 for such degrading conduct and refused a request by Yankee owner Jacob Ruppert for a stiffer fine for insulting his team. "Well," said Landis, "Casey Stengel can't help being Casey Stengel."

Stengel returned home to Kansas City a big man. "Even my father made a big fuss over me," he recalled. "He told me he used to stand by the window in the *Kansas City Star* and look at the news bulletins. 'See what my boy did, see what my boy did.' I think he was glad he let me play baseball."

"We used to sit around town in a couple of saloons," says Runt Marr, "and talk about that a lot. A lot of guys would hang around him and beg him to show them how he did it. He'd get a couple of beers in him and he would pantomime the whole play ending up on the floor sliding home in some dirty old saloon."

It has always been traditional in baseball—then and now—that instant baseball fame came from a great World Series play. The eyes of the public were always on the Series by press, radio, and later by television. Casey Stengel came into the Series a well-known player. He came out of it a famous player.

Some of the joy of the event was taken away from Stengel when he was traded by McGraw, ever the cutthroat pragmatist, to Boston on November 13. He went to the Braves along with teammates Dave Bancroft and his platoon partner (the Braves were getting one center fielder for the price of two) Bill Cunningham for Billy Southworth and Joe Oeschger.

Casey would actually get more playing time in Boston in 1924 with a .280 average in 131 games. He would play another dozen games with the Braves in 1925 before accepting a managerial and front-office job in the Boston organization with their Worcester team.

In managerial skills, Casey Stengel was a direct descendent of John McGraw. When Casey evaluated McGraw in later years he said, "He wanted you to be a fighter at the plate and not just give in to the pitcher, whatever happened. Stand in there, don't back off an inch, and get a piece of the ball. Something may happen.

"He also was very alert on when to start the runners, when to start double steals, and he was very good at not having you caught off a base. He hated to see you walk off sluggishly. He said the first two steps off a base, if the batter hits the ball, might make you be safe at third or safe at home plate.

"But after the lively ball came in he knew he had to cut down on the base running and go to slugging. He was the best manager I ever saw at adapting from the dead ball to the lively ball. At the plate he'd let you go for the slug on three and nothing, two and nothing, three and one if there were men on bases. If there weren't men on bases, he'd get very disturbed at you if you didn't stand up there and fight the pitcher, especially with two strikes. One day I took a called third strike—the man curved the ball and I was asleep at the plate. 'Why weren't you ready up there to fight on that pitch and get a piece of it before it got to the catcher's glove?' And I said, 'Well I thought . . .' And he said, 'Don't think for me. Act.' If you got three or four runs ahead of him at the start of a game that would drive him crazy, because then all he could do was try and catch up. He couldn't maneuver as much. John McGraw was one of the three best managers in all the years I played in the National League—him and Frank Chance of the Cubs and Fred Clarke of Pittsburgh. I learned more from McGraw than anybody."

He had completed fourteen seasons in the major leagues, batted .284, had sixty major-league homers, collected 1,219 hits, stolen 131 bases. He had been a regular most of the time and certainly was a better than average player in his era. He would not have qualified as a Hall of Famer on his playing record alone. But there was so much more to come after he moved from Boston to Worcester in 1925, a managerial career of some note and a long full life yet, as a linguist, entertainer, salesman, actor, and bon vivant.

Stengel took the trade to Boston calmly as he had taken

every other trade. The end was coming, but for once he felt there might be something even more important than his batting average.

Casey Stengel had fallen in love.

On November 18, 1923, from Kansas City, Missouri, he wrote a letter to Glendale, California, addressed to a girl he had met in August. Her name was Edna Lawson.

"I am now a member of the Boston Braves," he wrote. "I hope you will see fit to take your vacation in the East this year. Boston is a fine town with a wonderful river. I am looking forward very much to seeing you. I remain, your faithful friend . . ."

And the signature read: Charles "Casey" Stengel. Edna Lawson would be getting letters and postcards from Charles "Casey" Stengel for the next fifty years.

6. Wooed and Won

THE HOUSE ON CUMBERLAND AVENUE in Glendale is one of the most beautiful in town, with sprawling gardens, manicured lawns, and a huge driveway with two separate entrances. The master of the house, John Maximilian Lawson, banker, real estate developer, former mayor of Glendale, distinguished citizen, is the youngest of the four children of John William Lawson and Margaret Foruilly. The elder Lawson was born in Canada, raised in upper New York State, and moved to Menominee, Michigan, before the turn of the century. He made money in the logging business and moved west to California to expand his investments. There were four Lawson children, Mae, Edna, Larry, and baby John.

"I was spoiled, I know that," says John Lawson, as he sits on a couch in the den of his magnificent home. "There was nine years between me and Edna."

Edna Lawson was born August 31, 1895, in Menominee. She was a spirited young girl with shiny brown eyes, long, whispy, dark hair, and a strong interest in sports, with swimming, basketball, and tennis her main interests. She was always good in school with a special verve in arithmetic.

"We knew she would do something with figures," says John Lawson. "She liked that stuff and was able to stick with a problem until she got it."

The oldest of the Lawson children, Mae, was the better looking of the two girls, while Edna was the neater dresser, very careful about her appearance, slower to anger, a favorite of her mother in many ways.

"Edna was a very solid personality," says John Lawson. "She was the stabilizer of the family, very mature as a young girl and very secure in her own self. In some ways, she seemed more mature than her older sister."

In 1914, the elder Lawson suffered severe business reverses in the general business malaise in the country. He moved his family from Michigan to California that year and entered the real estate and building business. Edna finished school at Glendale High and, being a tall, willowy brunette, went into the movie business as an extra.

"The picture business actually started here in Glendale," says Lawson. "They opened up a couple of studios and began making silent movies, westerns mostly, and a lot of people in town played bit parts in them. Tom Mix was making a movie and he needed some people for one of those old blockhouse scenes and somebody ran up to Edna on the street and asked her to work in the picture for twenty-five dollars. She said, 'Why not?' and was an extra in that picture and about five or six others. Glendale was a prissy town then, everything close to the vest, very conservative, and getting into a picture like that was pretty exciting for a girl just out of high school like Edna. I remember going down there to watch them and it was funny seeing all those fellows walking around town wearing leather cowboy suits in that hot weather."

Edna never caught the movie bug and quickly ended her career as an extra. She took an office job, switched to another, and in 1920 went to work for the county of Los Angeles in the Hall of Records. She taught herself accounting and bookkeeping procedures, wrote clear letters, and was a faithful employee for a man named Howard Byron, who moved on later to become treasurer and tax collector in Los Angeles. It was a steady job, fairly interesting, important, and well-paying.

"Edna didn't go out all that much," says John Lawson. "She had a few boyfriends here and there but nothing real serious. She was very devoted to my mother and they spent a lot of time together around the house and in town when Edna was off from work. In those days it took a long time to get anywhere, so when she was off somewhere with my mother, that was about all the time there was between workdays."

Each summer Edna would take a two-week vacation and travel to visit family and friends in different parts of the country. One year she traveled back to Menominee, Michigan, where the Lawsons had a great many family members, and met Van Meusel, wife of Irish Meusel, an outfielder with the New York Giants. They became good friends, writing back and forth, seeing each other every summer, spending a great deal of time together.

"Van kept asking Edna to come east and visit her in New York during the baseball season," says John Lawson.

In the summer of 1923 Edna planned a vacation with friends in Portland, Oregon. It was a part of the country Edna had never seen and there were also some Lawsons living there. In early June, Edna received a letter from Van reminding her that the two girls had talked of spending some time together in New York.

"This might be Irish's last year with the New York Giants and the last time we can get together to see the Broadway shows and the night spots and major-league baseball," Van Meusel wrote. "Won't you please come east?"

Edna decided she would. She canceled the Oregon vacation. She borrowed a trunk from a co-worker at the Hall of Records, filled it with summer dresses, and headed east on the Union Pacific train out of Los Angeles.

Edna first went to Philadelphia where she was met by Van Meusel and another friend by the name of Ethel Chambers. The Giants were on a long road trip so Edna, Van, and Ethel went to the Chambers' summer place in Atlantic City, New Jersey, where Edna swam, walked on the beach, and devoured ice cream. "She loved sweets," says John Lawson. "She ate tons of candy but never seemed to put on a pound."

One day the name of Casey Stengel came up. Van Meusel, a leading matchmaker among the Giants, brought it up. She told Edna Casey Stengel was a handsome bachelor, a wonderful dancer, and a party fellow. "Van also told me he was a free spender and would make me laugh,"

Edna recalled with a smile years later.

The Giants opened a series at home and Edna went to the Polo Grounds with Van Meusel. She sat alongside the Giants dugout with Van and several other Giants wives. They were just behind the first dugout box occupied by Mrs. John J. McGraw, who faithfully kept score of the game. Edna didn't know much about baseball, but she was told to keep her eye on the fellow in center field, Casey Stengel.

"I didn't know enough about baseball to know where center field was, but I saw somebody out there between two other fellows, so I figured that must be center field," Edna said.

Once the game had ended and they had been introduced, Casey asked Edna if he could walk with her back to the Meusel apartment and offered to take the Meusels and Edna out to dinner and dancing.

"I can't tonight," said Edna. "I have a date."

"How about tomorrow night?" said Casey.

"That would be fine," she said.

Edna had been in New York only a couple of days at the time but had gone out for two straight nights with a young doctor from Brooklyn. This was to be the third night. There would never be a fourth.

"Edna had this handsome Jewish doctor from Brooklyn," Casey said years later, "and I swept her off her feet so the doctor never married anybody and went on to do some splendid operations while he was waiting for me and Edna to split up, but he's still waiting and I don't know how good his operations are anymore and why would you go to him if he couldn't concentrate on his work."

"The Jewish doctor was just a date, nothing serious," Edna said years later. "Casey always made it out to be more than it was because he wanted people to think he swept me off my feet and stole me away from somebody else. You know Casey, it has to be a good story or it wasn't worth telling."

(All attempts by this writer to find the Jewish doctor and verify the story were to no avail, since family members could not recall the doctor's name and Jewish doctors in

Brooklyn are as numerous as sand on the beach.)

The next night Edna and Casey went to dinner and then dancing, and the Jewish doctor was out of the picture forever. The following night a similar schedule was followed. For seven nights Edna and Casey ate dinner after the game, went dancing, went to a movie ("He held my hand for the first time," said Edna), talked about Casey's baseball trips, and made plans to meet again a week later in Chicago. The Giants were on the road there and Edna was staying with some family friends. This time Edna and Casey, without his teammates and their wives around, were able to get to know each other a little better. Two weeks after he met Edna, Casey Stengel, a thirty-three-year-old bachelor, asked Edna to marry him.

"I told him he was very nice, but I didn't know him all that well. I had to talk it over with my folks and I wasn't sure I wanted to get married right now," Edna said.

Casey, a gay blade, had never really had a serious romance before, and Edna, almost twenty-eight, never had a steady boyfriend. Casey was certain this was it, Edna knew she had to wait. Edna went back home to California without a promise. Casey sent letters and flowers. Edna sent him a shirt for Christmas. Casey sent her a gold pen.

During his playing days in Brooklyn and again with the New York Giants, Casey had many girl friends, but none that could take him away from total dedication to baseball. He had dated some Broadway showgirls, attended many happy parties with his teammates, was forever being fixed up by the wives of teammates as one of the outstanding bachelors in New York. They would always be flings, one-night stands, nothing that would sway Stengel from concentrating on improving his game on the field. He had been close to his mother, a gentle, soft-spoken, warm woman, and seemed to be seeking, without success, a similar woman as a wife. He could be abrasive, loud, profane, and argumentative on the field, but he was always cordial, respectful, and gentle with women. He took great care with his personal wardrobe, he was vain, he was always concerned about his appearance and enjoyed being admired by some attractive ladies.

"You'd see a lot of them around the park and why wouldn't ya if you was with the Giants," he said years later. "They all wanted to get to meet ya and we'd be in the hotels and they would be around the lobby and hope somebody might introduce them. But when you had McGraw for a manager—as strict as he was—there wasn't what you call a lot of free time for chasin' them what with McGraw sending the coaches up to check your rooms."

There was even one time when McGraw decided that some of his players were sneaking out of their hotel rooms at night and hired detectives to trail the players and report to him.

"It made me so damn mad when I found out he had three or four detectives chasing three or four of the players all over town and I didn't have a detective of my own," Stengel said.

Most of his teammates simply assumed that he was a confirmed bachelor and likely to remain so, a man so dedicated to baseball that there was little room in his life for anybody else. It may have stayed that way had he not met the lovely lady from Glendale.

Edna found Casey amusing, entertaining, a marvelous storyteller, a successful, famous young man. She was attracted by his honesty, his directness, his utter confidence in himself and in the future success of their relationship together. "He was kind, he was thoughtful, he was loving," Edna said years later, "and he was extremely considerate of my feelings on all matters."

"He came back to Kansas City that winter," recalls Runt Marr, "and talked about that beautiful girl he met in New York. He said he was getting married soon and would probably move away from Kansas City if he did. 'I guess I'm old enough, ain't I?' I told him I thought he was, what with his major-league career going downhill now."

Stengel was traded to the Braves that fall, wrote Edna letters about the cultural benefits of Boston, asked her to commit herself to him, and asked for the address of Edna's brother, Larry, a career army officer, now stationed in Belleville, Illinois, outside of St. Louis. He wrote Larry Lawson that he would like to visit him on Boston's first trip there in 1924. Lawson agreed and Casey took Edna's brother and his wife to the Chase Hotel in St. Louis for a marvelous dinner. It would help turn the tide for Casey in winning Edna's hand.

Years later the Chase Hotel, huge, ornate, and charming, would always be a favorite for Stengel. When he managed the Mets, the team stayed there. After a dinner in the Tenderloin Room, Casey and the writers—"My writers," he always called them—walked to the hotel lounge one night. Robert Goulet was the featured entertainer and when he saw Stengel, he stopped in the middle of a song, bowed, and introduced him as "one of my great heroes, one of the world's great heroes." Stengel, his eyes twinkling and his mouth squeezed together in a cute, embarrassed smile, looked at the handsome, dashing singer and said, "He has effeminate appeal, just like me," and sat down. He was seventy-four years old that summer. Then he drank with his writers until 5 A.M. in the Merry-Go-Round bar off the main lobby. "I'm dead at the present time," I told him as I took leave of him at the elevator. "I'll be down for breakfast at seven. C'mon down and I'll give you a story," he said. He was down at seven, according to the bell clerk and a waiter I checked with. I slept until 4 P.M. He was forty-two years older than I was that summer.

After the dinner at the Chase with the Larry Lawsons, Edna's brother wrote her that she should come visit him this summer and see that Stengel fellow again. "He is very charming and would make a good catch," Larry Lawson wrote.

Edna came back east in August, settled in at her brother's home, spent a good deal of time with Casey again when the Braves came west, and finally accepted his proposal.

Edna Lawson and Charles Dillon Stengel were married on August 18, 1924, in the parlor of Bishop Henry Althoff of St. Louis by Father Louis Ell, a Catholic priest, in a small Catholic ceremony witnessed only by Edna's brother and his wife. The newlyweds drove back to the Lawson residence and proceeded to send telegrams to their families. Several workers in the city hall had spotted Stengel, and the local reporter, quickly alerted, phoned the information to the Associated Press. It was on the news wires before any of family members had heard about it, a fact that disturbed the elder Stengel a great deal.

"That was a great love affair from the first day to the last," says John Lawson. "I don't think I have ever seen or heard of two people being closer."

Casey could be crusty, sarcastic, mean at times, but never with Edna. He was always courtly with her, a perfect gentleman, respectful, a sixteenth-century knight who would do everything except throw his jacket in a puddle to make her comfortable. He was always considerate of her feelings, kind and loving toward her in his worst times. Their affectionate glances and soft pats on each other's hands and face were sometimes embarrassing to outsiders. Since they were never to have any children, their devotion to each other was total. There were no rivals for their love and affection. She needed him and he needed her. He would make no decision without her. They would be as close as two people could get, their warmth and love for each other building each day of the more than fifty years they were married.

Mr. and Mrs. Charles Dillon Stengel—she always called him Casey and he always called her Edna—dined on the roof of the Chase Hotel that evening of August 18, took a midnight train, and arrived in Chicago the next morning for a series with the Cubs.

Edna went on to Pittsburgh with Casey and then on to New York for the first time as a married woman. They moved into Casey's old apartment at the St. George Hotel in Brooklyn and commuted by subway for the games against the Giants. When the season ended, Edna and Casey went to England, where Casey was playing in a barnstorming trip. The players were lined up one day in a field in London. King George V came over to shake hands with the American baseball players. "Nice to meet ya, King," said Casey Stengel.

"When they played before the king and queen I wasn't

Stengel meets King George V or vice versa. The King is the one in the hat in 1924 barnstorming trip photo.

too impressed," said Edna. "I wound up having tea with Queen Mary, but if there had been any better place to go I'd probably have gone there instead."

The European trip ended, the Stengels spent a week with Blanche and John McGraw in their Westchester home and then took a train to Kansas City where Edna met Stengel's father, mother, sister, and brother. From there, it was on to Glendale, California, where they decided to make their home.

"We had heard a lot about him, a famous ballplayer like that," says Jack Lawson, "but of course we had never met him. So when Edna wrote us that they were coming in on the train from Kansas City we all went down to the Union Pacific Station. I was a college kid then and there were my parents and sister Mae and her two children at the station. I remember seeing Casey get off the train and walk toward us with Edna and I guess what I remember most was the big hat he was wearing, that wide brim just about covering up his face. And he had on a big coat, one of the heavy, floor-length things they wore in those days and he walked sort of funny, bowlegged you know. But he seemed friendly, smiled and greeted us all so warmly."

Casey and Edna stayed with Edna's parents while their new house on Grandview was being completed. They moved into it that winter and lived in that home the rest of their lives. Casey busied himself each year with baseball; Edna would go back east for most of the season but both of them maintained separate interests through the years.

"Edna became very involved in the family business," says Jack Lawson. "We built houses and apartments and Edna was very good watching over the business end. She was not afraid to raise the rents and we had this one building with twenty-seven apartments and she took care of it all. She was a terrific business woman. Whenever we had any troubles with the Internal Revenue Service— everybody in business does—we sent her down and she took care of all the paper work and got things straightened out."

During the winters there would be dinner in their home or at the home of friends, or nights out at the Robin Hood or Damon's Steak House in Glendale. Casey would swim regularly in the pool out back, work out in the rose garden, or hit a tennis ball on the courts behind the house with friends and neighbors.

"Edna was really the spark plug of the entire Lawson family," says Jack Lawson. "She was a very strong woman, handled the family books, made sure everything was attended to. She ran their household, Casey and hers, handled all the business and saw he was taken care of."

Life was smooth, pleasant, and busy through the years. There seemed to be only one thing missing in the marriage: children. The Stengels never had any children of their own, though neighbor children, nieces, and nephews were always in attendance.

"I used to spend all my summers there because of the swimming pool," remembers young John Lawson, Edna's nephew and John (called Jack by the family) Lawson's son. He is forty years old and runs the family business now. "When Casey was away for the baseball season I would watch the house. My friends would come over and we'd swim and play tennis. In the winter we would come over and talk with Uncle Casey about the season. One time I was with my friend, Pete Lewi—he's a big lawyer out here now and the son of Charlotte Armstrong, the mystery writer—and he was playing the tuba. I was playing the trumpet and it was more noise than music. Casey would sit around and listen and say, 'You kids play real good. Now I'm gonna take a nap and listen in my sleep.' "

John Lawson saw Casey in some of his bad moods. "If he was sleeping and we came in and woke him up he would yell at us. He would scream but get over it fast. I think the angriest I ever saw him was when he was walking downstairs one time and the banister broke and he fell and hurt himself badly. He was very, very upset over that. He also didn't like the lights on upstairs when he was sleeping. One time, after we had left every light on in the house, he got up, unscrewed the bulbs, and hid them all away. Then he went back to sleep."

Why no children of their own?

"I think they simply never wanted any," says Jack Lawson. "Casey was a little old [*was* he born old?] when they got married and in those days it was considered dangerous to have children after thirty. Edna was also getting up there in age when they married [29] and I think they felt they didn't need children. Maybe Casey was too great a man, too busy with other things. They did so much, traveled so much, met so many people, they probably figured children would change all that and they didn't want to get involved with them. Casey traveled all summer with the team and was away a good deal in the winter with banquets and dinners and such, and children had no place. I never heard them discuss it and as far as I know, they never seemed to miss having children."

John Lawson, Edna's favorite nephew, says that Casey and Edna were warm and wonderful to him and his two sisters and Mae's three children.

"I don't know anything about their desires for children," he says. "It just never came up. That wasn't something you brought up with an aunt or an uncle like Casey.

I agree with my father that I don't think they ever wanted children. The only thing I know about the subject is that one time I was in the house and discovered contraceptives sitting on a dresser in their bedroom. I can't remember how old I was at the time, probably a teen-ager because I knew what they were, but Casey had to be in his sixties by then, so they were still sexually active even though they were concerned about not having any children."

The Lawson family situation changed dramatically in 1932 after a serious auto accident.

"It was the year of the Olympics in Los Angeles and we were all interested in it during that summer. My mother was not interested and she decided to take a trip up to Reno where she could visit her brother," says Jack Lawson. "He was a miner up there and they were in this big, black Packard along one of the narrow highways and they had a head-on collision. My mother's brother, Hank, was killed instantly and my mother was almost killed. She was in a hospital for months. She was a paraplegic when she came out and had to be carried everywhere. She had no control of her bowels and had to be attended to the rest of her life. Edna went up to Reno, stayed with her all the time, and finally brought her back to Glendale. She piled pillows up in the back seat of the car to get my mother comfortable and drove all the way back to Glendale by herself."

Jack Lawson speaks of his sister with much admiration. "She kept the family together then," says Lawson. "Edna got my father to build an addition on the house and my mother and father moved in with Casey and Edna. My dad was a successful builder and developer after he came out here, lost all his money in '29, began coming back around the time of the accident, 1932. He ran his business affairs and Edna ran the part of the business in my mother's name. There were a lot of family responsibilities after the accident and Edna handled all of it. She was a wonderful daughter. My mother died in 1944 and my father died in 1945. Edna took care of both of them until their final days."

After Casey became the manager of the Yankees in

1949, Edna and Casey lived every summer for the next twelve years in the Essex House across from Central Park in Manhattan.

"I spent a few summers up there with them," says John Lawson. "We would eat most of our meals out and that was exciting. I'd answer the phone in the apartment and it would be Dan Topping or Del Webb or George Weiss or some famous newspaper man. Just talking to those people was thrilling. Sometimes I would have to tell them Casey couldn't talk because he was doing his exercises, push-ups and sit-ups, on the floor of the hotel, and he had to call them back later. We would be ready to go to dinner and Edna would say, 'Let's go, darling.' Casey would be talking to me or to someone on the phone and ask Edna for a drink. She would fix him a triple Old-Fashioned and then we would all go down. I went to a lot of the games with Casey and once in a while I'd go on one of those shopping sprees with Edna, but I wasn't much interested in that."

John Lawson says he made several road trips with the Yankees. Washington was his favorite city. "The Yankees stayed in the Shoreham Hotel in Washington with this gigantic swimming pool. That was great fun. After a game I would be invited out by a couple of the players to join them at the bar. That was pretty thrilling. I remember that the players would see him in the hotel lobby and they'd say, 'Good evening, Mr. Stengel, how are you Mr. Stengel.' I didn't hear many of them call him Casey. It was all very respectful, like they were a little afraid of him."

In 1957, Jack Lawson and some friends got together to organize a new bank called the Glendale Valley National Bank. They collected one million dollars from investors to underwrite building projects in town. During the organization of the backers, Paul Burkhardt, a friend of Jack's, asked Lawson, "Why don't you put Casey on the board?" Lawson approached his brother-in-law, who checked with his bookkeeper Edna, and soon Casey Stengel, after paying $50,000 into the pot, was a member of the board of directors of the bank.

"I think that was a stroke of genius," says Lawson. "I

think we became the best-known little bank in the country because of Casey."

In 1933, Casey had written a will leaving part of his money to Edna, part to Edna's nieces and nephews (more evidence that they planned no children), and part to his own parents, brother, and sister. The will was never changed throughout his lifetime and all Stengel family heirs were deceased at the time of Casey's death. Upon Edna's death, the estate went to Edna's nieces and nephews.

"It's all in probate and a matter of record," says John Lawson, who handles the family finances now. "Casey left eight hundred seven thousand dollars in his estate and Edna left something over two and a half million dollars. Edna also had some personal property that was worth more than eight hundred thousand dollars. The entire estate will probably come close to four million dollars when it's probated and the heirs will share less than a million and a half after the government gets finished eating into it."

There was also another strange financial find when Casey died.

"We began checking through the home after Casey died," says John, "and we found thirty-five thousand dollars in cash. There was money in envelopes all over the house, five thousand dollars in a drawer here, ten thousand in a closet there, five thousand of it stuffed in a suitcase, more in the fireplace, and some of it even stuffed into pockets of his old clothes. Casey was a banker, but he didn't trust banks all that much. He just loved the feel of cash and always managed to have a lot around. As he became older and got ill, I think he forgot what he did with his money and I guess that's how so much of it accumulated."

Edna and Casey Stengel lived and loved for more than fifty years together, surviving the rigors of managerial defeats and the joys of victory, meshing as a perfectly balanced couple.

"It was not easy in the baseball business, but they learned to tolerate and appreciate each other," says Jack

Lawson, "as well as love each other. I don't think it would have been the same with children."

Casey Stengel came alone to spring training for the first time in fifty years at the Mets training base in 1974. He was asked how Edna, who had suffered a stroke, was faring. "She's no good from here up," he said, as he moved his hand upward from his neck. "She went crazy on me overnight." Then he turned away from this writer, his eyes filling with tears, his voice thin and weak, the fight and the fire burning out of him after a lifetime of togetherness. "I don't like comin' here without Edna," he said. "I miss her and why wouldn't ya after your whole life."

7. Why Wouldn't You Give It a Try?

IN THE SPRING OF 1925, approaching his thirty-fifth birthday, Casey Stengel knew the end of his playing career was near. "I don't think I can cut the mustard," he told his new bride. He had labored through the 1924 season with the Braves. He had batted a creditable .280 in 131 games, but his legs ached constantly, his knees were sore, and his back seemed forever to be going out of wack. "I felt that year like I was carrying a ten-pound sack of potatoes on my back," Stengel said later. He worked hard at the Boston spring training camp in St. Petersburg, was solicitous of Edna's adjustment as a baseball wife with endless boring hours alone in the stands as he took extra batting practice, and entertained her in the resort town's best restaurants, some of which he would still be frequenting forty years later.

The 1925 National League season opened quietly with John McGraw's Giants favored to win their fifth straight pennant. In the American League, all of the attention focused again on Babe Ruth. This time it was different. Ruth had collapsed in spring training (sportswriters covering the Yankees decided to make up a story for public consumption about overindulgence in hot dogs and soda pop, while they knew it was an overindulgence in sex and a social disease that knocked the Babe out) and his condition was baseball's biggest story that spring.

By early May, used only as a pinch hitter, Stengel had one single in thirteen at bats. The evidence was clear: Casey Stengel was through as a major-league player. Judge Emil Fuchs, who owned the Boston club, recognized something besides declining playing ability in Stengel. He saw that the veteran outfielder was one of the smartest baseball players around. He knew that Stengel understood the game on the field and understood its finances and business structure off the field. He was an exciting performer, well liked by the fans, dramatic, colorful, and dedicated. He would often rage at umpires, get heaved out of games, pay stiff fines, but always come back as enthusiastic and dedicated to winning as before. He was, in his upbeat personality, almost indestructible. There was no game he thought he couldn't win, no score too difficult to change, no life more wonderful than that of pulling on those colored socks, that knitted uniform, and that tight cap and playing the grand old game. He no longer was young enough to play it well, but he was certainly smart enough to teach it well. He had helped his younger teammates at Boston, and Judge Fuchs thought he would always be able to lead and instruct.

Fuchs called his veteran outfielder into his office. Stengel, fearing that this would be his release, was braced for the worst.

"How would you like to run our new farm club for us?" Fuchs asked. Fuchs quickly explained that the Boston club had purchased a new franchise in Worcester, Massachusetts. Fuchs wanted Stengel to run the club as team president, act as general manager, and play as much outfield as his aching legs could handle.

"Why wouldn't you give it a try?" Stengel said years later. "I wasn't doing much in the big league and I figured I could still play in the small league and run it, too."

Ever since his first days as a professional player, Stengel seemed a perfect managerial candidate. He studied the game. He was dedicated. He was always learning, absorbing, filing information. He had confidence in himself. He was unafraid to gamble on a ball field, to argue for his beliefs. He had gained a great deal of inside baseball knowledge at McGraw's feet. He had a most amazing memory for small facts about a ballplayer, where a man might hit a ball, what pitch he didn't like in a key spot, what a pitcher might throw, which players didn't do well in cold weather or on windy days. He had maximized his average baseball talent with his brain. He would do the same as a manager.

On May 12, 1925, he became the president-manager-outfielder of the Worcester club in the Eastern League. The league had gained a measure of fame when a strong first baseman by the name of Lou Gehrig graduated from the Hartford club after the 1924 season right to the Yankees.

Stengel took to managing the way a duck takes to water, with his mouth open, quacking, his eyes seeing in every direction, and his wings flapping.

"One day we were playing the Hartford club," Stengel recalled, "and Leo Durocher was at shortstop for them. He was hitting about .208 and while they were in the clubhouse at a meeting, I went out to his position and scratched .208 in the dirt in figures six feet long."

"I remember Casey from those days in Worcester like it was yesterday," says Ken Smith, a former newspaper man who now is the director of baseball's Hall of Fame in Cooperstown, New York.

"He was talking Stengelese then also. I'd ask him for the starting lineup and he'd do this thing with the names, stretching them out in two or three syllables, saying, 'My pitcher is Mr. Jon-es from Cincin-cincin-natt-tti, Oh-io.' Every time he made a newspaper man laugh," says Smith, "he helped sell tickets."

Stengelese was also a perfect way of avoiding answering questions Stengel did not want to answer. A tough, probing question, "Why did you hit for so-and-so?" would elicit a "Now wait a minute, for crissakes, and I'll tell ya," and thirty minutes later he still hadn't. And wouldn't. Stengel could be direct, especially with his players, if he wanted to. He once had a young pitcher on the Yankees, an intellectual, by the name of Mark Freeman. Freeman was on the mound, stretching with two runners on when he was attacked by a fly, swung his arms to get rid of it, and was called for a balk for breaking his motion. Casey stormed to the mound to inquire about the situation and when Freeman explained about the nasty fly, Stengel shot back, "If you're gonna pitch in the big league you're gonna have to learn how to catch 'em in your mouth."

Casey worked incredibly hard at his Worcester job. He played one hundred games as an outfielder and batted .320. He managed his club to a third-place finish. He ran the office, handled the payroll, made all travel arrangements, put in a long day, each and every day in Worcester. As president, he spent a great deal of time with his counterpart on the Yankee farm at Hartford, George Weiss.

"Casey and George got along real well," says Hazel Weiss, "but I don't think they were ever close friends. I think George respected Casey's ability on the field, but he knew Casey was a clown."

Hazel Weiss says George was no different at home than he was in his baseball office.

"He was just a serious man," says Hazel, who contrastingly was a good-time gal, who loved to sing and dance. "That was his nature. He simply was the boss and did his job, in the office or anyplace else. There could be only one boss in an office and one boss in a family."

At the end of the 1925 season, pulling one of the great triple plays in baseball, general manager Stengel released outfielder Stengel, president Stengel fired manager Stengel, and president Stengel resigned. He was a free agent and soon was hired to manage the independent Toledo Club in the American Association.

A Toledo lawyer by the name of Oscar Smith and his partner, John McMahon, were interested in purchasing the property in Toledo under Swayne Field, where the Mudhens played. The real estate seemed a good investment. The lawyers discovered that New York Giants manager John McGraw owned the park and the team. He wanted to sell both the team and the property, but the lawyers were reluctant to get into the business end of baseball, having no background. When they told McGraw of their fears he said, "I think I can recommend the best man for you in the operation of the ball club. He can handle and develop players, manage the club properly, and in addition has business ability. He will produce a successful operation for you and one that will appeal to the public."

That man was Casey Stengel. McGraw had recognized that Stengel, with his gift of gab, his leathery face, his unending patience, and his endless energy, could win the press and the public to his cause under any circumstances. Casey had always been comfortable with sportswriters as a player and catered to them—knowing full well how vital they were to a successful baseball business—upon becoming a manager.

"One of the most important things about Casey was that he knew how to win over the sportswriters," says veteran sports editor Sy Burick of the *Dayton* (Ohio) *Daily News*, who knew Stengel from his days in Toledo. "Unlike most managers he always took the trouble to find out who you were. He may never know your name, but he could recognize you. Whenever he saw me for forty-five years he would say, 'And how are things in Dayton, Ohio?' That was his way of telling you he knew you.

"I saw Casey once in the early 1970s and after he said, 'And how are things in Dayton?' he looked at me," says Burick, "grinned like a Cheshire cat, and said, 'Have you seen that man who managed from behind the telephone pole lately?' A manager named Ducky Holmes had been thrown out of a game in the 1920s and hid behind a telephone pole at the end of the field giving signals. Casey hadn't mentioned that to me in forty years."

Because of his combativeness, a flaming temper, a desire to excel as a manager, and hopes of getting picked to handle a big-league club, Stengel fought with umpires, opponents, and rowdy fans. He was suspended more than a half-dozen times in his six seasons at Toledo, had several fights with fans, was actually arrested once on a charge of assault and battery after allegedly slugging a fan in the stands (the charges were later dropped for lack of evidence), and had to be escorted off the field by police after attacking a player on the Columbus team for grabbing one of his players. Unwisely this act occurred in the home park of the Columbus club and *The New York Times* reported, "Police quelled the crowd

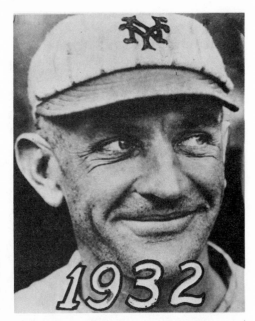

Casey as a Brooklyn Dodger coach in 1932 posing in his old New York Giants uniform for a gag.

and escorted Stengel to the clubhouse and later to a taxi."

Part of all this was his nature. Part was a calculated attempt to call attention to himself, sell tickets, excite the fans, take the pressures off a losing team. Stengel's most volatile arguments with umpires always came in losing games. His dirt-kicking, cap-throwing, loud-cursing act with the Yankees in later days was copied by his successor, Ralph Houk. "It never failed to wake us up," said Houk. "You never do it when the other team is asleep," Stengel once told this reporter with a wink, "only when your team is."

After paying his dues, learning his trade, and enriching his managerial image as a rabble-rouser, Stengel was rescued from the minors and returned to the big leagues by a phone call early in December of 1931. It was Max Carey, the new manager of the Brooklyn Dodgers and a former teammate of Casey's at Pittsburgh, who called him and asked, "Would you like to coach for me at Brooklyn?"

He was back in Brooklyn, back home with a team

known as the Daffiness Boys, because they seemed more inclined to wild play and good times than to winning many baseball games.

"Casey was a very good coach with young players," said Al Lopez, the team's catcher and a lifelong Stengel friend. "He would go out to Ebbets Field early in the morning and hit fungoes for hours with anyone who wanted to improve. He was serious on the ball field. He might talk for an hour without letting up, but he wasn't trying to be funny. He was offering advice and you had to learn how to pull it out."

Lopez, shortstop Glen Wright, and Stengel would often dine together after a game. Their favorite spot was a place called the Three Star Restaurant near the Brooklyn Bridge. It was famous for lamb chops. Stengel put on his favorite suit one night, had his shoes shined in the boot-black parlor of the St. George Hotel, where he lived (Edna was back home visiting her family in Glendale), and put on a fedora with a large feather. After dinner the three Dodgers journeyed across the bridge in Stengel's car to Speakeasy 101 in Greenwich Village. This was in 1932 during the depths of the depression with Prohibition adding to the general malaise. Stengel knocked on the door and a small panel was opened in the entrance to Speakeasy 101. "Come right in," said a man behind the door, "we know your face, Mr. Stengel."

Stengel's face had always been his passport. On a trip to Mexico with the New York Mets in 1964, the traveling party had been held up an hour while Edna Stengel searched for her passport with her photo. The customs official said to Stengel, "Señor Stengel, you don't need a passport, you have your face."

So Stengel, Lopez, and Wright entered the Speakeasy and listened to the piano player and the violin player the rest of the evening. At one point in the conversation, while Stengel was explaining to Lopez how McGraw called pitches for his catchers, he suddenly stopped in mid-conversation. "Wait a minute for crissakes," he bellowed, "I know you." He was looking across the room at an Oriental waiter. He had last seen him in Tokyo a dozen years earlier on a barnstorming tour. "He was our bat boy," Stengel said.

"The waiter came over, Stengel asked him how he had gotten to the States, the boy explained he came to visit an aunt in 1927 and stayed, and Casey reminded him he had been a good bat boy," said Lopez. "Then Casey picked right up and said, 'And when McGraw wanted the curve ball he put his hand . . .'"

Stengel traded Lopez to Boston in 1936, but they remained good friends. The Braves were playing the Dodgers and Lopez and Casey went for dinner at Joe's, a restaurant under the Brooklyn Bridge, famous for the best home-fried potatoes in Brooklyn. A journeyman Dodger outfielder by the name of Randy Moore was with them. Stengel asked Moore what he would be doing after his baseball career ended. "Well, my father-in-law has some oil wells back home in Naples, Texas. I might get involved in that." Casey said he might be interested in putting a few bucks into some oil wells, too, if there was room. "Let's put the Mexican in it, too," said Stengel.

"Casey was fired by the Dodgers the next year and was out of baseball," said Lopez. "Moore had broken his leg and quit. He went into the oil business and one day he called Casey. He asked if Casey was serious about investing. Casey said he was, got Edna to approve a ten-thousand-dollar investment, and went in with Moore. I went in for a thousand bucks."

Soon the wells were producing oil. Stengel, for the first time in his life, had steady income outside of baseball and had become a wealthy man. "I did all right, too, with my little share," Lopez said.

The financial independence had given Stengel the kind of security baseball people rarely had. He could take a job on his own terms and he could leave it with pride intact. Randy Moore's oil wells assured Stengel of that.

The nation was in the bottom of the depression when Stengel arrived back at Ebbets Field in 1932. World War I veterans, with overseas caps and laced puttees, were selling apples for a nickel outside the entrance to Ebbets Field. Stengel was paid $7,000 as a Dodger coach, $1,500 less than he was making as the Toledo manager. He could afford the pay cut because Edna Stengel, wise in the ways of investment, was successful with her family's real estate interests back in California. Stengel, a proud man, didn't like to admit that Edna's money kept him living in style. Years later he was asked by this reporter what it was like in Brooklyn in those days for him.

"My wife takes care of my money and hers, too," he growled. "Why wouldn't she when she's a good book-keeper. You never saw them throwin' no benefits for me, for crissakes. How could you make any money when so many of them were sellin' apples and you had a job that didn't pay so good?"

Stengel enjoyed the coaching job. He was still a Brook-lyn celebrity and would spend much time before games leaning against the low walls of the grandstand talking with the fans. Unlike any team in baseball history, the Brooklyn Dodgers were a source of incredible public pride. As one of the five boroughs of New York City, Brooklyn had little personal identification save for the Dodgers. The rivalry of the Giants, Dodgers, and Yankees made baseball a hot New York topic. Yankee fans were Republicans. Giants fans were middle-class small busi-nessmen. Dodger fans were out-of-work laborers. Stengel was a great source of joy to them. When he was named the manager of the team on February 23, 1934, to succeed Carey, it was a very popular choice. Carey still had a year to go on his contract. "Will he be paid off?" Stengel asked his new boss. "That's not for you to worry about," said Steve McKeever, the club president. "If you don't want the job fifty others will take it."

He took it. Carey was paid off.

The lead sports article on page eight of the *Times* the next day, February 24, 1934, had an eight-column head-line reading: LAYTON DEFEATS COCHRAN IN FINAL FOR WORLD'S THREE CUSHION BILLIARD TITLE and ex-plained how Johnny Layton of Sedalia, Missouri, de-feated Welker Cochran 50–23, at the Capitol Academy in New York. John Kieran's "Sports of the Times" col-umn was a study of the titanic battle of milers in the impending AAU indoor meet at Madison Square Garden.

Brooklyn Dodger baseball was not all that important on a February day in the judgment of *Times* editors. The baseball public and the baseball writers knew otherwise. Baseball writer Roscoe McGowen's article at the top of page nine in that day's edition began, "Charles Dillon (Casey) Stengel became the ace of a new deal for the Brooklyn Dodgers yesterday when he signed a 2-year contract as manager succeeding recently deposed Max Carey."

The signing took place actually at the bedside of business manager J.A. Robert Quinn, who was ill in his apartment at the New Yorker. Stengel would receive a salary of $12,000 a year for 1934 and 1935. Sportswriters were summoned to the New Yorker and Stengel was introduced to them as the new Brooklyn boss.

"For more than two hours in another suite Stengel answered questions from all sides at the same time, some seriously and some with the quaint wit that has made him famous among baseball men," McGowen wrote. "He takes his job with utmost seriousness and Brooklyn fans may be assured that while the club has hired a colorful personality it has not engaged a clown [that word again]." Stengel wore a blue suit, a blue tie, and lustrous black patent leather shoes. His hair was combed and plastered down with grease. He answered a few questions humorously pointing out, "This here team is going in for the N.R.A."—not meaning Roosevelt's National Recovery Act —"this here team will have a new riot act."

The reporters all laughed and Stengel grew serious, using his change of pace as well as his famed change of face. "Every one of the gentlemen directing this club wanted me to be the manager. I will be the manager, too. Damned if I don't think I know a few things about baseball and I think I can teach baseball. I know I've got ballplayers who can help the club and help me and I can help them. That's what I want to do. The boys have got to play hard for me. That's all I ask," Stengel said.

Somebody asked the new manager about Hack Wilson,

the veteran outfielder who held the National League home run record of fifty-six with the Cubs in 1930, but had been losing ground as a Dodger due to age (he was thirty-four), heavy drinking, and overweight. "Hack is all right, but he will have to qualify for his job. Everybody will," Casey said, "but gee, fellows, you know all this just happened to me and I haven't had time to think. It might be different if I was looking for this job and had been trying to get it, but I never dreamed of it." Somebody asked Stengel about Carey and Casey said, "Max and I are friends. I've played this game square and come in here clean and that's what makes me feel so good about it. I think Max knows that too."

Stengel finished sixth with the Dodgers in 1934, fifth in 1935, and seventh in 1936. Then, with a year remaining on his contract, he suffered the same fate as his pal, Carey. He was excused for the 1937 season with full pay.

By 1938, the Ebbets and McKeever interests were losing so much money on the club they decided to bring in new money and new people. Larry MacPhail would soon be summoned from Cincinnati to run the Dodgers and, after his first Brooklyn pennant in 1941, they would never again be a shoddy franchise. So, in effect, Stengel's Dodger teams were the bottom of the losing Dodger era.

"I think he was a hell of a manager even though we didn't win much," says Tony Cuccinello. "He was a teacher and there wasn't a guy on any Stengel team who wasn't a better player for having played under him."

Cuccinello, seventy-three, lives in Tampa, Florida, now, plays golf regularly, and attempts to empty the Gulf of Mexico of fish.

"I was married in 1932 and I took an apartment on Church Avenue in Brooklyn. Casey lived nearby at the Bossett Motel. Ken Strong, the Giants football player, and Stan Lomax, the broadcaster, were good friends of mine. We'd get together often, all of us, in Casey's apartment in the hotel. Edna would prepare dinner and we'd talk baseball all night. Casey never ate much, just took a couple of drinks, started talking, and that would be it for the night."

Cuccinello remembers Stengel as an aggressive manager, always in the game, always hollering from the bench at the opposition, always fighting for his players.

"We were playing the Cubs one day and they were a real good ball club," says Cuccinello. "They had won in '32 and still had most of the same guys in '34. We were getting the hell knocked out of us, 10–1 in the first game and about 12–2 late in the second game. Casey was up and down that bench screaming like it was 1–1 in the ninth inning. The rest of us were pretty quiet. The big Chicago pitcher, Lon Warneke, the guy with that high kick, had nailed a couple of our guys. Stengel thought we were too timid about it. 'Do I have anybody here who will take a crack at them?' All of a sudden, Van Mungo, our best pitcher, says, 'I'll take a crack at them, skip.' He got up, picked up his glove, and went to the bullpen. He threw a few pitches and Casey called him in. He hit Gabby Hartnett right in the ribs with his first pitch. Mungo was a little smashed when he did that, see, because he had pitched the day before and he was known to take a drink once in a while after a game. I don't think Mungo could ever do anything wrong in Casey's eyes after that."

"I guess you could say I was Casey's boy up there," says Mungo, who now lives in retirement in Pageland, South Carolina, after a movie theater he owned burned down in 1960 and he decided not to rebuild. Mungo joined the Dodgers as a fireballing nineteen-year-old in 1931.

"I was just a kid when I came to the club and Casey took care of me. I had this big Ford in '34 and I'd often drive Casey to the park. Then I'd wait for him after the game and drive him and Edna home. Every few days Edna would come to the park with a present for me, a tie, a set of cuff links, a shirt, a pair of socks, things like that."

Casey loved to tease Edna, and Mungo remembers one afternoon he nearly frightened her to death.

"We had lost a tough game and I was driving and Edna was sitting in the front seat with me and Casey was in the back seat, real quiet and unhappy over the loss. We're going along like that and all of a sudden we hear the door open and close real quick. Edna turns back and doesn't see Casey. She thinks he's jumped out of the car. 'Stop the car, stop the car,' she starts yelling. I slow down and Casey pops his head up and says, 'Somebody looking for me?' He was under the seat on the floor."

Mungo had become a hard drinker in later years, but Casey always understood. "It ain't drinkin' that kills ya," Stengel once said, "it's stayin' up all night trying to get it." Stengel once caught one of his young players with the New York Mets sneaking a lovely redhead up to his hotel room at 4 A.M. He had been out with his writers and saw the player. He said nothing. The next day he held a clubhouse meeting. He went over the other team's hitters and suddenly said, "You gotta learn that if you don't get it by midnight, chances are you ain't gonna get it, and if you do, it ain't worth it."

Mungo said he always felt warm toward Stengel, followed his managerial career with the Yankees later on, and sent him a congratulatory telegram after his 1949 win.

"He was a good fellow, good-natured to his players, with a lot of spirit. The worst thing ever happened between Casey and me was that I never helped him win. That's my only regret," said Mungo.

Other than Mungo, the pitchers on the 1934 Dodgers were a sorry excuse for a staff. For example, there was a thirty-year-old journeyman right-hander named Walter Beck, better known as Boom-Boom Beck, for his propensity for giving up long drives that would rattle against outfield fences, boom, boom, boom. Beck was pitching in Philadelphia's Baker Bowl one day with baseballs rattling against the metal fences with ridiculous regularity. Stengel could take it no longer. He marched to the mound.

"Walter, give me the ball," Stengel said.

"No, Casey, I still have good stuff. I can get this guy out."

"Walter, give me the ball and go take a bath."

Beck, angered at the removal, turned and fired the ball on a fly against the outfield fence. Veteran Hack Wilson, alerted by the noise and assuming it was another of Beck's boom-booms, chased the ball down and fired it to second base.

"Then the other players and the fans commenced laugh-in' and Beck was pretty mad. He walked in the dugout, kicked over a water bucket, and nearly broke his toe," Stengel later said.

Casey had developed just the proper touch for removing unwanted pitchers. A young left-hander named Tug McGraw once protested when Stengel wanted to take him out of the game. "I can get this guy out, I did last time I faced him," said McGraw, then in his rookie season with the Mets. "Yeah, I know," said Stengel, "but it was in this same inning."

The Dodgers rattled along, sort of like Boom-Boom's pitches, for most of the 1934 season. Their solace would come in in the final two games of the season.

The hated New York Giants were in first place most of the year. They were led by crusty manager Bill Terry. Before spring training that year, Roscoe McGowen of the *Times*, preparing a scouting report on all National League clubs, had asked Terry his opinion of the Dodgers. Said Terry: "Is Brooklyn still in the league?"

"I really said it," says Terry. "That wasn't newspaper talk. It made a lot of money for both of us."

Terry, eighty-one, lives in Jacksonville, Florida, where he is still an active partner, with his son, in an automobile dealership. A Hall of Famer with a lifetime .341 average, he was the last National Leaguer to bat .400 with a .401 mark in 1930. Babe Herman batted .393 in 1930 and didn't win the batting title.

"Casey and I became good friends later on," Terry says, "but that crack really started something. We had played together in '23 and in '24 he went to Boston. He wasn't much of a ballplayer by then. He couldn't hit left-handed pitching, his fielding was slow, and his legs and arm were gone. But he was a funny fellow, kept everybody alive on the bench, and contributed as much to a ball club off the field as some guys do on the field."

Terry's crack wasn't needed to make the Giants hated in Brooklyn, but it didn't hurt. The Giants suddenly saw their lead slipping away in the final days of the 1934 season. The Cardinals, under the leadership of Frank Frisch, were driving. The Giants had led by six games on Labor

Day. With two games to go, they had fallen back to a flat-footed tie with St. Louis. The Cardinals were to beat the Reds two in a row, while the Dodgers of Casey Stengel, for heaven's sake, with Van Mungo, beat the Giants on Saturday, and Al Lopez and Tony Cuccinello, combining for seven hits, beat them Sunday.

Brooklyn fans, salvaging the hot-stove-league season if not the regular season, rushed on the field and hoisted Stengel and Lopez on their shoulders. Cuccinello, the other Sunday hero, had hurtled quickly into the dugout, knowing full well as a native New Yorker what the game meant in Brooklyn.

The fans cheered and whistled and hollered until Stengel, finally released from their grips, popped out of the dugout and took a deep bow. No bird flew from his cap this time. They wouldn't go home and the noise grew as time passed. Edna Stengel, at home at the hotel, set about the task of preparing drinks and a buffet dinner. She knew Casey would not come home alone this night. He came out of the clubhouse, tripping out of the rotunda, signing autographs, talking constantly, moving toward the subway because the fans had surrounded all of the Dodger cars. Casey enjoyed every second of it, loving the loving he was getting from the Brooklyn fans, and thrilled it had saved the season. It would be considered Brooklyn's greatest triumph over the hated Giants and would not be paid back in full until seventeen years later when Bobby Thomson homered to give the Giants the 1951 pennant.

Years later Stengel sat at a hotel bar in Cincinnati and recalled that day. "He wasn't what you would call the sweetest guy," he said, of Bill Terry, "and those games did nothing for his appetite. Why wouldn't you win them if you can and give your team something to think about that isn't losses and it was amazin' the way the fans poured out of the stands and rode the subway with you, till you had to get off and didn't."

The two wins over the Giants provided some solace for the fans but did little for the Dodgers' and Stengel's record. The club finished sixth, won seventy-one games and lost eighty-one, and went to spring training in 1935 with about the same prospects.

The Dodgers assembled for spring training at Daytona Beach on March 1, 1935. The most interesting addition to the team was a short, stocky right-handed hitting outfielder by the name of Stanley Bordagaray. He was of French ancestry and was immediately labeled Frenchy. Stengel had a habit of calling all players of French ancestry through the years Frenchy and even went so far as to call a young black player named Danny Napoleon by the nickname of Frenchy. When Napoleon, a rookie with the Mets in 1965, won a game against the Giants with a double, Stengel greeted sportswriters in the clubhouse by shouting, "Vive la France."

Bordagaray arrived in Florida wearing a beret, a Van-Dyke beard, and a handlebar moustache. "It looked like a little French waiter joined the club," said Stengel. Bordagaray's wife, Dorothy Duncan, was a gorgeous redhead and she got as much attention in camp as the new outfielder.

"The beard was dark brown," says Bordagaray, who is clean shaven now. "It came to a T. There had been some contest in my hometown in California over the winter for beards and I had grown it for that. When it came time for spring training I just left it on. I was making three thousand dollars a year playing baseball, so I figured I could at least have fun while I was not getting rich."

Stengel was angered by the beard. He thought it made Bordagaray look like a clown. "If there's gonna be a clown on this club," Stengel said, "it's gonna be me." Stengel almost always resented any player who played up to the press. He felt that this was his private preserve as manager, team spokesman, and salesman.

"One day Casey came to me and asked if I would shave it," said Bordagaray, now a recreational director for the city of Ventura, California. "We were in a losing streak and I told him if he thought it would help us win, I'd go along."

The beard went, but the losing streak stayed.

Bordagaray didn't need the beard to draw attention to

himself. He played with verve, diving into bases, the Pete Rose of his day, running through stop signs at third where Casey coached, laughing and telling jokes, and amusing his teammates with his tales of racing against horses in a minor-league promotion, a common practice of the day after the Dodgers had put 1932 Olympic hero Jesse Owens on display at Ebbets Field against a four-legged speedster.

One day Bordagaray hit a line drive off the wall in right field and raced to second base with a double after a head-first slide. Billy Jurges, who was the Chicago second baseman, walked over to Bordagaray and said, "Let me knock the dust off the base." Jurges stepped on the base, suddenly lunged at Bordagaray, and tagged him out. Casey shot out of the dugout and began arguing with the umpire. "How could he be out if his foot was on the base?" The umpire said Bordagaray had taken his foot off the base.

"Finally Casey gave up and we're walking back in together. 'How the hell could he tag you out if you was standin' on the base?' I said, 'Well, Casey, I was standing there tapping on the base and I guess he tagged me in between taps.' "

Stengel and Bordagaray often had screaming matches on the Dodger bench. Unlike his managerial hero, McGraw, Stengel tolerated screaming matches with his players.

"You couldn't win an argument with him and you would always wind up with a fine," says Bordagaray. "I had a good time playing for him. Nobody who played for Casey Stengel would ever forget him. How could you?" Nobody could forget Bordagaray, either. He once explained to Casey why he didn't slide on a close play by saying, "I didn't want to break the cigars I had in my pocket."

With first-baseman Sam Leslie having a good year, Bordagaray adding to the offense, and Mungo winning sixteen games, the Dodgers moved up a notch to fifth place in 1935. Stengel was making a strong effort to rebuild the club with youngsters. On all his clubs he liked to have youngsters as regulars, with veteran pitchers and veteran infielders on the bench. Once in a while he would pick up a skilled old outfielder to help his young players. Late in 1935 the Dodgers purchased the contract of Johnny Cooney.

Cooney, born in Cranston, Rhode Island, had pitched and played the outfield for the Boston Braves from 1921 through 1930. Then elbow surgery apparently ended his career and he drifted to the minors. Stengel brought him back to Brooklyn and he played ten more major-league seasons.

"Not a lot of people know this," he says, "but Casey and I played in the same opening day outfield in Boston in '24. He had come over from the Giants and was in right field and I started in center. We were in the dugout before the game and he came over to me. He winked and said, 'Kid, anything hit between us, you get. Old Case is saving his dogs.' He could still hit at the end. I remember one game he hit two home runs, one to left and one to right, so don't let anybody tell you he wasn't a good ballplayer because he was."

Cooney, who lives in retirement now in Sarasota, Florida, was grateful to Casey for bringing him back to the big leagues.

"The arm was bent all out of shape," he says. "I could only stretch it out halfway and the elbow could fit in a bureau drawer. They took thirteen pieces of bone out of the elbow and had to chisel some pieces away with a machine. My left arm was always a lot shorter than my right after that operation. I went up to Boston with him when he managed there and I coached for him at Kansas City. He once put me into a game to play second base left-handed. I told him, 'Casey, I can't play second. I'm left-handed.' He said, 'Put the glove on your wrong hand and fool 'em.' So I did and they never hit a ball to me."

Cooney, who hit only two home runs, both in 1939, in 3,372 major-league at bats, was a marvelous contact hitter. He had only 107 strikeouts in his entire career.

"I wasn't a big fellow [five feet ten and one hundred sixty-five pounds in his playing days], but he taught me how to concentrate on hitting down on the ball, hitting it through the infield," Cooney says.

Stengel would yell, "Butcher boy, butcher boy" to his smaller hitters. It simply meant he wanted them to hit down on the ball, like a butcher cutting meat from his butcher block, instead of lifting useless fly balls to the outfield.

"He picked me up when I was down," says Johnny Cooney. "He was one great guy. Make sure you make it known how much I owe the man."

The Dodgers trained quietly in Daytona Beach again in 1936. Most of the stories in the New York papers that spring concerned a certain highly touted rookie on the Yankees by the name of Joe DiMaggio.

Babe Ruth had been traded to the Boston Braves in 1935, played in twenty-eight games, and quit on Sunday, June 2, 1935. On that afternoon, across the country in San Francisco, his successor as the big man of the Yankees, DiMaggio, had hit a home run, a double, and three singles in lifting his average to .414. He was already owned by the Yankees and was playing his final season as a minor leaguer for his hometown San Francisco Seals. DiMaggio would hit .398 for the Seals and come to the Yankee camp in St. Petersburg the following spring as the most exciting rookie since Lou Gehrig. Gehrig was then at his peak but would soon be overshadowed by DiMaggio in his later days as he had been through all of his earlier days by the great Ruth.

Even the Brooklyn Dodgers, in training in Florida, were shocked when it was learned that DiMaggio had burned his foot in a diathermy machine and would miss the opening game of the season. Casey Stengel, who never failed to read the sports pages every morning, knew of the youngster's problem. He also knew how to solve it. "If I had him, from what I hear," Stengel told Frenchy Bordagaray, "I'd play him on one foot."

Instead, he had to play the veteran Cooney on two feet, the undisciplined Bordagaray, and a journeyman named George Watkins in his outfield. Buddy Hassett was an improvement at first base with a .310 average, Bordagaray batted .315, and third-baseman Joe Stripp hit .317. Mungo won eighteen games, Fred Frankhouse (Casey called him Frankfurterhouse) won thirteen games, but the rest of the pitching staff wasn't much.

The Dodgers slipped back to seventh place in an eight-team league, won only sixty-seven games, and lost more money. The owners were restless. Stengel still had another year to go on his contract, but he could see the handwriting on the wall.

"When you look at the standings and you see you are near the bottom," he said years later, "you know the owners are preparing to commence firin' you. They looked and they did."

On October 3, 1936, after the third game of the World Series between the New York Giants and the New York Yankees had been completed with a 2–1 Yankee win on Frank Crosetti's scratch single off Fred Fitzsimmons, a press release was handed out to reporters at the Series headquarters in New York's Commodore Hotel. In seventeen words Casey Stengel's career as the manager of the Dodgers was finished. "The Brooklyn Baseball Club announces that Casey Stengel will not return to Brooklyn as manager next year," the statement read. Team secretary John Gorman handed out copies and fled the pressroom.

At that instant Stengel was walking over from the Waldorf-Astoria Hotel to the Commodore, some ten blocks away, after being notified of the move by Dodger vice-presidents Jim Mulvey and John Gilleaudeau. The Dodgers, knowing full well Stengel was an extremely popular figure, were hopeful they could avoid the criticism of the press over the move. Stengel, always aware of his standing with the press and slick at getting them quickly on his side, walked into the lobby of the Commodore, ran into a couple of his newspaper buddies, and quickly held an impromptu press conference.

"They told me the club hadn't done so well," he shouted. "They hadn't made much money, you know, and they decided unanimously to make a change. They didn't say who will follow me though. [It turned out to be Burleigh Grimes.] I've tried hard enough to do my part in fulfilling the contract and I expect the Brooklyn club to try at least as hard to take care of its end of the bargain."

"My services were no longer required," Stengel reminisced years later about the Brooklyn firing, "so I commenced being unemployed, which I was before in baseball numerous times. The Brooklyn people were honorable about it and a check was in my mailbox at all times."

The Series ended October 5, 1936, with the Yankees beating the Giants in what turned out to be the first of four straight—a record to be broken some years later by a well-known jug-eared Yankee manager—and attention shifted back to Stengel.

Brooklyn and New York sportswriters, whose rivalry was as heated as that between the teams, agreed on one thing that October. Casey Stengel deserved more than just a few perfunctory columns in the press and a gold watch. He deserved a party and they gave him a dandy one in the New Yorker Hotel. It ran well into the next morning and Stengel later described it as "one of the most splendid parties any disposed manager could have which is usually not a good reason for a party but I've had many of them."

The writers knew Casey had gotten a raw deal. The Dodgers were a lousy team when he took over and a lousy team when he left. The management was tightfisted, concerned always with the pressures of the banks, and afraid of failing. They would not spend money for players, had no farm system of note, and did little to help Stengel succeed. Ebbets field was the smallest park in the league and generated the least income. It would be shown, however, with the arrival of Larry MacPhail, that money could be made with the Brooklyn franchise.

The hall was overflowing as the celebration started and a good many of them were still there well after midnight. Stengel and some close friends among the writers were still going strong at 4 A.M. There was an air of warm conviviality all around.

"This is a splendid party for a deposited manager," said Stengel, stumbling on his adjectives, "and I want to thank all you pressmen and baseball people for attending, which

I know wasn't easy considering the work you just put in for the World Series. I want to thank Mr. Joe McCarthy for attending and congratulate him for a wonderful win and Mr. George Weiss for bringing him some good players and some of my Brooklyn players here, Mr. Buddy Hassett and Mr. Otto Miller, which is one of my best coaches. We didn't do all that well in Brooklyn if you've been watching the standings since we are not occupied with games in October like the better ball clubs and when that happens, the ownership commences looking for a new manager, which is the way, when maybe they oughta commence looking for players like Joe DiMaggio and them fellows McCarthy has over there in Yankee Stadium. I wanna thank you for all these words and for that clock which you gave me so I can get to work on time wherever I have a new job."

Steve Owen, the coach of the football Giants, stood up and said, "This is the first time I've ever seen a man get an award for being discharged."

Stengel invited all his pals to drink with him until the booze ran dry, and he left the New Yorker with that clock under his arm as the sun came up. The huge clock would sit in a prominent place on the bar in his den for the rest of his life and it was there, shiny and still running, late in 1978. Right next to the group photo taken that 1936 night.

So Casey Stengel, forty-six years old and a failed manager in his first big-league chance, was out of work. He would collect $15,000 for not managing the Dodgers in 1937, as Max Carey had collected $10,000 for not managing them in Stengel's first year of 1934, a business practice that may have indicated why the Dodgers were always on the threshold of financial extinction.

He spent the winter at home in Glendale, journeyed to Texas in the spring to examine his oil properties with Randy Moore, journeyed up to Brooklyn to sit in the stands, eat peanuts, banter with the fans, and kid with the press, accepting his unemployment with the same good humor he had always shown. He was also thinking seriously about getting out of the game he had given his life to for more than a quarter of a century.

His managerial career in Brooklyn would always be something special to Casey Stengel and years later he would bring up those days with the Dodgers as years of much affection. He would refer to his favorites as "the fella with the moustache [Bordagaray] and the fella which caught as good as any of them [Lopez] and the fella which throws a ball through a brick wall [Mungo] and the fella with the twisted arm and wouldn't strike out and why would you if you couldn't hit a ball over a building [Cooney]." And he would refer to Brooklyn as "the borough of churches and bad ball clubs, many of which I had" in his later ramblings.

Casey and Edna would live the good life that year of 1937, away from the pressures, financially secure, away from the losing ball clubs. He would visit some of his favorite restaurants on their occasional trips to New York, attend vaudeville and theater, many times as a first-nighter, with Edna looking sleek and gorgeous in her latest finery and Stengel, in cap and bow tie, a dashing figure of a middle-aged man. One of their favorites was Al Jolson, and they attended an opening at the Palace and heard the great entertainer walk to the footlights and say, "You ain't heard nuthin' yet."

Casey liked that a lot. He knew people still had a lot more to hear from him. Even in New York. He decided he would take another baseball job if one came along. He could, with his newfound financial security and his Dodger pay for a year, remain comfortably unemployed in 1937. Managers were always being hired and fired. He expected he would soon receive a call to return to his trade.

8. If Ya' Got the Horses

CASEY STENGEL was not in baseball in 1937. At forty-seven he was unemployed. Did he miss it?

"You're damned right I did," he told this writer years later. "If it's your work and you ain't doin' it, you miss it, right?" Right.

So when Bob Quinn, whom Stengel had known as business manager in Brooklyn, offered him the job of managing the Boston Bees (soon to be Braves again), he jumped at the chance. Quinn, as general manager of the Boston team, hired Stengel for the same reason the Dodgers had hired him. He thought he could manage a baseball team and he thought he could attract some fans. Few managers have ever been honestly sure they helped sell tickets. Stengel could and always would say it. His character had been firmly set in the public mind by now, a rambunctious, garrulous, ebullient manager who would light a fire under his team or burn up trying. Boston had finished fifth under Bill McKechnie in 1937 and when McKechnie was grabbed off by Cincinnati, Quinn turned to old pal Stengel.

Edna and Casey were having breakfast in their rented home in Omaha, Texas, where they had spent a good part of 1937 examining their oil wells. Casey was sitting at the kitchen table, sipping a cup of coffee, reading the sports pages of the *Dallas Morning News.* The phone rang. It was Bob Quinn. He got right to the point.

"Casey, do you want to come with us next year?" Quinn asked.

"I'd be delighted," said Stengel.

"OK, you've got the job," Quinn said.

"I'm delighted, thank you. We'll fool a lot of the boys."

Quinn said he would make the announcement later in the day to the press and Casey could come to Boston in a couple of weeks to sign a contract.

The *Times* reported on October 25, 1937, under a headline stating: BEES PICK STENGEL FROM MORE THAN 150 APPLICANTS TO MANAGE TEAM IN 1938 that Stengel had been selected and quoted Quinn as saying, "I turned down Casey's request after McKechnie resigned. I wanted Donnie Bush of Minneapolis or Gabby Hartnett of the Cubs."

Announcing that he was no better than a third choice and also suggesting he really didn't want him because he had already turned him down, Quinn felt obligated to explain his selection of the ousted Brooklyn manager.

"He may have the reputation of a clown [not again], but I've worked with him for two years," said Quinn, "and I know he can be as serious as anyone and he's loyal. Don't sell Stengel short. He can fool a lot of people. Casey will make players hustle. He's a good man for mixing up plays. He won't be afraid to holler for a hit and run or a bunt and he's not afraid to try something new."

What Quinn didn't tell the press was that Stengel had agreed to put $50,000 of his newfound oil money into the Boston operation. It was probably as good a reason for his selection as any other. His finishes at Brooklyn, sixth, fifth, and seventh, would hardly make him a choice the Bees had to have.

Stengel had a few old pals on the Boston club in 1938 —Al Lopez behind the plate, Tony Cuccinello at second, Johnny Cooney in right field, and a center fielder named DiMaggio (only this one was a strikeout specialist named Vince) and a left fielder named Max West, a husky, left-handed hitting rookie from Alhambra, California.

"I first met Casey about '35 or '36. I was playing sandlot ball around Glendale," says West, now retired after years in the sporting goods business in California with home-run king Ralph Kiner. "I was probably fifteen when Stengel saw me hit a couple out and came up to me after a game and said, 'Whew, you can hit a ball with some pop,

After sitting out a year and getting rich from his oil wells, Casey returns in 1938 to managing in Boston. Stengelese spoken with a broad A was something to hear.

sonny.' Then he spent some time with us when he was out of baseball in '37, sat us down on the grass in some old park and began lecturing on the finer points of the game."

The crosstown rivals, the Boston Red Sox, had a big, skinny slugger they were touting by the name of Ted Williams.

Stengel had first spotted Williams in 1937 playing in the Pacific Coast League in San Diego. He saw the great natural skill in the skinny slugger, and after being hired by Boston in October, he tried to convince Quinn to buy him. The price was too high for the Bees and Williams wound up crosstown with the Red Sox. Stengel would always be a strong admirer of Williams. Williams would return the compliment.

"I have always been a great admirer of Casey Stengel's," Williams said after his retirement. "He was a great manager and showed great strength of character. I don't think anybody contributed more to baseball than Casey Stengel. He ranks right there with Ty Cobb, Babe Ruth, and Judge Landis."

Williams admired the small things Stengel could do in a game. When Stengel was managing in New York, a Boston sportswriter complained the Red Sox lacked leadership because no player would go over and slow down a pitcher in trouble like Gil McDougald did with the Yankees. Williams bellowed, "McDougald, you think so, eh? You know the real reason he went in there? Probably because Casey Stengel rubbed an earlobe or picked his nose to signal for McDougald to get out to that mound and slow that son of a gun down until he could get another pitcher warmed up."

The closest thing Stengel ever had to Williams was West.

"He can hit a ball over a building and through the wind," Stengel told Boston sportswriters. He was suggesting West was strong enough to conquer the cruel breezes of the Charles River near Braves Field.

"I was the youngest guy on the Braves that year," says West. "Casey watched out for me and he told the older players, Lopez, Cuccinello, Cooney, to keep an eye on me. The whole league didn't have three rookies that year besides me."

West remembers the sound of Casey's voice. "I can hear it now, even with my eyes closed. He was always yelling on our bench. Years later I finished up with San Diego in the Pacific Coast League. Casey was with Oakland. I would be across the field and I would hear that voice. 'Hey you, get up there and hit.' It wasn't any quieter."

Boston turned out to be Brooklyn with a different accent. West had some trouble adjusting to big-league pitching and hit only ten homers. DiMaggio batted .228 and led the league with 134 strikeouts. Jim Turner won fourteen games but lost eighteen. Another ex-Dodger, Joe Stripp, led the club in hitting with a .275 mark. The Braves finished two games over .500 with a 77–75 record. The only satisfaction for Stengel with his fifth-place finish was the fact the Dodgers, under Burleigh Grimes, won sixty-nine games, lost eighty, and finished sixth.

The Braves fell to seventh place in 1939 and gained permanent possession of that position with seventh-place finishes in 1939, 1940, 1941, and 1942. When war broke out on December 7, 1941, Casey told Edna, "I'm going back into the navy and paint ships again." Instead, President Franklin D. Roosevelt gave baseball the go-ahead as a morale builder and Stengel stayed on as the Boston manager.

One of the better players on his 1942 team was a stocky, young left-handed hitter from Brooklyn by the name of Tommy Holmes. He would go on to set a National League record for hitting in thirty-seven consecutive games, until broken by Pete Rose's mark of forty-four in 1978. Holmes now works in the sales promotion department of the New York Mets. He is sixty-two years old.

"I was playing sandlot ball in Brooklyn when Casey first saw me," says Holmes. "I was with the Bay Parkways semipro team and I hit a few homers. Casey pushed the Braves to make the deal with the Yankees, my original organization. 'I remember you,' he said, when he first got me. 'You can hit a ball into the east wind.' I guess he thought I'd hit some homers in Boston despite the winds."

He did manage twenty-eight homers in 1945, but he was mostly a spray hitter.

"We had Paul Waner, a great hitter, on that '42 Boston club. I was a lead-off hitter and he wanted Waner to help me use the bat. One day he came to me and said, 'Now he [Waner] will take a drink once in a while, but he can hit the lines. Listen to him and you might learn six or eight things.' Waner worked with me and really helped. Casey had more baseball brains in his little finger than any other manager I knew had in their whole body."

Victories were rare for the 1942 Braves (59–89 was Stengel's worst record until he took over the New York Mets two decades later) and each one was savored. His most important victories always came over the Pirates because they were managed by his close friend, Frank Frisch, a former New York Giants teammate. They would scream at each other across the field and then go out to dinner together. Casey always saved his best pitcher, knuckleballer Jim Tobin, for the opener of a Pittsburgh series. He had a catcher named Clyde Kluttz who couldn't hit much but could handle that butterfly. The best hitter on the team was Ernie (Schnozz) Lombardi, a big, lumbering two hundred thirty-pound receiver who could hit like mad, didn't like catching, and hated to run. He would have made a fantastic designated hitter. Lombardi won the batting title that year with a .330 average, a hell of an achievement for a thirty-four-year-old who couldn't run a lick.

"It was a blistering hot day," recalls Holmes, "and Lom was sitting in the cool of the dugout before a game against the Pirates. He knew Tobin was starting, he wouldn't catch, so he never took his glove to the dugout. All of a sudden Casey comes over to him and says, 'Schnozz, would you catch for me today? I need your bat. I gotta beat Frisch, I gotta.' Lombardi just curled up in the dugout. There was no way he would catch Tobin, no sir. Casey kept after him. 'Just this one time, just this one time.' Then Lom, who was a softhearted guy said, 'OK, just this one time,' and he starts putting on his gear."

Vince DiMaggio, whom Casey had traded over to the Pirates, was Pittsburgh's lead-off hitter. Lombardi squatted down and gave the sign for, what else? The knuckleball. It was all Tobin threw.

"He swung on the first pitch, got a piece of it, and fouled it back into Lom's head," says Holmes. "Lom took off the mask, shook the bees out of his bonnet, and got back in there. Here comes the second pitch and Lom catches that one in the cup. Now he's rolling around on the ground, holding his privates. Now another knuckleball, the hitter swings and misses, the ball flies by Lom's ear and rolls to the screen. Lom turns and gives chase. He gets near the screen, trips, falls on his ass, and collapses after he lobs the ball back. Now he pulls off his mask and throws it to one side. Then he pulls off the chest protector and throws it to the other side. Then he pulls off his shin guards and deposits them on the ground. Lom starts unbuttoning his shirt and heading for the bench. He's quit. Casey gets up and screams, 'Road apple, you left all your equipment out there for someone to fall over.' Then he starts laughing and we all get hysterical and Casey says, 'If you don't play

I'll cut my jungle [jugular] vein,' and he starts making cutting motions across his neck. Lom came out and I can't tell you if we won or lost, but we didn't stop laughing for a week."

Casey loved Lombardi, but he was not above making fun of him. In another game against the Pirates he gave the big catcher the bunt sign. Lombardi followed orders and bunted toward Bob Elliott at third. "He starts for first," says Holmes, "and he's puffing and snorting all the way down the line and the crowd is screaming. Elliott charges in, gets the ball, and makes a long, underhand throw. The umpire puts the safe sign down and Lombardi is on first. I look over to third and Casey, who was coaching there, is flat on the ground in a dead faint. It was fantastic. A couple of pitches later Casey gave him the steal sign and Lombardi stole it. He really did."

Ernie Lombardi stole eight bases in his sixteen-year major-league career. One came in 1942. You could look it up.

Casey's 1942 Braves was his worst club until his days with the Mets. They had some good hitters in Lomardi, Holmes, and West, who had now developed into an important slugger, but they had little pitching. Tobin and Al Javery led the staff with twelve wins. In the early days of the season, Stengel missed out on two youngsters. They were to come back a half-dozen years later after service in World War II and pitch Boston to a pennant. Fans in Boston would forever remember the 1948 cry, "Spahn and Sain and pray for rain." Johnny Sain was used in relief that year. Warren Spahn pitched four games and was sent to the minors. He would become the winningest left-handed pitcher in baseball history and pitch again for Casey Stengel twenty-three years later with the Mets.

"I played for Casey Stengel before and after he was a genius," says Spahn.

As Spahn's career blossomed after the war, Casey was often reminded he cut Spahn and sent him to the minors in 1942.

"That's how smart I was and it was the worst mistake I ever made in baseball," he said.

"Casey was a mean son of a gun then," remembers Spahn. "If we lost, he made us keep our uniforms on and sit at our lockers thinking about our mistakes. Then he'd let the regulars dress and make the rookies go back on the field and work on fundamentals."

Warren Spahn and Casey Stengel would meet again twenty-three years later with some interesting results. For now, Spahn was back in Hartford and the Braves were back in seventh place.

Casey Stengel brought his Boston Braves north in 1943 with little hope of improvement. Military service was cutting deeply into the baseball team, with weak clubs like the Braves hurt more than stronger clubs. The song was right about the Braves. "They were either too young or too old."

The Braves, like the Dodgers, were always on the threshold of financial disaster. Stengel had been talked into investing $50,000 of his own money into the club. In exchange, he would get some say in trades and other business aspects of the team. It was hoped they could keep the franchise solvent until the war ended and some of their best prospects returned from service.

The day before the 1943 season opened the Braves and Red Sox played an annual charity game. With Ted Williams and many of the Red Sox stars off in service, the Braves won the game. Stengel, tripping the light fantastic that night after his triumph over the local rivals, had walked from Fenway Park to the Kenmore Hotel, where he lived. He was almost there when it began raining. A heavy mist had blown in off the Charles River. Fog covered the area. A wartime dimout, with black tape covering the top half of all automobile headlights, made visibility difficult. He was hunched over as he crossed Kenmore Square, a newspaper held over his head against the rain. He was caught in the middle of the square, cars on both sides of him. He stepped back and was struck by a taxicab turning into the square. He was rushed to Massachusetts General Hospital, where inexperienced orthopedic surgeons, with the medical cream away in service, botched the job. He had suffered a severely fractured left leg.

The cast was not placed properly on the leg. He suffered a staph infection. He remained in the hospital for six weeks and doctors considered amputation. Finally, he started to recover.

Stengel had been placed at first in the hospital's maternity ward because of the shortage of beds. One good friend, Frankie Frisch, wired him in care of the psychiatric ward, deciding that is where Casey Stengel would most need help. He received the message. It was all in a kidding vein. The most bitter line of all was written by sportswriter Dave Egan in the *Boston Record*. He nominated the cabdriver, who hit Stengel, as "the man who did the most for Boston baseball."

"I think Casey cried when he read that," Edna Stengel once said. "He was flat on his back, he was worried about his health, and he cared about the club. That was cruel. Why would somebody write that?"

Stengel never completely recovered from that accident. His leg remained twisted slightly and he never could walk without the indication of a slight limp. He also retained a knot in his leg that never disappeared. Years later, in showing the knot to this writer, he said, "That's where the cab got me. It's an apple, but it ain't a road apple, that's something which is different."

Out a good part of the 1943 season with the bad leg, Stengel began losing his appeal in Boston. His jokes had worn thin, his team was as bad as the first day he took over in 1938, and new ownership, led by construction millionaire Lou Perini, wanted a change. They suggested general manager Bob Quinn find a new manager for 1944. Quinn stuck by Stengel. Quinn suggested it would be unfair to fire a manager for being hit by a cab, but he relayed Perini's sentiments to Casey.

"I don't want to handicap anybody. I won't stay," he told Quinn. At the termination of his contract in 1943, he resigned. He collected his full pay, was paid off dollar for dollar on his investment in the club, and he returned home to Glendale, California.

Casey Stengel was out of baseball. To Casey, to Edna, to Edna's family, to the press and public, it seemed the end of the line for the weary old manager. He was almost fifty-four years old, had never finished higher than fifth in nine managerial seasons in the big leagues, and no longer needed a job with his oil wells producing and Edna shrewdly building a small fortune with the financial acumen of a J. P. Morgan.

If Casey Stengel's career in baseball had ended after 1943, he would have been remembered casually by serious fans as a fair player, a character, a wordsmith, an entertaining personality on the baseball scene for more than three decades. But there was to be more of a public life for Stengel, the best of his public life yet to come. It all began casually in Chicago when manager Jimmy Wilson was fired early in 1944. Phil Wrigley, the chewing gum man, wanted Charlie Grimm to replace Wilson. Grimm was running the Cubs' farm club in Milwaukee. As soon as Grimm could find a successor he could move to Chicago. He called his old pal, Casey Stengel. He knew that Casey could double as general manager and field manager.

"I had complete confidence in him," says Grimm. "Everybody in baseball knew that Casey had enormous energy and would give you all he had. I didn't know if he could win or not. I told him we had a pretty good club. 'If ya got the horses, we'll win,' he said. I remember years later, after he won six or eight pennants with the Yankees, asking him if he was a different manager than he had been in earlier years in Brooklyn and Boston. 'I got the horses,' he said. That was all there was to managing."

Farm club owner Bill Veeck, stationed with the marines in Bouganville (where he would lose a leg to the recoil of a cannon), almost had apoplexy when he heard Grimm had turned his Milwaukee team over to Stengel. He fired off a letter to Grimm. "You've hired a clown," he wrote. Grimm sure had, a clown who made newspaper people and fans laugh, increased attendance by some two hundred thousand fans, and won his second pennant in professional baseball. Then he quit again, making the announcement to newsmen at a season-ending party at 4 A.M.

Stengel knew that with the war nearing an end Veeck would return to active ownership of his club and pick his own manager. Casey also knew that he would be more attactive to a big-league club—if another opening occurred—available and a recent winner. It was a calculated risk, but Stengel knew the machinations of baseball, he had friends all over the country, he was locked into a network of informers from so many teams, and he figured a resignation on top would be more impressive than a firing by Veeck a few months later.

Casey went back to Glendale again. He was available for new employment and nurtured the idea that some big-league club might come knocking. The big-league club was the Yankees. They wanted him to manage their farm club in Kansas City. Stengel jumped at the chance after George Weiss, now running the Yankee farm system, offered him the job in 1945.

Stengel returned to his hometown with much joy. His parents had both died before the war, but his sister Louise and his brother Grant were still around. He was a minor celebrity in Kansas City, enjoyed renewing old friendships and spending nights at the bar of the Muehlebach Hotel. He also renewed an acquaintanceship with an old Kansas City politico he had known in the early twenties by the name of Harry S. Truman. He attended several banquets in Kansas City where the new President of the United States was speaking. Truman would later throw out the first ball at a Washington opener when Stengel managed the Yankees, laughing as Stengel said, "Give 'em hell, Harry." A huge gold toy cannon, a gift from Harry Truman, sits on a mantle in the den of Stengel's Grandview Avenue home in Glendale.

Stengel finished seventh with the Yankee farm club at Kansas City, resigned another job, and went home. This time he felt it was for good. Edna missed her family. Casey felt he was getting too old at fifty-five for minor-league managing and the major leagues obviously had forgotten him.

While he pondered his future, a man named Cookie de Vincenzi, who had just sold the Oakland club to Brick

Laws, called and told him the managerial job was open at Oakland. Was he interested in the position? He certainly was. Oakland in the Pacific Coast League was a strong franchise. Most of the Coast League franchises were strong, with Los Angeles and San Francisco eventually leading the way into big-league baseball, and Oakland following. Edna Stengel was all for the move. At fifty she was getting a little weary of the cross-country journeys each summer and wanted to spend more time with her family.

Stengel finished second in 1946 with the Acorns, dropped to fourth in 1947, and won the pennant in 1948 with 114 victories. No Stengel team would ever win more but, of course, no Stengel team would ever win less than the forty wins recorded by his 1962 New York Mets team. Managing baseball teams was definitely a roller coaster experience.

The 1948 team would catapult Stengel to the Yankees. It was a veteran club with so many old players the local press began calling the team The Nine Old Men, in the same way that political writers referred to Franklin Roosevelt's aged Supreme Court nine. Stengel's juggling of these sometimes weary bodies led the press to applaud his managerial magic and address him as The Old Profesor, for his magnificent teaching skills. It would come out Old Perfesser in New York later on.

"We had some good players on that club," says Cookie Lavagetto, who got his nickname (he was born Harry Arthur Lavagetto in Oakland in 1912) as a nineteen-year-old playing for Cookie de Vincenzi, the team owner, in 1932. He went on to a distinguished big-league career and returned to Oakland in 1948.

"Our team included Ernie Lombardi, Nick Etten ["Nick Etten's glove fields better with Nick Etten out of it," wrote Joe Trimble of the *New York Daily News,* when a ground ball stuck in Etten's glove on the field], George Metkovich, Maurice Van Robays, and Jim Tobin. We knew how to play," Lavagetto says.

Lavagetto played third base and was also assigned an off-the-field task. He was to keep an eye on a rambunc-

A photographer's dream, Stengel poses as he counts noses on two famous schnozz's of the day, Billy Martin and Ernie Lombardi. The Oakland team won the pennant, of course, by a nose.

tious young infielder by the name of Billy Martin.

"Casey asked me to room with him," says Lavagetto. "He wanted me to teach him some baseball, watch over him, teach him the ropes."

"He really had a fantastic baseball mind," Lavagetto says of Stengel. "He just never missed anything. He seemed to be able to be in six places at once."

Cookie's charming wife, Mary, and Edna Stengel spent a great deal of time together. Mary Lavagetto says no two people ever were as close as Casey and Edna.

"She was the perfect foil for him," says Mary Lavagetto. "He played off her, but she was smart. She knew when to put her foot down and make him stop."

Stengel had sent a young Oakland pitcher by the name of Spec Shea to the Yankees and another pitcher by the name of Gene Bearden to Cleveland. He had produced an exciting team in Oakland, he made money for his owners, and he had decided that 1948 was to be his final year in baseball. "After it's over," he told Edna that summer, "we're going home for good."

Casey's fate was being settled three thousand miles away that summer in New York. George Weiss, unhappy with Bucky Harris because he had gone against the book in losing a 1947 Series game to the Dodgers when he walked the winning run, because he was losing, and because he was drinking heavily, wanted a change.

Weiss convinced Dan Topping and Del Webb, who were intimidated by Weiss because they believed he was the one indispensable man in the organization (an idea always fostered by Weiss wherever he worked), that a change was necessary. He told Topping he had no one in mind but would scout around. He had tried to move Stengel into the job before Harris was hired in 1947 but had less control then with Larry MacPhail running the club for Topping and Webb. He would certainly move to Stengel now if he could sell him to the owners. "What about DiMaggio?" asked Topping. "Too valuable as a player," said Weiss. "Boudreau does it," said Topping. "Boudreau isn't DiMaggio," said Weiss. There the matter rested until late September. Weiss, a thorough man, talked to Brick Laws. He talked to Paul Krichell, his most influential scout, and to Bill Essick, his West Coast scout. He talked to other baseball people on the Pacific Coast. He got nothing but glowing reports about Stengel—sharp, dedicated, energetic, and still selling tickets, the consensus seemed to be. Weiss called Jim Turner and told him to be available for a coaching job with the Yankees. Then he went to work on Topping after asking Laws to soften up Webb. Topping, a stiff, hard man, was afraid of Stengel's image as a clown. He wanted a winner. "Casey will win with the club," said Weiss, "and he'll make money."

Topping, worn down by Weiss' persistence, bought it. Weiss first phoned Casey in early October after newspaper speculation had presented Casey Stengel's name frequently. After all, it was a baseball friendship that went back to 1925. On Sunday, October 10, Weiss called Stengel again in Glendale and said, "Come to New York and we'll talk about the manager's job."

Casey and Edna flew to New York, were met by George Weiss, transported to the Waldorf-Astoria Hotel by limousine, met with Dan Topping, and signed a two-year contract for $45,000 a year. Two days later, with the 1948 World Series ended and the Knights of Columbus band marching down Fifth Avenue, Casey Stengel was introduced to the press as the fifteenth manager of the New York Yankees.

Who could imagine what wonders lay ahead for this gnarled old man as he walked to the microphones that day and thanked Bob Topping for a job given him by Dan Topping? All that could be sure is that years later, after his Yankee retirement, when he sat behind a desk at the Glendale Valley National Bank with a sign reading, "Stengelese spoken here," he would be described by one sportswriter as "the man who did for English what Winston Churchill never could—kill it."

9. You Think
I Was Born Old?

THROUGH THE EXCITEMENT, pressures, and successes of the 1949 season, the new manager of the Yankees lay back with the players. He was always available for the press, especially the sportswriters who traveled with the team and were called "My writers" by Stengel. He would pose for any picture, the more comical the better, holding an umbrella on a rainy day, signing autographs for a pretty girl with a lecherous wink as a favor for a movie publicity man, wearing a wild hat or playing a bat like a banjo. He would turn on for out-of-town sports columnists, on their occasional visits to the Yankees, rattling off a trail of Stengelese for them as payment for their attention.

David Condon of the *Chicago Tribune*, a husky, jovial, cigar-smoker, was one of his favorites. When he asked Stengel about his pitching staff early in March of 1950, Casey began, "I know'd you'd wanna check that so I looked it up. Why woundn't ya use all the ones you got if ya needed hitting especially since my own fellas which is new and how do you know what they can do if they hadn't played a game for ya since it don't count yet and they don't get paid."

Those who had been around Casey for a while knew he simply wasn't ready to name names of his starters this early in spring training. While other managers would say, "It's too early to say," Stengel would perform his act. The reporter would smile. The Stengelese would be recorded as well as it could be. A column would be written later about this funny man with the funny grammar. Casey had

Edna and Casey are honored after 1949 championship with parade down Glendale's main street. Next to Duke Morrison, a well-known Glendale druggist's son, who became known as John Wayne, Edna and Casey were town's favorite people.

ducked a question without hurting anyone's feelings. He was a brilliant strategist and could play the press the way Heifetz played a violin.

His pregame and postgame interviews with the press always were wildly amusing, win or lose, simply due to his mischosen language.

In 1949 he was restrained with the players. He criticized them only on occasion. He did it gently. He picked his spots. In the spring of 1950, flushed with the success of 1949, his confidence in dealing with his players was restored. He knew now, given "the horses," he was a fine manager. With the confidence came more arrogance. The true personality of the man, secure, in control, masterful in maneuvering, came to the surface.

"That was a different Stengel who came to spring training in 1950," recalls Phil Rizzuto. "The victory had changed him. In 1949 he let us manage ourselves to a great extent. The famous play when DiMaggio was on third in a big game against Boston and I squeezed Joe home with a bunt was our own play, me and Joe put that on alone. After that he wanted to control every play himself, he wanted the credit. It seemed like he wanted to spend more time with the writers and less time applauding the players. Casey started thinking *he* was the New York Yankees."

On the day before spring training opened officially in 1950, Stengel sat on a bench outside the Yankee clubhouse at St. Petersburg. He was surrounded by "My writers." His two favorites were a crotchety old cynic from the *World Telegram and Sun* named Dan Daniel, who described everything he didn't like as "bush," and John Drebinger of *The New York Times.* While Daniel was almost always caustic, Drebinger was almost always kind. Daniel made honesty and integrity a fetish. Drebinger would bend an elbow or freeload a meal if he thought it would win him a story. His favorite trick was hiding behind a potted palm in the lobby of the team's Soreno Hotel headquarters in hopes of gently slipping into view as the team traveling secretary appeared, in time to buy breakfast. Drebinger's appetite was enormous. He would eat anything, including a melted cheese sandwich once stuffed with yellow Western Union copy paper he gleefully downed while writing hurriedly on deadline.

Drebinger, Daniel, and Stengel were each closing in on sixty years of age that spring, even though none would admit documentary evidence into the argument. Stengel's true birth date became a running gag because a variety of record books listed different birth dates, July 30, 1889, July 30, 1890, and July 30, 1891. No birth certificate was ever found and Stengel later insisted the accurate date was the 1890 date.

"I was riding in a cab one time with Casey and Edna," recalls Bob Fishel, a former Yankee public relations director and now an assistant to American League president Lee MacPhail. "For some reason or other we got on Casey's birthday. 'I was born July 30, 1890, and you could look it up,' said Stengel, knowing full well that no official document had ever recorded his birth. Edna turned to me sweetly and said simply, ' '89.' Casey got so goddamn mad. He shouted at her, 'Who asked you?' She never lost her composure. Just said over again, ' '89.' "

The 1890 date became more or less the accepted date and Stengel, Daniel, and Drebinger often celebrated birthdays together on Yankee road trips. Drebinger, a bouncy, gregarious fellow, was hard of hearing. He wore a hearing aid and Stengel loved to tease him about it. They knew each other well from Casey's days in Brooklyn. Stengel regularly played the same gag on Drebinger.

"I'm gonna give you my opening day lineup now," he announced, as the writers, all of whom had been informed he was about to nail Drebinger again, gathered around. "My opening day pitcher is Mr.——" Suddenly, Drebinger couldn't hear a thing. He saw Stengel's lips moving with the names of Yankee players, but he was missing them. He turned up the volume on his hearing aid. Stengel became more frenetic in his recitation with his pantomime in full flower. "Goddamn batteries," shouted Drebinger, as he pulled the hearing aid from his chest and flung it to the ground.

In 1950, the Yankees had opened an early spring camp in Phoenix, Arizona, for ten days before the Florida camp. They sent a half-dozen of their West Coast players there before the big camp opened. The purpose of the camp was to give personal instruction on baseball fundamentals to many of their better prospects. Stengel called the camp "an instructural school," and attended for a week.

"I was out there for a week," he told his assembled writers. "I had some of my coaches [Bill] Dickey and [Johnny] Neun out there with me. I knowed I won the pennant last year cause I was standing near that electric pitching machine and before the arm could hit me, Dickey and Neun yelled for me to watch out. If I hadna won, they woulda said, 'Let it hit the old bastard.' "

As defending world champions, the Yankees didn't need much help in 1950. Casey and George Weiss were still determined to rebuild with younger players, ready for the day when the pitching staff would grow old and when the veterans, DiMaggio and Henrich, would be gone. Two youngsters caught everybody's eye that spring. "If they are as good as they say they are," wrote Milton

Gross, in the *New York Post*, "the Yankees will have a tough time sending down two youngsters, Ed Ford, a left-handed pitcher, and Al Martin, a second baseman."

Ed Ford, a blond, wisecracking, tough-talking left-handed pitcher from New York City, had written Stengel a letter in the later stages of the 1949 season.

"I was at Binghamton and having a good year," recalls the Hall of Fame pitcher better known now as Whitey Ford. "The Yankees were having a tough time winning the pennant and I thought I could help. Casey relayed a message through one of the scouts that he would see me in 1950 if I was as good as I said I was."

He was good, but Stengel had Reynolds, Raschi, Lopat, and left-hander Tommy Byrne as starters. He sent Ford out for more seasoning and brought him back in June.

The other cocky kid who showed up that spring, Al Martin, was born Alfred Manuel Pesano in Berkeley, California. His father deserted his mother and she remarried a man named Martin. The mother worked and the boy was raised by his maternal grandmother who took one look at the scrawny, big-nosed baby and called him, "bellis," short for "belissimo," the Italian word for beautiful. The other kids on the street thought his grandmother was calling him "Billy," and he acquired that name. "I didn't know my name was 'Alfred,'" says Martin, "until I started school and the teacher kept hollering, 'Where's Alfred Martin?' and some other kid nudged me."

A spunky kid with more guts than ability, Martin battled his way through school baseball and signed with the Oakland Acorns of the Pacific Coast League. In the final weeks of 1947 and in 1948 he played for Casey Stengel.

"I got there late in '47," recalls Martin, "and the veterans were getting all over me for my big mouth and my big nose and how skinny I was. They also needled me about my batting average at Phoenix, .392. Casey heard them kidding about the light air in Arizona and how balls fly out of those small parks."

"I don't care if he done it in Africa, it's still .392," Stengel said.

"That really touched me," said Martin, "how he would

stick up for a young fellow like me."

Martin had first come to Stengel's attention in 1946. He had tried out for the Oakland club as a seventeen-year-old. Stengel, always talented with a fungo bat, took him on.

"He started hitting me hot grounders, the manager of the club, this very famous baseball man, and I was thrilled. He was hitting them as hard as he could, hoping I'd miss them or ask out. I got every one. Finally he threw his fungo bat in the air, walked away, and said loud enough for me to hear, 'You can't get one past this skinny kid.' I was so excited I couldn't stop shaking."

Casey and Edna Stengel never had any children of their own. Billy Martin, fatherless for most of his life, became Stengel's surrogate son, each feeding on the other, each needing the other, their personalities, attitude, and drive closely linked. It was McGraw and Stengel, teacher and pupil, all over again.

Al Martin, with a newly bobbed nose, arrived from California at the Yankee camp in St. Petersburg, quickly informed the sportswriters his name was Billy Martin, and went out to dinner that first evening with none other than Joe DiMaggio. It was almost unheard of.

"I was a cocky kid," Martin says. "Nothing scared me. Not even the Big Guy. DiMag came up in front of the other players and said, 'Let's have dinner tonight, kid.' After that I was considered Joe's bobo. We'd walk into the clubhouse together a lot. When Joe came in it was like a senator or president coming in. He would walk by a guy and say, 'Hi, kid' and the guy would say, 'Hi, Joe' and it would continue like that down the line. Then he'd come over to me and say, 'Hi, Dago,' and I would say, 'Hi, kid' and we'd both get a big laugh. When Joe quit I got the last bat and last pair of spikes he ever used in a game."

A journeyman player at best, except for a few emotionally charged World Series performances, Martin managed to stay close to the Yankee stars, to DiMaggio, to Mickey Mantle later on (now his closest friend), to Whitey Ford, to Yogi Berra, and always, to Casey Stengel.

"He thought by hanging around the stars he would

become a star," said Minnesota owner Calvin Griffith, one of many baseball people who fired him. "It couldn't work. He might have thought he was a star. Nobody else did."

It was Stengel's strength as a manager that he spent more time with the fringe players than with the stars.

"The first fifteen guys on a club you don't have to bother with," he once said, in explaining his managerial philosophy. "They're always playing and don't need the manager. The next five play once in a while, so you gotta spend some time buttering them up. The last five you gotta be with all the time, because they may be plotting a revolution against you."

Ralph Houk, the former Yankee and Detroit manager, now living in quiet Florida retirement, played in only ninety-one games in his Yankee career. He spent his early youth in the Yankee bullpen.

"Casey always spent a lot time with me," says Houk. "He loved talking to the younger players. That was his way of including them. I was sitting on a train one day and he comes up to me. 'Hey, catcher'—he always called me 'catcher'—'what do you think of the hit-and-run play?' I was just a kid then and I didn't want to disagree with him and we didn't use it much, so I told him I didn't think it was worth a shit. 'You're fulla shit and I tell you why,' he begins, and starts telling me how McGraw thought it was a great play and now he does thirty minutes on McGraw and the Giants and the hit-and-run play. A week later he sees me again, 'Hey, catcher.' Now I'm ready for him. Sure enough, he asks me about the hit-and-run play and I'm smiling and saying what a great play it is and all of a sudden he starts hollering, 'Now wait a minute, for crissakes, it's a horseshit play and if you listen I'll tell you why.' Damned if he didn't do thirty minutes on how McGraw hated it."

Stengel's energy was boundless. Through the spring training days of 1950, he would arrive at the park shortly after 7 o'clock, change quickly into his uniform, study the overnight medical reports gathered by trainer Gus Mauch, meet with his coaches at 9, discuss the two-a-day schedule with them, and move on the field for the 10

o'clock workout. Like McGraw he was a tremendous or-
ganizer, determined that his players would be moving at
all times, unlike other managers who allowed players to
lounge at the batting cage for minutes on end until their
hitting turn. His players would work hard on calisthenics,
would work in the field, would take laps around the park,
would be in constant motion until their hitting turn came.

After the first workout there would be a half-hour break
and a light lunch of juice, soup, and milk would be available for the players. Stengel would meet again with his
coaches. The afternoon session would be run until 2
o'clock. Then, when the players were excused for golf,
rest, or a cold beer, Stengel would meet with the press.
Then he might have a drink or five in the pressroom at
the hotel, take Edna to dinner, return to the Soreno bar
for a nightcap with coaches or press, and retire for three
or four hours sleep. Sometimes his tired eyelids would fall
and he would sit on the bench, his eyes closed, his ears
open, napping lightly while his coaches handled the drills.

"He could probably see more taking a nap," says Ralph
Houk, "than most managers could see wide awake. One
time, on a hot spring day in 1950, we were running a new
play he devised for a pick-off. He was always coming up
with new plays. I looked over at the bench and could see
he was asleep, his head down, not looking at us. I was in
my catching gear doing this play and the sweat was pouring off me in the heat. Somebody banged a bat on the
bench, he jumped up, looked at the field, and said, 'The
hell with it, we don't have the players here to make it
work.' "

Casey Stengel had ways of getting reluctant players in
shape. One of them was to run them in ways they never
expected. That is why he showed them so many trick
plays in the spring and never used them in the season. He
also showed them many plays he did use. As a brilliant
teacher of baseball skills, he forced all his outfielders to
throw relays high. It was something he learned from
McGraw.

"When you throw them low, the infielder has to bend
down and loses a step in relaying the ball home. Throw it

Stengel watches as old pal Harry Truman, another well known man from Missouri, throws one lefthanded to open 1950 baseball season. *(Photo courtesy of the Stengel family.)*

high and the relay home may get your man and you might win the game," Casey explained.

The Yankees broke camp in 1950 and took the train north for the opening of the season. Joe Collins had become the first baseman, Coleman was at second (Martin was on the bench and soon would be dispatched to Kansas City for a month), Rizzuto was at shortstop, and Billy Johnson, who had been hurt by a bitter holdout, was at third. Bauer, DiMaggio, and Woodling were in the outfield and Berra was a full-time catcher.

Rizzuto, who had his finest year in 1950 and would win the American League Most Valuable Player Award, recalls the season with much unhappiness.

"I don't know what happened," he says. "Casey just seemed to be a different person, playing to the writers, second-guessing the players, talking behind everybody's back. One day we were playing the White Sox. They had a fine shortstop named Alex Carrasquel. We have this clubhouse meeting and Casey says, 'Now don't anybody hit the ball to Carrasquel.' Sure enough, we get a couple of guys on one inning, Bauer is up and damned if he doesn't hit to Carrasquel, who starts a double play and we lose the game. Casey stars raving on the bench, 'I told ya not to hit it to Carrasquel, I told ya not to hit it to Carrasquel.' How the hell could you help it?'"

Casey was a perfectionist, driving his players hard, demanding excellence from them at all times, pushing them to limits they didn't think themselves capable of. He knew a ground ball to shortstop was never a good place to hit the ball.

One of the most skilled hitters Stengel had was Gene Woodling, a magician with a bat. Woodling was a very selective hitter, sometimes spotting a pitcher two strikes in hopes of getting a pitch he could pull for a long hit or a home run. The Yankees were playing St. Louis and Lou Kretlow was pitching for the Browns. He started the game by walking the first two hitters on eight pitches. Then Woodling was up.

Casey is standing on the bench hollering, "He's wild, he'll walk the whole ball park." Just then Woodling, who almost always takes two pitches, swings at the first one and grounds into a double play. Casey falls down the dugout step, bangs his knee against the concrete step, and begins screaming at Woodling. Woodling, no shrinking violet, begins screaming back at Casey. Woodling spent the next five days on the corner of the bench.

Casey demanded total obedience on the field. There could be only one manager on a team, one leader, one spokesman for a club. On the Yankees it was Stengel. Some of his more high-strung personalities such as Woodling would chafe at his directions. In 1949 Stengel was pretty much a laissez-faire manager. From 1950 onward, Stengel ran the game with an iron hand, more and more controlling every play, calling the signs, dominating the personality of the players, closely following the strict on-field guidlines of McGraw.

Off the field it was different. He was a hell-raiser himself, was a hell-raiser as a player, and allowed the players great freedoms. He rarely abused a man for late nights or loud drinking or chasing women. He could accept any-

Duke and Duchess of Windsor visit Yankee Stadium in 1950 and join Edna Stengel and Yankee co-owner Del Webb in club box behind Yankee dugout.

thing as long as his men were ready to play.

"Off the field he allowed us to police each other," says Woodling. "If a guy was drinking too much or not taking care of himself, we got him back in line. One word from me or from Bauer or a look from DiMaggio and the guy would be humble."

Bauer once grabbed a Yankee rookie by the shirt after he reported to the park drunk.

"If you ever come to the park like this again, I'll break your head," Bauer said, "now get the hell inside, take that uniform off, and go home." When Stengel inquired about the absence of the player, Bauer came up to the manager and said, "You won't need him today." Casey winked and understood. The Yankees beat Philadelphia 11–3 that afternoon.

Martin rejoined the Yankees in June, told Coleman he would have his job by July, and sat next to Stengel whenever he wasn't playing, which was almost every day. Ford was called up in June, was bombed in Boston in a relief effort, pitched and won in Detroit, and quickly established himself as a class pitcher with a 9–1 rookie record and a 2.81 ERA. DiMaggio was having his last great season at thirty-five with a .301 mark, 122 RBIs, and 32 home runs. Rizzuto batted .324 and fielded like a dream, Bauer hit .320, Yogi hit .322 and learned how to catch, and Johnny Mize hit 25 home runs in 274 at bats as a part-time player. Raschi, Reynolds, and Lopat won 51 games among them and the Yankees won the pennant by three games over Detroit. It was two in a row for Stengel.

The Yankees played the Philadelphia Phillies Whiz Kids in the Series. Raschi outpitched relief pitcher Jim Konstanty, a surprise starter, in the first game, with a 1–0 win. Then Reynolds beat Robin Roberts in ten innings, 2–1, the Yankees won the third game 3–2 on Coleman's ninth inning hit, and Ford, with one-out relief help from Reynolds, beat the Phillies 5–2 to seal the sweep.

Casey Stengel, who had never won a pennant in the National League, now was 2 for 2 as an American League manager.

"I think the 1950 pennant was very important to him," says Yogi Berra. "A lot of people win it once. Sometimes you can be lucky. To win it twice you had to be good."

There would be little quiet in the spring of 1951. The Yankees had arranged to shift training camps from St. Petersburg, Florida, to Phoenix, Arizona. George Weiss got the idea that the Yankees could make more money playing in Arizona as World Champions than they would in Florida, where they were known and familiar. Weiss was always on the alert for a chance to make a buck.

"I was holding out that spring," recalls Eddie Lopat. "I had won eighteen games and Weiss offered me a two-thousand-dollar raise. I wanted ten thousand. I was only making twenty-six thousand dollars. It was a hell of a fight and I think he finally gave me five thousand. Years later I found out Topping and Webb used to give him a top budget figure for payroll. Anytime he came in under that, he got ten percent of the difference. You could see why he tried to hold salaries down."

Despite their success, the Yankees were not the most highly paid players in the game. The payroll of the Boston

Red Sox, under the generous hand of owner Tom Yawkey, was always higher. Yankee player salaries were held down by Weiss for his own financial gain and that of his employers by a simple method. He negotiated with players by telling them their World Series money figured as part of the salary.

"He'd give you this bull that you'd make six or eight thousand dollars in Series money," says Eddie Lopat, "so he could keep your salary down. Once I said, 'What if we don't win? Will you make up the difference?' He said, 'We'll win.' That was the end of it."

Salary figures were always leaked to the press by the club. They were always higher than the player actually received.

"The players were always afraid to let their salaries be known," says Tony Kubek, who arrived at Yankee Stadium in 1957, "because they were embarrassed."

Players who went over Weiss' head to Dan Topping or Del Webb did better. Yogi Berra had a habit of agreeing to terms the night of Yankee pennant victory parties. Stengel always pushed him to Topping, who was generally in a wonderful mood on those occasions, when Yogi complained about being underpaid.

Now the Yankees were in Arizona in another of Stengel's "instructural schools." Casey was looking for a pitcher to replace Whitey Ford, who had been drafted into the army. The Korean War was on and the draft would have an impact on baseball, albeit not quite the same impact as the complete mobilization of World War II.

Three youngsters, who had attended the "instructural school," were asked to stay on as the big camp opened March 1. One was a hard-throwing right-handed pitcher, twenty years old, from El Monte, California, by the name of Tom Morgan. Another was an infielder by the name of Gil McDougald, a thin, bony-faced line-drive hitter with a wide open batting stance.

The third youngster to come out of the "instructural school" in 1951 was a well-muscled, blond nineteen-year-old from Commerce, Oklahoma, named Mickey Charles

Mantle. He was so young, so powerful, so full of potential as a great player that Stengel was almost overwhelmed with excitement.

"Now I don't want you to write that the kid is going to be making the Big Guy move or anything like that," Stengel told the sportswriters. "He's strong, he's got a chance, and why wouldn't you like him if you had him."

Mantle was incredibly shy, a country boy with little more than a passion for baseball and not much experience. Billy Martin quickly took him under his wing. Joe DiMaggio, already revealing to some of his friends that this would be his final season, seemed too distracted. He and Mantle said little in the clubhouse, though DiMaggio did help Mantle in the outfield as the youngster broke in.

"I think all the fuss started in Arizona after the first few exhibition games," recalls Ralph Houk. "Mickey hit some balls that were unbelievable. He was doing it right-handed and he was doing it left-handed and light air or not out there, nobody had ever done things like that before."

Mantle soon became the darling of the press. They hounded him and harassed him. They wrote about his tremendous power and his incredible running speed. The pressure was enormous. He grew shier than he had been. DiMaggio was quietly pushed into the background as he worked hard to get in shape. His back hurt, a knee was bothering him, and both his heels were giving him some pain.

"I think Mickey was afraid of Joe," says Jerry Coleman. "How could you not be? He was coming in to play center field, everybody knew that. Casey didn't help the situation much. He raved about Mickey and hardly ever mentioned Joe to the writers. I don't think DiMaggio was jealous of the kid or anything like that, I just think he felt that he had already done it and the kid hadn't and he deserved to go out as the the number-one guy."

With Mantle getting most of the attention and Di-Maggio pretty much left alone, the Yankees came to Brooklyn for an exhibition game before the season opener. Mantle sat on the bench before the game, penciled into Stengel's lineup as the right fielder. Casey walked up to the kid.

"C'mere, I wanna show you something," he said.

Mantle jumped up, stuffed his glove in his back pocket, and followed Stengel out toward right field. Stengel began talking of his days at Ebbets Field, how he had played for the Dodgers, how he had learned how to play the tricky right-field wall at Ebbets Field, just two hundred ninety-seven feet from home plate with the wall and the screen above meeting at a strange angle.

Now Stengel was at the fence with Mantle behind him. He pulled a ball from his pocket and began throwing it off the wall, first high, then lower, finally at the angle, watching the ball come off in strange ways. Mantle carefully studied his manager's whirling motions.

"Got it?" Stengel asked.

Young Mantle seemed transfixed. Finally he said, "Gee, Casey, I didn't know you played here."

"For crissakes," bellowed Stengel, "you think I was born old?"

Mantle's name was put on the Yankee roster the day before the 1951 season opened. The minimum salary was $6,000 a year, but Stengel had asked Weiss to give this special rookie $7,000, and Weiss, growling a bit, had finally gone along. Stengel would go out of his way to help young players. He knew they would always remember it. He was planning for the future.

There has never been a purer baseball talent than Mickey Mantle. "He had it in his body to be great," Stengel said.

His physical ability was exceptional, a compact five-foot eleven-inch, two-hundred-pounder with enormous shoulders and chest. If power was all there was to the game, nobody could have doubted Mantle's greatness. But there was more. Driven by a father who wanted more for his son than the black soot of the zinc mines where he worked, he had controlled Mantle's young baseball career every step of the way. Stengel, who was nearly sixty-one that spring, was more of a grandfather image to Mantle than a father image. Mantle's father, Elven "Mutt" Mantle, was not forty years old when he died later that year. Stengel felt responsible for this untried nineteen-year-old. He knew he had it in him to be exceptional. Mantle's biggest problem was his uncontrollable emotions, his flaming temper, his reckless intensity on and off the field. Mantle's worst enemy was his own makeup.

Mantle had hit some prodigious home runs, had gotten some big hits as a rookie, but was striking out at an alarming rate. In June Stengel decided to send Mantle back to the minors hoping he would relax without the pressures of New York. When he reported to the Yankee farm club at Kansas City he told his father, "I'm quitting." His father embarrassed him by saying, "Go ahead if you want. You can work in the mines the rest of your life."

Stengel had been pained to send Mantle out, but he knew it was for the youngster's own good and his own. If Mantle was as good as he thought, his natural ability would bring him back. It was the only solution to the strikeouts, the sulking, the thrown bats, the unfulfilled potential.

He would come back later that season, finish strong, and go on to a brilliant Hall of Fame career. Stengel would grow impatient with Mantle's immaturity and Mantle would be angry at Stengel's prodding, but they would have a warm relationship for years.

"He used to get mad at me sometimes," said Mantle, "and I guess I used to get mad at him, though I wouldn't show it when he was around."

Mantle, who had a mean streak in him, would be one of the Yankees who would do much to undermine Casey's authority in later years. He would talk behind his back, make fun of the old man's ways, and generally lead players into quiet rebellion against Casey. "Ralph Houk is the best manager I ever played for," says Mantle, without a second thought.

After another bitter pennant race, the third in three seasons for Stengel's Yankees, they edged Cleveland by five games for the third straight pennant. Stengel's team was marvelous in the stretch, built around the pitching of Vic Raschi, Eddie Lopat, and Allie Reynolds. Raschi won

21 games, Lopat won 21, and Reynolds won 19. Bauer led the club in batting with a .296 mark. Berra hit 27 homers and won the MVP award. DiMaggio, in his final season as player, though he would not officially announce his retirement until December, batted .263 on painful legs and sore knees.

The big talk in baseball when the Series opened was still about the Miracle of Coogan's Bluff. Bobby Thomson had hit a three-run homer in the bottom of the ninth inning to give the Giants a 5–4 victory over the Dodgers in a National League playoff. The Giants won the first game, the Yankees won the second, the Giants won the third, and then it rained.

"I put the whommy on the Giants," Stengel told the sportswriters. "I needed the rain to bring my big pitcher back."

The day off allowed Stengel to bring back Allie Reynolds, who pitched a strong game for a 6–2 Yankee victory at the Polo Grounds. The Yankees won the next two games and Stengel had his third World Series in a row, a feat turned in only once before in baseball history by Joe McCarthy's Yankees in 1936, 1937, and 1938. That club also added a fourth World Series to its consecutive triumphs, in 1939, and that would be Stengel's goal now.

On October 11, 1951, Casey and Edna Stengel finished packing their belongings in the hotel suite at New York's Essex House, across from Central Park, and called for their favorite bellboy, Tommy Addazio.

"I don't think Casey ever knew my name," says Addazio, now retired after nearly forty years at the hotel. "Edna always did. She'd always say hello, do the tipping, and ask me about my family. Casey always wanted to know if I had any ballplaying relatives who could play like DiMaggio."

Addazio says he would often knock on the door to bring up a meal or a pot of tea, or take the bags down if the Stengels were leaving on a trip.

"Most of the time I would get in there Casey would be in a chair reading the sports pages. This one time I came in after Edna opened the door and Casey is on the floor, wearing just his shorts and a T-shirt. He was doing push-ups. 'Forgot to finish my exercises,' he said. I almost passed out. He musta been sixty or sixty-five years old then and he was doing push-ups like a kid. He was some strong guy."

"When we were all together in Oakland with him," says Mary Lavagetto, wife of Cookie Lavagetto, who coached for Casey in Oakland and with the New York Mets, "we used to call him Popeye, the Sailor Man. He just seemed the strongest man in the world and a little strange like Popeye."

"I was always amazed at his physical strength," says John Lawson, Edna's nephew, who lived near the Stengels in Glendale. "He would come up to me, grab me by the wrist, and say, 'Wanna wrestle with Uncle Casey?' I never did, no matter how old he got."

Stengel also talked with his hands. When he wanted to make a point, he would poke a finger into a man's chest and say, "You're fulla shit and I'll tell you why." One time he poked his finger into a young sportswriter's chest—this young sportswriter—and left a red mark on the chest that didn't go away for two days.

Stengel never stopped thinking of himself as a physical person. Even in his later years he could grip a man with a handshake that would crack knuckles. He could hold on to a reluctant listener until the blood was choked off. He had long fingers and could rub dirt on and off a baseball with one hand. He put those fingers to work scratching his name in his large, sprawling letters on more than five hundred Christmas cards in 1951.

As Stengel prepared for his fourth season as Yankee manager, he knew this year would be different. He would be shooting for Joe McCarthy's record of four straight championships and he knew he would be attempting it without Joe DiMaggio. On December 11, 1951, DiMaggio had made it official. He had retired. Stengel had flown to New York for the occasion. DiMaggio had turned thirty-seven in November and his body, ravaged by the incredible pressures of his selfless efforts on behalf of the Yankees, had simply broken down.

"I remember one day we were playing in 1951," says Eddie Lopat. "It was a hot afternoon in Washington. We had a doubleheader. Yogi had played the first game and we had won. Then he sat out the second game, Charley Silvera played, failed to hit with men on bases, and we wound up with a 3–3 tie called by darkness. When it was over, me and the Chief had to hold DiMag under his arms and almost drag him into the clubhouse, he was so weak. He comes in and sees Yogi, all calm and cool after resting, at the food table. He just looked at Yogi and said, 'You shoulda caught both games.' Then he just stared at him. I think DiMag's impact was so enormous that Yogi didn't miss a game for weeks after that."

Now DiMaggio was announcing his retirement. The press releases had been handed out, the announcement had been made in the Yankee offices, and the first question was, "Why are you quitting?" DiMaggio simply said, "I no longer have it."

The Yankees had tried to persuade him to stay on as a part-time player and pinch hitter for a couple of more years and had actually drawn up a 1952 contract for $100,000, which now sits unsigned in a glass case at the Baseball Hall of Fame in Cooperstown.

Years later, as the waves licked against the dock across from DiMaggio's Restaurant on Fisherman's Wharf in San Francisco, DiMaggio's older brother, Tom, the unofficial family spokesman, was asked why Joe had really quit that day when he still could make $100,000 for a part-time season. At first he just shook his head and wouldn't answer the question. Then he turned back and said quietly, "He wasn't Joe DiMaggio anymore."

There is no denying there had been some friction between DiMaggio and Stengel. The years had colored the case. Stengel spoke only with high praise of DiMaggio from the day of his retirement on. DiMaggio was always warm to the old man in later years. But there had been some bitterness, some anger, some animosity between the two and each one, respectful of the great skill of the other, could now breathe easier apart than they ever had in three seasons together.

Stengel stood at the microphones that December day in the Yankee offices and said, "I just gave the Big Guy's glove away to the Hall of Fame. He was the greatest player I ever managed."

As Stengel greeted his 1952 Yankees, it was obvious there had been a changing of the guard. Mickey Mantle, apparently recovered from knee damage suffered when he had slipped and fallen in a drainage ditch in Ebbets Field during the World Series, was now moved to center field. Jerry Coleman, a World War II Marine Corps fighter pilot, was scheduled for call-up again for duty in the Korean conflict and would soon be gone. Billy Martin, who some facetiously suggested had notified Coleman's superiors as to his availability, was now the second baseman. Gil McDougald had won the third-base job permanently. Veteran Johnny Sain, picked up late in 1951, would be an important spot pitcher.

DiMaggio was home in San Francisco. He had been signed to do a pregame television show for the Yankees and would be in New York early in April. For now, he sipped tea each morning in his family restaurant, played golf, spent the early evenings playing cards with friends, and dined in many of San Francisco's most pleasant restaurants. One day he saw a picture in a newspaper that interested him. It was of a ballplayer named Gus Zernial, a slugger with the Philadelphia A's, who trained that spring in Pasadena, California. With Zernial was a Hollywood starlet. DiMaggio later saw Zernial at a charity exhibition baseball game. "How come I never get to pose with beautiful girls like that?" DiMaggio kiddingly asked Zernial. The Philadelphia slugger explained that a press agent named David March had arranged the picture. DiMaggio made a phone call and a date was arranged.

The name of the starlet was Marilyn Monroe.

The fact that DiMaggio had departed the Yankees posed major problems for Stengel. DiMaggio was slipping as a player, but he could not easily be replaced. Stengel was uncertain Mantle could play center field on his bad knee and experimented with journeymen Bob Cerv and

Irv Noren before going to Mantle. More importantly the players would miss the Big Guy's leadership.

"It just wasn't the same ball club without Joe," says Rizzuto. "It is impossible to measure his hold on the team, his impact, his status. His leadership was essential. A lot of us thought we wouldn't win without Joe."

Casey was not among them. Aging players are always difficult for a manager to handle, especially ones as proud and laconic as DiMaggio. In some ways Stengel felt freer as the Yankee manager after DiMaggio retired. There was now only one Big Guy on the Yankees. His name was Stengel. He would run the game and make sure the players ran themselves.

"The thing a lot of people forget about our Yankee teams," says Lopat, "is we were together. We didn't play for individual records. We played for winning. Guys stayed on top of other guys. Casey didn't bother much with discipline. He knew we disciplined ourselves. One time Mantle was in a hitting slump. You know how he was when he wasn't hitting, bats flying, helmets flying, water coolers getting whacked, things like that. This one time he had his head down in the outfield thinking about his slump (Joe Garagiola once said of a baseball slump, "It's like a cold. If you work on it it will go away in two weeks, if you don't it will take fourteen days.") and somebody hit a line drive that got by him as he lollipopped after it. He came in after the inning, Bauer stared at him for a minute and said, 'You sick, kid?' Mantle just shook his head and curled up in the corner of the dugout. He played ball after that."

Billy Martin, with Coleman flying jets in Korea, suddenly emerged as a leader of the team. DiMaggio led by deeds, Martin led by words. He fought with the umpires. He fought with opposing players, starting field fights with Clint Courtney of St. Louis, stepping on his glasses, and with Jimmy Piersall of Boston, telling him he should be locked up in a crazy house, as well as with other players around the league. Stengel, who had spent his early professional career as a player doing much the same thing, maximizing his talent with his tongue, egged Martin on.

The relationship grew deeper and stronger between the two of them.

The Yankees won the pennant again in another tough struggle with Cleveland. They finished with ninety-five wins to the Indians' ninety-three and went into the World Series in 1952 against Brooklyn. The Dodgers, apparently suffering no lasting effects from the traumatic loss to the Giants and Bobby Thomson in 1951, won the flag by four games.

The 1952 World Series is remembered for a single play. Casey could talk about it for hours, describing the movement of half-a-dozen players in detail, reciting the reaction of the Dodgers in pantomime, creating a moment that was frozen in time, talking endlessly about it in a style of his own, best described some thirty years before the play by Ring Lardner who said, "Casey Stengel could talk on any track, wet or dry."

Brooklyn won the first game of the 1952 Series 4–2 behind Joe Black. Vic Raschi had evened it up 7–1 with a three-hitter. Preacher Roe had beaten Eddie Lopat in game three 5–3, and Allie Reynolds had come back to win game four 2–0. Carl Erskine had survived a five-run Yankee fifth inning in game five for a 6–5 eleventh-inning win, and Raschi and Reynolds had teamed for a 3–2 win in game six to tie it. Now it was game seven. The Yankees led 4–2 in the seventh. The Dodgers loaded the bases. Bob Kuzava, a left-hander, came in to relieve. Lopat had started, Reynolds had relieved him, and Raschi had relieved Reynolds as Stengel urged his weary pitching staff on, seeking that fourth straight Series triumph. Now it was Kuzava against Duke Snider. The count went to 3–2 and Snider popped out. The hitter was Jackie Robinson, a fiery competitor and a victim of Stengel's biting tongue. Stengel, always looking for a man's weak spot, had yelled "duck-ass" at Jackie, making fun of the strange way Robinson ran. Robinson had stared at Stengel and now ground the dust from the bat. The Ebbets Field crowd was roaring as the count went to 3–2. Kuzava threw a soft curve at Robinson. This reporter asked Stengel years later to describe the play.

Machine gun style, this is what it sounded like.

"We had this left-hander, Gazzara [Kuzava] and they had that brilliant Mr. Rob-A-Son at the plate and all of a sudden, whoops, here comes a slow ball when you expect a fastball, and why wouldn't you tap it into right field if you wuz right-handed, but Mr. Rob-A-Son tried to hit the ball over the building and instead he hit a ball up the shoot, excuse me, as hard as Ned in the third reader, and Mr. Collins, which was my first baseman was counting his money so he never seen it and Mr. Berra, my catcher, is standing with his hands on his hips yelling for Mr. Collins and Mr. Gazzara did the pitching and he ain't about to do the catchin', so that leaves the second baseman, and you know who that is, to come in, lose his cap, and get it before it hits the grass, which if he did would be kicked because he was runnin' so fast and almost tripped over the mound which was a mountain in Brooklyn to help them sinker ball pitchers, Mr. Erskine and them and McGraw used to do that too, and why wouldn't ya, if you had spitters in the staff, but my rooster caught it and it didn't hit off his schnozz like a lot of them would have." Then he stopped and said, "Get it?"

"I didn't know it was a good catch," Martin said later, "until I heard Casey talk about it."

The sight of the skinny second baseman racing in for that little pop-up made "Movietone News," and made Billy Martin a heroic baseball figure.

Kuzava got by the next two innings, the Yankees won the game 4–2, and Casey Stengel had managed the Yankees to four straight World Series championships. He was now in a class with Joe McCarthy, four straight championships of the world, with a chance to stand alone in 1953.

The Yankees would be stronger in 1953 because Stengel's young left-handed pitcher, Whitey Ford, had now returned from service.

As Stengel and the Yankees drove for their fifth straight pennant, Ford quickly emerged as the pitching leader, Mantle the batting leader, and Martin the team leader. Ford would win 18 games, Mantle would hit 21 homers and knock in 92 runs, and Berra would bat in 108 runs with 27

Two famed ex-athletes, West Point football player Dwight
Eisenhower and Central High's Casey Stengel, meet at 1953
opener.

homers. Mantle also hit the longest homer of his career early that season, a drive off left-hander Chuck Stobbs in Washington, measured at five hundred sixty-five feet by publicist Red Patterson's suddenly available tape measure.

The Yankees had an eighteen-game winning streak from late May through early June in 1953 and a nine-game losing streak in late June that brought them back to the field.

"Every day during the winning streak," remembers Billy Martin, "the old man would chew us out for something. I mean he could remember a play a week earlier that we hadn't done right in a 10–1 game or a ball that hit the wall and was played into a triple when it might have been a double. Growl, growl, growl. That's all he did. And we kept winning, winning, winning. It was just the opposite in the losing streak, he was quiet and gentle. I hardly knew it was Casey."

During the losing streak, Stengel berated the press (he even locked them out of the clubhouse once), fought with the umpires, was grouchy with Edna, wouldn't eat properly, and stayed up all hours of the night. But he never let on to the players how severely he was taking the defeats.

"As long as they're playin' their hardest," he said years later, "you can't do a thing. Making them feel bad don't help them win."

"If there was any one great skill Casey had as a manager," says Eddie Lopat, "it was in knowing when to pick his spots. He didn't have a degree, but he was one of the greatest doctors of psychiatry I had even seen."

The Yankees won the pennant in 1953 by a comfortable margin of seven games. No team had even won five pennants in a row, not Joe McCarthy's Yankees or John McGraw's Giants or Connie Mack's A's. Only Casey Stengel's Yankees did that and he gave credit to his favorite manager, McGraw.

"What I learned from McGraw I used with all of them," he said. "They're still playing with a round ball, a round bat, and nine guys on a side."

The Yankees won the World Series four games to two.

Billy Martin had an outstanding Series with an average of
.500 and hit two homers, as did Mantle and McDougald.
Carl Erskine of Brooklyn turned in the outstanding pitching feat with fourteen strikeouts in a 3–2 third-game win.
Johnny Mize sat on the Yankee bench all game second-
guessing his teammates for swinging and missing at Erskine's curves, which often bounced in the dirt.

"He's killin' worms, he's killin' worms," Stengel yelled
at Erskine. "Lay off the pitch."

"Make him get it up," said Mize.

Then Mize was sent up to pinch-hit for Vic Raschi in the
ninth inning. Erskine had thirteen strikeouts and had two
strikes on Mize. He threw a ball that bounced in the dirt,
Mize swung and missed it, and Martin, never one to miss
a chance to needle, shouted, "Make him get it up, make
him get it up," as Mize trudged unhappily back to the
bench.

In the last of the ninth inning of the last Series game of
1953, with the score tied 3–3, Hank Bauer walked, Mickey
Mantle beat out a hit, and Billy Martin singled to center
to win the Series.

Stengel raced out of the dugout to hug Martin as he
came back in. The Yankee Stadium crowd of 62,370 stood
and applauded. Edna Stengel sat in her seat behind the
Yankee dugout and cried. Hazel Weiss, sitting in the next
seat, gave her a big hug.

Five pennants in a row. Five world championships. The
most outstanding managerial feat in baseball history.
Casey Stengel, who had feared he wasn't man enough for
the job of managing the Yankees that October day of 1948,
now realized he had the best managerial record ever in
Series play. All season, as the Yankees won, he was funny
and gay and entertaining. As they lost he was crotchety
and angry and ill. He was putting on his "change of faces"
as fast as the fortunes of the Yankees changed.

Suddenly, at sixty-three years of age, when most men
are considering retirement, he was sitting on top of his
profession. He was no longer a clown, he was a genius. In
cold type, a quarter of a century later, the five Yankee
championships in a row, seem improbable. He had some

great players to be sure, but he maneuvered all of his players, platooned, motivated, guided, and stole games better than any manager ever did. He had DiMaggio at the end of his career and Mantle at the beginning of his. DiMaggio had been a better player before and Mantle would be a better player later. Berra was probably at his peak in those seasons, and Reynolds and Raschi and Page and Coleman certainly were. But Bauer and Woodling and Joe Collins and Bobby Brown and Irv Noren and Bob Cerv were hardly more than average players. It was Stengel's handling of these players, his understanding of their personalities, his cleverness in using their skills, his wisdom in calling on small details, that made the Yankees winners. Stengel once said after a pennant win, "I never coulda done it without my players." A quarter of a century later it seems obvious "his players never coulda done it without him." Stengel had learned his trade well through his playing days, his managerial days at Brooklyn and Boston, his apprenticeship for the Yankees in the minors. When he had the horses, as Charlie Grimm suggested, he could finally ride them to victory.

He had become an important public figure with this last victory. His face was as recognizable as any face in America. In the twilight of his years, when the life cycle is usually descending, Casey Stengel's star was ascending madly. He had always been loved. Now, finally, he was admired.

Douglas MacArthur, another well known West Point athlete and
speech-maker, meets Stengel after his recall from Korea.

10. The Señor Beat Me and You Could Look It Up

A MAN IS OFTEN TESTED by the friends he keeps in a lifetime. Casey Stengel had a legion of friends, many, including Runt Marr, Dutch Zwilling, and Harold Lederman, the jeweler, dating back to his days as a Kansas City schoolboy. There were some few friends in Glendale, mostly Edna's friends to be sure, that Stengel would dine with on occasion while on the road. He would be courteous, generous, always picking up the check, warm, and giving. But his real friends, his true friends, the ones he felt most comfortable with, the ones he could drink late with, argue with, laugh with, had to have some connection with his life's work, baseball. They might be ex-teammates such as Zach Wheat in Kansas City, ex-players such as Al Lopez in Florida, club officials, retired opposing players, newspapermen. They had to know a curve ball from a billiard ball, a home run from a run home. They had to be tuned in to Stengelese and know what Casey meant when he said, "run, sheep, run" or "butcher boy" or "road apple," or "worm killers." For more than four decades one of his closest friends was Al Lopez, a catcher on his 1932 Dodgers, a fellow investor in Texas oil wells, and in 1954 an opposing manager with the Cleveland Indians.

The idea of the game was to win, but the joy of the game was even greater when one could beat one's good friends. There was something special to beating a Frankie Frisch at Pittsburgh or an Al Lopez in Cleveland.

Cleveland, under Lopez, had a strong team in 1954. Three future Hall of Famers—Early Wynn, Bob Lemon, and Bob Feller—anchored the pitching staff. Two other starters, Mike Garcia and Art Houtteman, were first rate. Cleveland had the two best relief pitchers in the game in Don Mossi, a jug-eared left-hander always nominated on all dugout "ugly teams," and Ray Narleski. Hal Newhouser, who had won 118 games in five seasons with Detroit from 1944 through 1948, was a spot starter. The offense was solid with Bobby Avila, Al Rosen, and Larry Doby, the league's first Negro player.

"If I don't win the pennant this year," said Stengel, in the spring of 1954 despite the obvious Cleveland threat, "they oughta commence firing the manager."

After five straight championships Stengel felt contempt for the rest of the American League. Most of his young players, Mantle, Martin, Berra, Ford, were approaching their peak years. The team had been improved with a husky first baseman out of Purdue named Moose Skowron and a handsome third baseman out of California named Andy Carey, as famed for his prodigious appetite as for his lucious-looking wife.

"Lopez says he can beat you this year," a reporter goaded Stengel before the Yankees broke camp.

"Did the Mexican say that?" Well, tell the Señor, unless my team gets hit by a truck and my brain rots, he ain't gonna win because the Yankees are," Stengel said.

Cleveland got off fast. So did the Yankees. Cleveland continued hot and the Yankees slipped back. Vic Raschi, traded away to St. Louis after a holdout, was gone. Phil Rizzuto showed signs of slipping after being the regular shortstop since 1941, Jerry Coleman didn't hit much, and Mantle, who had undergone his second knee operation, was late in coming on. The Indians were so hot none of this really mattered.

"We'll catch 'em," Stengel convinced the press.

The Indians beat the Yankees twice in a Cleveland doubleheader on September 12 and never were challenged again. They won 111 games, the best record in baseball history, and were feted with a parade downtown across Euclid Avenue in Cleveland with the lake breezes blowing through the open convertibles filled with happy Indians. The Yankees, meanwhile, won 103 games, the most ever under Stengel. It was not enough.

Through the entire chase Stengel, true to his fashion, never lost hope. He never quit on his team, played every game as if that victory would reverse the inevitable. On the bench during the Cleveland doubleheader loss he stood up for eighteen straight innings, nearly six hours, shouting and cheering his club. "You gotta be awake, you gotta be awake," he shouted as any Yankee got on base. He walked up and down the bench constantly. He rolled his fists over and over each other in a sign that he wanted more speed from his base runners. He slapped himself hard in the chest as he implored his hitters to drive a ball against a wall. He cupped his hands and yelled at the opposing pitchers with his screeching voice. "Butcher boy, butcher boy," he screamed at Hank Bauer as Early Wynn, a huge right-hander, threw high fastballs. When Bauer popped up one of Wynn's blazing fastballs for the final out in the doubleheader loss, Casey mumbled, "road apple," his word for fool, and trudged into the clubhouse. Then he began planning his next day's lineup so he could muster a new drive on the Indians. This time it was not to be.

The Yankee pennant-winning streak was over at five straight. Stengel was a loser for the first time in the American League. There was at least one consolation. He had been beaten by a friend.

Years later, on quiet summer nights, Stengel would sit at some hotel bar and talk about his 1954 Yankees. He would try to explain how a team could win 103 games and not win a pennant. Then he would say, "We had a splendid season, but the Señor beat me and you could look it up."

In the spring of 1955 a former platooned outfielder by the name of Casey Stengel, now a second-place manager, searched for a strong right-handed hitter for the Yankees. Despite the Cleveland victory in 1954, the Yankees, with 103 wins, were still fundamentally a sound club. Stengel believed he could make them stronger with another right-handed hitter, another platooned player.

"He was carrying that platooning to ridiculous extremes by then," says Phil Rizzuto. "One game he had me, Willy Miranda, and Billy Hunter platooning at shortstop and none of us came to bat. He was taking me out all the time. I move up to hit and I'd hear Casey screaming from the dugout, 'Hold the gun, hold the gun.' That would make me so damn mad. He always waited until I was in the batter's box."

Yogi Berra and Mickey Mantle were the power leaders of the team and Casey always felt the switch-hitting Mantle was a better hitter left-handed, even if he did seem to have more power right-handed. "Right-handed," he would say, as he ran his hand across the letters of his uniform, "Mantle is blind up here." He would like to have a strong right-handed hitter to place in the lineup between Berra and Mantle. He found him that spring of 1955 in a six-foot two-inch, two hundred ten-pound catcher-outfielder from St. Louis by the name of Elston Howard. He was a strong line drive hitter with enormous hands and thick wrists. He could hit a ball hard to any part of the field. He had won the Most Valuable Player Award in the International League at Toronto. He was the perfect Yankee rookie, soft-spoken, well-mannered, well-educated, dedicated to excellence, a proven team player.

He also was a black man.

In 1954 the Supreme Court of the United States had struck down the long-held principle of "separate but equal" schools in the Brown decision, and Blacks were on the move in every area of American life. Baseball had been integrated in 1946 with the signing of Jackie Robinson, who was the Rookie of the Year for the Dodgers in 1947. One by one, teams signed Negro players. The Yankees said nothing. They refused to comment publicly on their racial attitudes. There was nothing in the backgrounds of millionaires Dan Topping or Del Webb, the team owners, or George Weiss, the general manager, to indicate they cared to deal with the question, let alone solve it. Pressures grew. Marchers demonstrated outside Yankee Stadium. In 1954 Howard, staying away from the team in the private home of a St. Petersburg Negro doctor, trained with the Yankees before being sent to Toronto. The situation was repeated in 1955 as Howard fought for a spot on the club.

"We had an exhibition game in Miami," remembers Howard. "There still weren't a lot of black players in baseball. I was at a black hotel, the Sir John, on the day we played the Dodgers. I walked in and I saw Robinson, Campanella, Newcombe, and Gilliam. 'Oh you guys stay here, too.' Robinson said, 'Not much longer.'"

After a strong spring and proven ability to play the outfield, first base, and catch ("Casey called me a three-way platoon," says Howard), the first Negro player to make the club went north with the Yankees.

Stengel announced to the writers that Howard had made the club. He said he would use him in three positions, platoon him with Irv Noren at the start, make him his number-one right-handed pinch hitter. Howard could hit, hit with power, field, and throw. The only important baseball skill he lacked was running speed.

"When I finally get a nigger," Stengel told the press, "I get the only one that can't run."

It was a remark that would be repeated over and over about Howard through the years. Was Casey Stengel a racist?

"I never thought so," says Howard, now a Yankee coach. "I never felt any prejudice around Casey. He treated me the same as he did any other player."

Casey Stengel was born in Kansas City in 1890. People born in Kansas City in 1890—except for some few exceptions—called black people "niggers." He would use the term frequently, sometimes even resorting to the more derogatory "jungle bunny" when he spoke later of lesser black players he had with the New York Mets—Choo Choo Coleman, Joe Christopher, and Charlie Neal.

Howard says he never felt anything less than a Yankee around Stengel.

"I remember in the World Series he would scream at Newcombe and Robinson and Campanella from the bench. I never heard him scream racial things. I also heard him scream at Hodges and Reese and Snider in the same way," says Howard.

Jackie Robinson, to his dying day, insisted that Stengel was a bigot. "He never gave black players an equal chance," Robinson said.

Robinson's close friend, Howard Cosell, agrees.

"He was a doddering old man and a racist who should have been retired twenty years before he was," says Cosell. "Jackie always thought he was a bigot."

Casey Stengel always thought Cosell was a bore. He tried to keep his players from going on his show in its earliest days and refused to be interviewed by Cosell when Cosell and Ralph Branca had a pregame show with the Mets. Cosell is less than an objective observer about Stengel's racial attitudes.

Left-handed pitcher Alvin Jackson played for Stengel for four years with the Mets. He is a black man, the pitching coach in Boston, and one of the few black coaches in the major leagues.

"He never treated me with anything but respect," says Jackson.

Stengel was a man of his times, a nineteenth-century white midwesterner who had to be pulled kicking and screaming into the racial liberalism of the twentieth century.

Says Howard, "I don't think he ever cared about your color if you wore the Yankee uniform with pride."

Howard wore it with pride. He remembers Stengel in the lobby of the Muehlebach Hotel in his native Kansas City early in 1955.

"I had stayed in a black hotel the first time in," Howard recalls. "Now on the second trip Casey came to me in the lobby and said, 'Just get your key like everybody else.' I walked up to the desk, the key was there with my name on it, and I went to my room like everybody else. Then I was so frightened I double locked my door and put a chair against it. The phone rang and it was Phil Rizzuto, my great white father. 'Come on down and have dinner with me in my room.' After that it was all the same for everybody. I asked Casey about it later. He said he went to George and said, 'Howard's one of my players, ain't he? If he don't stay here, we don't stay here.' That settled it."

There would be a number of other black players, Suitcase Simpson and Hector Lopez, most notably, during Stengel's Yankee tenure, but the Yankees would never be considered leaders in the integration of baseball. It is ironic that after the fall of Casey Stengel's Yankee empire under general manager Ralph Houk, starting in 1965 with most of Stengel's players now gone or too old, the Yankees would not come back as an American League power until 1976 with fifteen Blacks on that twenty-five man roster.

There were no movers around the Yankees in Stengel's time for black players. Topping, Webb, Stengel, and traveling secretary Bill McCorry, a crotchety old retired player who said "No nigger will ever have a berth on any train I'm running," all would have been happier if the social change had never brought the pressures upon them. Significantly, it was Lonesome George Weiss who supplied the players and actually put them in Yankee uniforms and it is at Weiss' doorstep that the "No Niggers Need Apply" sign must be hung.

Through it all, even though he was being badgered on one side by militant blacks calling him an Uncle Tom and on the other side by racists (the hate mail reached a crescendo in 1963 when Howard won the MVP title and was pictured in most every newspaper in America with his light-skinned wife, Arlene, who many viewers decided must be white), Howard survived. He thanks Casey for it.

"He made me feel part of the club," says Howard. "He made me feel I was a Yankee. The Sunday night before the 1955 season opened [publicity director] Bob Fishel called me and said I was to go on the Ed Sullivan television show with Casey. I went to the studio and there was Casey and Johnny Kucks and Tom Sturdivant. We were the three rookies who had made the club. He was bragging about the three rookies and then he tells Sullivan, 'This is my three-way man here, the best I ever got at a lotta positions and he can do a number of things which a lot of them can't.' Sullivan just stood there staring at him. I felt pretty good with all that bragging about me."

The only thing about Stengel that angered Howard was the platooning.

"Sometimes he'd take me out for a pinch hitter against a right-handed pitcher and I'd go home and let off steam at Arlene and she would just say, 'Stay calm, your time will come.' She probably understood the old man better than I did," says Howard.

The Yankees won the pennant and were scheduled for a barnstorming trip through Japan.

"I didn't want to go," recalls Howard. "I wanted to be home with Arlene. She was pregnant with our first boy. He said I could work on some things over there and he would let me stay in contact with Arlene by phone. He paid the bills for the phone and also picked up the hospital tab. Arlene's room was filled with flowers from the Yankees."

Stengel sat down next to Howard one night at the hotel bar in Japan. He began talking about Satchel Paige, the great Negro pitcher, who had been brought to the big leagues by Bill Veeck.

"He starts telling me how he faced him in the twenties and what a great pitcher he was and this went on into the night and I'm falling asleep and he's going a mile a minute. I said, 'Casey, I gotta get some rest,' and he says, 'Now wait a minute for crissakes,' and he's off and running again. Then I protested that I had to play the next day and he tells me he won't play me. Then we finally quit about 5 A.M. and I'm dead and I remind him he said he won't play me and now we go to the park and sure enough the old bastard has my name on the lineup card. When I complain to him, he says I would only play two innings. I played all nine and felt like a dishrag for three days."

Toward the end of the trip, Howard told Stengel he needed a raise now that he was a father. Stengel told him he would see what he could do.

"We get back home," Howard says, "and I get my contract for 1956 and it calls for the same seven thousand I got in 1955 and I'm really pissed off. I sent it back. It was nearly March and I'm at a banquet in St. Louis with Stan Musial. I tell him about my contract and he says, 'Just sit back and wait. You'll hear from them.' Finally, a few days before spring training a new contract comes for fourteen thousand dollars. I sign it real quick and send it back. The first day I asked Casey, 'Did you help me get that?' He just winked."

Howard says Casey Stengel's greatest strength was that he was a player's manager.

"One time we lost a few games and George Weiss was angry because some of the players were staying out late. We have a clubhouse meeting and Casey is going over the hitters and all of a sudden he says, 'And George has the detectives after you, so watch your step.' The detectives followed Tony Kubek and Bobby Richardson into a church and then into a malted milk parlor. Casey was always looking out for his players," says Howard.

Elston Howard, closing in on a quarter of a century as a Yankee now, leaned back in his chair. His voice grew thin and choked. He said, "Casey Stengel was a good man, good for the game, good for the press, good for the public. If you busted your ass and played hard for him, he was good for you, too."

Howard batted .290 in 97 games as a Yankee rookie. The Yankees won the pennant by three games over the Indians. They finally lost a World Series to the Dodgers in seven games with Johnny Podres shutting the Yankees out 2–0. It set off the largest demonstrations of joy in Brooklyn since V-J Day. Howard ended the Series with a ground ball to shortstop Pee Wee Reese, who threw to Gil Hodges at first for the final out. Don Hoak, at third base in place of Jackie Robinson, would always recall the instant, if not totally accurately.

Years later, while Hodges was managing the Mets, Reese and Hoak, both out of baseball, got together in a hotel bar. They drank late into the night. They began arguing about the last play, Hoak kidding Reese that he had made a bad throw and was saved by Hodges, Reese insisting the throw was on the mark. "Let's call Gil," said Hoak. They dialed the San Francisco hotel where the Mets were staying on a road trip, called for Hodges' room, and awakened a sleepy manager. "Gil, this is Hoak," said the third baseman. "I'm here with Pee Wee." Hodges caught the slurred words quickly. "It bounced," he said, and hung up the phone.

Casey Stengel had signed a new two-year contract with the Yankees in 1955. Now he had won his sixth pennant in seven seasons. Rumors circulated that George Weiss, unhappy at the loss of the Series, might ask Casey to step down.

Casey Stengel was past sixty-five. The lines in his face were deepening. His voice would grow more gravelly after a couple of drinks. He was sleeping less at night and more on the bench. Some players were complaining openly about his sarcastic tongue. He had suffered through several long colds during the season. He seemed more and more testy when his age was discussed. When a reporter showed him a clipping from a newspaper letters-to-the-editor column suggesting after the Series loss to the Dodgers (a sin among Yankee fans) that Stengel was finished and should be retired, he shouted, "You expect me to go into a goddamn fainting spell over it?" Then he stormed off.

Two weeks after the season ended the Yankees reassembled for the month-long exhibition tour of Japan. Casey Stengel, a Japanese favorite from his trip there more than thirty years earlier, was anxious to go. He could try out new plays, spread the gospel of baseball, and sign checks while Edna bought enough Japanese goods to rebuild one room of the Glendale house in a Japanese motif.

Unhappy about playing more baseball after a losing season, the Yankees hardly looked forward to the trip. But as soon as they got to Tokyo things changed. They found some of the finest restaurants were easily affordable. They turned on to saki, the Japanese rice wine. Their wives went on wild shopping sprees with the $500 in Japanese money they were given to spend. There were a couple of interesting moments while the Yankees whipped through the Japanese undefeated. One day the team met Japanese Prime Minister Hatoyama. He asked if any of the players had ever been in Japan before. Hank Bauer, the ex-Marine, nodded that he had.

"When was that?" asked the Japanese Prime Minister.

"When I landed on the beach at Iwo Jima," Bauer said.

On the final day of the trip a full-page picture of Casey Stengel, obviously asleep on the bench, holding a pair of bedroom slippers in his hand because the regimen was to take off the baseball shoes, change to slippers, and dress in the hotel, ran in the *Stars and Stripes.*

Was Stengel embarrassed?

"Why should I be embarrassed?" he bellowed. "We won all the games didn't we?"

George Weiss was impressed. He signed the sixty-five-year-old manager of the Yankees to another two-year contract.

11. Some People My Age Are Dead at the Present Time

CASEY STENGEL had learned to drink bourbon in Shelbyville, Kentucky, in 1910. He was still brushing up on his skills in 1956 in St. Petersburg, Florida.

The night had ended in the morning with Casey, his coaches, publicity man Bob Fishel, and a few hearty newspapermen closing the bar at the Soreno Hotel. After an hour or two of sleep, with the first light of day cracking through the sky, Stengel was jolted awake by a phone call.

"Casey, this is the Colonel," said coach Jim Turner. "I'm in the clubhouse. I think you oughta get down here."

"What the hell for, it's still night, ain't it?"

"I'll explain when you get here," Turner said.

Stengel got out of bed, showered, put on a Yankee jacket he kept in his room, drove to Miller Huggins Field, and entered the clubhouse. Don Larsen, a pitcher the Yankees had acquired from Baltimore after a 3–21 season in 1954, was seated on a bench. His head was in his hands. Stengel saw a huge bandage on his forehead. Turner sat nearby.

"I was driving along this winding road," Larsen says now. "I guess I had a few. It wasn't that. Mostly it was that I was tired, spring training, the hot sun every day, the workouts and all. You understand."

As Larsen explained it at the Yankee Old-Timer's Day in 1978, he had fallen asleep at the wheel of his car and hit a telephone pole ("Which jumped out on the road at him," Stengel would say later) and crashed into a bakery truck at 4 A.M., when bakery trucks are often on the road and pitchers usually aren't. Larsen was taken to a hospital

179

for fourteen stitches in his scalp and then on to the local police station on charges of drunken driving. He was allowed one phone call and made it to the Colonel. Turner then called Stengel.

When the writers arrived for the workout, already alerted to the incident, Stengel put on one of his greatest performances with double-talk so convoluted few remembered what the occasion for the press conference was.

"I was grateful for that," Larsen says. "I knew he stuck up for me. I always tried to pitch my hardest for him after that."

Larsen was 11–5 for the 1956 Yankees and started the second game of the World Series on October 5, 1956. He was wild, hit hard, and left in the second inning. He dressed quickly, went to a Manhattan bar, and told his friend Arthur Richman, a *New York Daily Mirror* sportswriter, he was quitting baseball. "Wait," said Richman, "you'll get another chance." On October 8 he started again. This time he was magnificent and pitched a 2–0 perfect no-hit, no-run game, the only time it has ever occurred in World Series baseball history.

"Casey was very happy for me," says Larsen. "I remember him dancing on the field to congratulate me."

Casey was happy that Larsen had vindicated his judgment. George Weiss, who could take a snort with the best of them, frowned on public drinking. He wanted Larsen disposed of after the Florida crash incident. Stengel fought for him and saved him, mostly because Weiss realized the Yankees were not all that deep in pitching.

Stengel had done more than his share of drinking in his own playing days. He understood the pressures and the pain of playing and understood that athletes turned to booze or women for relaxation. Some of then turned to both.

Joe Page, a dashingly handsome relief pitcher in Stengel's early Yankee years, walked through the Soreno Hotel lobby in the early hours one morning to be met by Casey Stengel and trainer Gus Mauch. Page had this lovely blond on his arm and was feeling no pain.

"Drunk?" asked Stengel.

"Me too, skipper," said Page.

"I don't think I ever saw Casey drunk," says Lee Mac-Phail. "He used to have a glass in his hand all the time, but while other people were drinking, he was talking."

"Casey drank for sociability," says Al Lopez. "That was his way of staying up all night with people. On the field he was a teacher. Off the field he was a talker."

On January 1, 1969, in his eightieth year, he was arrested for drunken driving in Glendale after driving his 1960 black Cadillac into a tree at 4 A.M. He was fined $302 by Municipal Judge Lee B. Stanton. This writer phoned him the next day and asked why he was fined $302.

"I ain't allowed to talk about the accident by my lawyer," he shouted into the long-distance phone to New York, "but around here if you do eight or nine different things wrong in a car, they fine you three hundred two dollars."

In every baseball season some old faces leave and some new ones replace them. Baseball players die twice.

They die the day they are cut, released, fired, waived, dismissed, or any number of euphemisms for a manager telling a man he is no longer good enough or young enough, and they die the day their life ends. The first death hurts so much more. In 1956 one important Yankee was "to die."

It creeps up on a man for a year or two or three, the fastball he can only foul off now, the curve ball that slips off the end of his bat, the ground ball that sneaks under his glove, the fly ball that just outmaneuvers his glove. Baseball is a game of small, sharp, graceful athletic movements, a ballet with ball, with perfect reactions, perfect coordination, and impeccable timing necessary for success. No one can hold back the destruction and evaporation of skills, as caused by the relentless march of time. For some, it comes sonner than for others. Few handle it gracefully. Joe DiMaggio did. Sandy Koufax did. Hank Aaron did. Willie Mays did not, Mickey Mantle did not, Warren Spahn did not, Stan Musial did not. In their aging years they grew testy, more suspicious, angered at their passing youth, angered at their managers and the press, afraid of the future.

On August 25, 1956, Yankee shortstop Phil Rizzuto was on the field at Yankee Stadium taking pictures of old ball-players as the Yankees celebrated Old-Timer's Day. The Yankees were moving easily to another pennant, the seventh in eight seasons under Casey Stengel. Clubhouse man Pete Sheehy walked to Rizzuto and said, "Casey wants to see you."

It was to be the worst shock of Phil Rizzuto's life. He was to be released as a Yankee. It was a chore Casey Stengel found the most distasteful of all his managerial chores. He could tolerate a man's drinking with a smile. He could whisper into a player's ear how a venereal disease could be cured. He could cut a man he didn't know very well without a problem ("He once cut shortstop Fritz Brickell," says teammate Clete Boyer, "by asking him if he could run, and when Fritz said he could, Casey said, 'Then run down to the station and catch the five o'clock train to Richmond.' "), but he couldn't cut old established players. He knew their families and had danced with their wives at pennant parties. He had frolicked with their kids and fought for salary raises for the players.

"I remember when we sent Ralph Terry back to the minors," says Lee MacPhail. "Casey called me from Baltimore. He asked me to take the train down from New York and tell him. He just couldn't tell him himself."

So, unaware of what was ahead of him, Rizzuto walked into Stengel's office that summer day in 1956.

"I couldn't imagine what he wanted," says Rizzuto, now a Yankee broadcaster. "I didn't even consider a release when I saw George Weiss sitting with him."

Rizzuto, the 1950 MVP, now nearing thirty-eight, was given a Yankee roster as he stepped into Stengel's office.

"We got a chance to get [Enos] Slaughter and make him eligible for the Series," said Stengel. "But we gotta cut somebody. Take a look at our list and see who we should cut."

Rizzuto studied the Yankee roster. He didn't know why he was being asked to help on this decision, except that maybe Weiss and Stengel wanted the opinion of a veteran player.

"We don't use [Charlie] Silvera, so maybe he should be the one," Rizzuto said.

"Nah. What if Yogi gets hurt and I gotta catch Howard and I need Silvera?" Casey said.

"What about [Rip] Coleman? You're not pitching him much," said Rizzuto.

"Can't do that. He can start and relieve and we don't have a lot of them can do that," he said.

By now Rizzuto was starting to get the message. "The old son of a buck couldn't come out and say it," Rizzuto says now. "Finally Weiss said, 'We would like to release you.' And Casey immediately says, 'We'll pay you and put you back on the roster after September. You won't be in the Series, but you'll get a share and get a ring and we'll see you again next spring.' I had heard enough. I got up and walked out."

Rizzuto showered and dressed quickly. George Stirnweiss (an old-timer who would later be killed in a train derailment) drove him home. He stayed incommunicado for several days.

"That was probably the best thing I ever did. Nobody could reach me and I couldn't say anything I would regret later. I'm sure that's why I got the broadcasting job. I didn't bad-mouth the Yankees and George and Casey publicly. Let me tell you, holy cow, I sure felt low. The first call I got after I started answering my phone again was from Buzzie Bavasi in Brooklyn. He wanted to know if I would play with their Montreal farm club."

Even now, more than twenty-three years later, the memory of that day still stings.

"I know the press and the photographers always fussed over Casey," says Rizzuto, "but not all the players loved him, you oughta know that."

One player who loved him was hurt by him. On May 15, 1957, Billy Martin was given a birthday party at the Copacabana in New York with Mickey Mantle, Yogi Berra, Whitey Ford, Hank Bauer, and rookie Johnny Kucks and all their wives. Sammy Davis, Jr., was entertaining. The Yankee group, seated at a ringside table, heard a racial remark made at Davis. Bauer told the drunk, "Shut the hell up" and the drunk, obviously blind with booze, challenged Bauer to "make me shut up." Tempers grew edgier and finally Bauer followed the drunk into a men's room corridor. Stories differ on what happened next, but the result was a drunk with a broken jaw and Ford and Berra restraining Bauer. The Yankees quickly left, but Leonard Lyons, a show business columnist for the *New York Post*, saw the commotion. He found out what had happened and his story was front page the next day. The Yankee management was livid. All of the players were fined $1,000, except for rookie Kucks, who was hit with a $500 fine. Weiss, without any evidence other than his own prejudice, decided Martin was the culprit. He had never liked Martin, calling him an "un-Yankeelike Yankee," and worked to get rid of him. Stengel fought against it. Weiss convinced the manager he had outlived his usefulness with the club and besides, said Weiss, "We have young [Bobby] Richardson ready to play second base."

On June 15, 1957, Martin was traded away from Stengel and the Yankees to Kansas City.

"I was with the club when the deal was made," says Lee MacPhail. "Casey couldn't tell him. I had to tell Billy he was no longer a Yankee. He couldn't stop crying."

"I have to admit that trade hurt me badly for years," says Martin. "I expected Casey to fight hard for me and keep me. Casey didn't fight hard enough to keep me and that hurt. I didn't talk to him for five years. People were trying to get us together. Mickey and Whitey also said I was Casey's boy and I should talk to him. Finally, I was scouting for the Twins and he was with the Mets, and he was seventy-two or seventy-three and I saw him in a hotel at the winter meetings. I looked over and he was surrounded by sportswriters and I thought, 'I won't be able to live with myself if he dies before I can talk to him again.' I went over like nothing happened, said, 'Hi, Casey,' and he looked at me, winked, and said to the writers, 'Let me tell you about this here fella, he caught a fly ball for me . . .' We never mentioned it again."

In 1959 the Yankees had a journeyman backup catcher to Yogi and Howard by the name of John Blanchard. Yogi was catching one hot summer day and Al Kaline hit a high fastball off Art Ditmar for a long home run. Casey, who never wanted a high fastball thrown to a good hitter, was livid. He began screaming to Yogi from the bench. "What the hell kind of pitch was that to throw him?" He quickly turned to Blanchard. "Get your gear. I'm gettin' Yogi outta there." Blanchard, who enjoyed hitting but detested catching, slowly put on his equipment, the shin guards, the chest protector, the sponge in his glove, the mask. The inning ended and Yogi and Casey screamed at each other on the bench. Yogi went back out and Blanchard sat in his full equipment because Casey told him to. The game continued. The heat increased. Blanchard sat. Finally, Yogi hit a two-run homer in the eighth inning, caught the Detroit ninth, and came to the dugout smiling with the win. As the final Detroit out was recorded, Blanchard, still sitting in his gear, the sweat spilling out of his body, took a bucket of ice water and dumped it over his head.

It was no wonder that in 1965 when Blanchard was traded away from the Yankees he cried uncontrollably. Mickey Mantle, his close friend, tried to console him by saying, "John. This is a break. In Kansas City, you'll get to catch every day."

Said Blanchard, "That's what I'm crying about."

With help from Larsen and Whitey Ford and Mickey Mantle (who had his best year in baseball with 52 home runs, 130 RBIs, and a .353 average)—all of whom could open and close a bar—Stengel won again in 1956. Larsen pitched his perfect World Series game and Casey Stengel had his sixth World Series triumph in eight seasons as Yankee manager.

Two fine-looking youngsters—Bobby Richardson, a marvelous second baseman, and Tony Kubek, an excellent shortstop and outfielder—joined the Yankees that next year as Billy Martin, a month after the Copa incident, was traded away to Kansas City. Richardson and Kubek,

"I wasn't born old," Casey reminds Mickey Mantle, after the blond slugger wins 1956 Triple Crown. Casey wasn't a bad player, either.

nondrinkers, religious young men, were frightened by Stengel's tough talk and late-night habits. Kubek remembers his reactions to Stengel with mixed emotions.

"He could be mean and intimidating," says the NBC sportscaster, "but he could also be very kind. When I got married he sent me a personal check. I was so thrilled I held on to it. One day months later I was short of cash and exchanged it in a drugstore. Then I got a note from Casey, 'I told you take your wife to dinner, but I didn't say to take her to a drugstore.' "

Like all of his players, Kubek never questioned Stengel's incredible attention to details.

"I was playing my first game in center field as a Yankee on a rainy night in Cleveland. I slipped going for a fly ball with the bases loaded and three runs scored. Casey came to me after the game and said, 'Let me see your shoes.' I lifted them up and he saw the spikes were worn down. I was a rookie and I was wearing a pair I had had since high school. He said, 'Young man, go out and buy a pair of shoes and I'll pay for them, but after this you're on your own.

This time it's my fault, but if it happens again, it's your fault. And it will cost you money.' I bought a new pair of shoes and it never happened again."

Stengel always had one personality for the regulars, driving them hard, staying on them, pushing them to excellence they themselves never thought they were capable of, and one for irregulars. No player was more of an irregular than Darrell Johnson, a bullpen catcher in 1957 who got into twenty-one games.

"Casey would get all over the stars, Mickey and Whitey and Yogi, but he hoped the others would learn from it," Johnson says.

"I guess Yogi was his favorite, his assistant manager. He always made fun of him, kidded him, but he really loved him. One time Casey was doing an imitation of Yogi on the bench while he was batting. He stuck out his lower lip and talked funny like Yogi and did some of Yogi's bouncy, walking steps. Then Yogi homered and when he came back to the bench I said, 'To me you look like Tyrone Power,' and Yogi said, 'I don't hit with my face,' and Casey just fell off the bench," Johnson recalled.

Casey showed how much he cared about Johnson by a ritual he performed each and every day.

"He would wait in the runway outside the clubhouse after a game until I got in from the bullpen," says Johnson. "Then he would say, 'You did a hell of a job out there today. Everything all right?' Then he would go on in."

Johnson always answered the bullpen phone when it rang with instructions from the dugout.

"This one day the phone rang and I heard Jim Turner say, 'Get Trucks ready,' only he had said, 'Kucks.' I told Trucks they wanted him up and he began to throw. Sure enough, they want the guy in the bullpen. Casey is at the mound waving and Trucks marches in. By the time Casey realizes it isn't Kucks, it's too late. Now he's pissed at me, at Kucks for not being in, at Trucks for being in, at Turner, at everybody. He storms back to the dugout. Trucks starts to pitch. He strikes out the first guy. The next guy hits into a double play. The game is over, he's waiting in the runway same as always, and says, 'You're one hell of a manager.' "

The Yankees won the 1957 pennant by eight games over Chicago, now managed by Al Lopez, and went into the World Series heavy favorites against the Milwaukee Braves. An ex-Yankee farmhand named Lew Burdette won three games for the Braves, an ex-player for Stengel's Boston Braves, Warren Spahn, won the other, and Milwaukee defeated New York four games to three. The Braves' offense was led by a young center fielder named Hank Aaron who batted .393.

In the four years between 1954 and 1957, the Yankees had won only one World Series. It was true that they had won three straight pennants, but some Yankee people were stung by the Series loss to the Dodgers in 1955 and now the Braves in 1957. Stengel was closing in on sixty-eight years of age, the lines deepening in his face, his voice growing more hoarse and gravelly, rumors of naps on the bench more frequent, more players talking behind his back about his caustic tongue, his Stengelese more entertaining to the sportswriters than his bosses. A cabal of anti-Stengel players, encouraged by some privately critical remarks made by Topping, was growing.

Another factor was surfacing. Ralph Houk had been sent to Denver in 1955 as manager of the Yankee farm club there. He had finished third in 1955, second the next two years, and won the Little World Series in 1957. He was thirty-eight years old, a loyal Yankee employee, and Topping's man. Topping was fond of him personally and admired his distinguished war record. Topping wanted Ralph Houk to manage the Yankees, the sooner the better.

George Weiss advised him that Houk wasn't ready. He needed more experience. He suggested that Topping bring him back to New York in 1958 as Stengel's coach and groom him as Casey's successor. It was secretly agreed upon by Topping, Webb—a silent partner in most of this—and Weiss, that if the Yankees didn't win the Series in 1958, Stengel would be forced out and Houk would be brought in. Casey could see the handwriting on the wall. He knew why Houk was being brought back to New York. He made no public fuss about it. As long as he managed the ball club, he would be in charge. Houk would be there, a distant threat to be sure, but not a consideration for the present. Stengel understood the inner machinations of a ball club better than most. The manager must have authority over the players, but the front office must have authority over the manager. It was just the way things worked. If Topping and Webb and Weiss wanted Ralph Houk around, Casey would accept him.

"I never was told I would manage the Yankees," Houk says. "I was just told I would be a coach under Casey and that would be it."

Baseball people are impressionable, more insecure than people in outside business, because their successes and failures—winning and losing—are so easily measurable. Somebody whispers that a man will make a good manager, some sportswriter prints it, and an image is born. Topping whispered that Houk would make a good manager, the press swallowed it, and Houk became labeled as the heir apparent. Immediately, he became more desirable as managerial material to other clubs, with Boston, Detroit, and Cleveland courting him for the next three years.

The Yankees were horrendous in the spring of 1958 with Casey concerned that he was about to see the collapse of his team. Gil McDougald was slowing down at second and Bobby Richardson wasn't ready. Tony Kubek was awkward at shortstop. Yogi Berra had crossed into the danger zone, thirty-three years old. Mickey Mantle and Whitey Ford seemed more concerned with parties than with pitches and pitching.

The nights at the Soreno bar grew longer and Stengel would often drive away many of the writers with his seemingly endless chatter. His face grew more craggy and he suffered sleepless nights, sometimes walking on the streets of St. Petersburg at 3:00 or 4:00 in the morning, sitting on a bench with some grizzled old resident, also unable to sleep, and arguing about the price of potatoes in 1900. He was drinking more and enjoying it less, his stomach gurgling each morning as he breakfasted in the coffee shop of the Soreno on black coffee, dry toast, and the *St. Petersburg Times.*

Suddenly, there was even more pressure on Stengel and the Yankees. After more than two years of constant rumors, the Brooklyn Dodgers and the New York Giants had fled New York City and moved west to California. The city was stunned. The National League did not have a franchise in New York for the first time since the league was formally organized in 1876 when Bobby Matthews turned in a 21–34 pitching record for the original New York Mets, seventh-place finishers with a 21–35 season log, something their successors would certainly understand almost a century later. National League president Warren Giles, acting unconcerned about the absence of a New York franchise, said, "Who needs New York?" City officials, led by Mayor Robert F. Wagner, would soon establish a committee to investigate the possibility of a new franchise in New York, with a man named Bill Shea at the head of it. The Yankees had drawn 1,497,134 fans in 1957. In 1958, as the only team in town, they would lose attendance and draw only 1,428,438, a factor that would weigh heavily in the demise of Casey Stengel's Yankee career.

For now, as the season opened in 1958, with Ralph Houk coaching at first base, with Stengel suffering from acute stomach pains, advancing age, and terminal grouchiness, the Yankees forgot about spring training and played serious baseball. Moose Skowron was a revelation at first base with his marvelous ability to hit right-handed home runs over the short fence in right field (and when he couldn't play to be replaced by a man named Marvelous Marv Throneberry, who would enter Casey's life again later); McDougald was clever and steady at second; Kubek matured as a shortstop; Andy Carey was the third baseman; and Bauer, Mantle, and Norm Siebern were in the outfield. Siebern would later have an excruciating time in left field, the sun field, in October during the Series, with Stengel berating him publicly for blowing a fly ball hit by Red Schoendienst. Wordsmith Yogi Berra would forever explain Siebern's October problems in the shadowy Yankee Stadium high sky by saying, "It gets late early out there."

Bob Turley led the staff with twenty-one victories ("He don't smoke, he don't drink, he don't chase women, and he don't win," Stengel said, earlier in the year after a tough Turley loss), Whitey Ford was 14–7, and Ryne Duren, who was to later announce he was an alcoholic, was the relief pitcher with the thick glasses and blazing fastball. "He takes a drink or ten," said Stengel of Duren, "comes in with them Coke bottles [thick glasses], th'os [Stengel never pronounced the *r* in throw] one on the screen and scares the shit out of 'em." Duren had a 2.02 ERA, a 6–4 record with 20 saves, and 87 strikeouts in 75 innings in his first year as a Yankee.

On July 9, 1958, with the Yankees breezing to another pennant, the season was halted as the country watched Charles Dillon Stengel perform on center stage in Washington, D.C. A Senate subcommittee on antitrust and monopoly had begun serious investigation into the workings of baseball's long-argued reserve laws, whereby players were controlled for life until sold, traded, or released. Baseball had enjoyed privileged business status by a Supreme Court ruling in the 1920s, and periodically, some congressional figure would get his name in the papers by suggesting a review of this outrage. Senator Estes Kefauver of Tennessee, a defeated vice-presidential candidate with Adlai Stevenson in 1956, had high hopes for 1960. The 1958 hearings would focus more attention on the senator, always available for a photo in his coonskin hat. Casey Stengel was asked if he would appear as a voluntary witness before the committee. Some notable players, including Ted Williams, an astute political observer as well as the game's greatest hitter, and Yankee slugger Mickey Mantle, unsure what an antitrust committee actually did, also were on hand for the 10 o'clock hearing.

"The room was jammed," says Mary Lavagetto, wife of Casey Stengel's pal, Cookie Lavagetto, then the manager of the Washington Senators. "Casey seemed very jumpy.

He stood outside the hearing room and chain-smoked, lighting one cigarette with another before he was called. He was extremely nervous and talked very little. He was dressed so neatly, his hair plastered down, and appeared as cute as I ever remember him. I sat there in the front row behind the witness tables with Edna. She was scared to death. We held hands on the bench."

The clerk of the committee introduced the proceedings and Kefauver gaveled it to order. Stengel was asked to move into the witness chair. He sat down in front of the chairman. He was twenty days away from his sixty-eighth birthday, his face deeply wrinkled, his suit slightly ill-fitting, and his new blue tie, bought for the occasion only that morning in the hotel shop by Edna, tucked inside his jacket. He held his glasses in his hand, and as Kefauver began to talk, Stengel slipped the glasses on, one of the few times he was seen with them in public.

"Mr. Stengel," said Kefauver, in his deep Tennessee drawl, "you are the manager of the New York Yankees." Casey nodded from his seat and did not say a word. "Will you give us very briefly your background and your views about this legislation."

Casey bent low to the microphone in front of him, cleared his throat, and began an oration, which in some circles was to become as famous as Horatio's or Lincoln's.

"Well, I started in professional ball in 1910. I have been in professional ball, I would say, for forty-eight years. I have been employed by numerous ball clubs in the majors and in the minor leagues."

His voice, thin, nervous, soft at the outset, now began to ripen. He was warming up. He increased his volume and the speed of his delivery.

"I started in the minor leagues with Kansas City. I played as low as Class D ball, which was at Shelbyville, Kentucky, and also Class C ball and Class A ball, and I have advanced in baseball as a ballplayer."

Now he was in full gear, the motor driving, his confidence returned, his audience completely attentive, the television cameras grinding, Kefauver holding a grin on his leathery face.

"I had many years that I was not successful as a ball-player, as it is a game of skill. And then I was no doubt discharged by baseball in which I had to go back to the minor leagues as a manager, and after being in the minor leagues as a manager, I became a major-league manager in several cities and was discharged, we call it discharged because there is no question I had to leave."

"By now the smiles and the giggles had turned into loud laughter," says Mary Lavagetto. "Everyone was laughing so hard it was difficult to hear everything Casey said."

Now Casey Stengel was more like Casey Jones, chugging along in high gear, roaring down the track, moving like an out-of-control steam engine, from his playing career to his minor-league managerial career, to his big-league managerial career to the railroad business, into night baseball, the weather, the fact that he was not a stockholder in the Yankees, with some side switches to Kankakee and the problems of making money with Sunday baseball.

Some legislation had been drawn up to exempt baseball, football, basketball, and hockey from current antitrust laws. The committee was actually considering bills H.R. 10378 and S. 4070. Senator John A. Carroll, a member of the committee, then asked, "The question Senator Kefauver asked you was what, in your honest opinion, with your forty-eight years of experience, is the need for this legislation in view of the fact that baseball has not been subject to antitrust laws?"

Said Stengel, "No."

The audience howled again. Now the hearing was in a shambles. Even the court clerk, a prune-faced man with thin bifocals, began to squeeze in a wide smile. Senator Carroll, waiting for the room to grow quiet again, then asked a complicated legal question filled with ipset dixit, ad damnum, sui generis, and other Latin legalese. "Do you call that a clear expression?" the senator asked.

"Well," said Casey, with a dramatic pause, "you are going to get me there for about two hours."

The laughter was uncontrollable. Senator Kefauver, knowing full well now he had met the enemy and it was

"Now wait a minute, for crissakes," bellows Stengel at 1958 Congressional hearings highlighted by a lecture in Stengelese. Rapt attention is paid by Mickey Mantle (left) and Ted Williams. Mantle agreed with everything Stengel said.

the English language, smiled and said, "Thank you very much, Mr. Stengel. We appreciate your presence here."

Casey got up to a standing ovation, walked to the bench behind the witness chair, his face filled with satisfaction, his eyes glistening, his mouth pursed in a boyish smile.

"Mr. Mickey Mantle," said Senator Kefauver, "will you come around?"

Mantle, wearing a new suit, a striped tie, and a silly expression on his face, walked to the table. His crew cut was neatly brushed and his manner was comfortable. Casey had done enough groundwork to ease his appearance.

"Mr. Mantle," Kefauver began in a serious tone, "do you have any observations with reference to the applicability of antitrust laws to baseball?"

A small grin escaped from the edges of his mouth and he said, slowly, "My views are just about the same as Casey's."

Now the hearing room exploded in laughter again. Stengel sat back in his chair and winked at Edna. Kefauver smiled and said, "I believe this would be an appropriate time to adjourn."

That evening, the Huntley-Brinkley report devoted nearly two minutes to the hearings. David Brinkley almost broke up uncontrollably after the film ran at the end of the program. Casey Stengel had become an instant television star. Editorials appeared in many newspapers around the country. Letters poured into Yankee Stadium. Stengel imitated Kefauver's drawl for his writers and Mantle spent twenty minutes entertaining teammates on Stengel's performance.

The legislation never got out of the committee.

Soon Stengel was back in the Yankee dugout, pushing his troops hard, driving for his ninth pennant to tie him with Joe McCarthy for the most in league history. The Yankees had run away from the league early, racing to a seventeen-game lead in early August, only to fall back as a result of illness and injuries to key players. The lead slipped to eight games, but then the Yankees recovered, as they always seemed to do when threatened, and won it by ten games. It was Stengel's ninth pennant in ten seasons, tying McCarthy's record with the Yankees making Stengel the equal of the winningest manager in league history. The only mark ahead was McCarthy's ten pennants, nine with the Yankees and one with the Chicago Cubs in 1929, and old skipper John McGraw's ten with the Giants.

The Yankees clinched in Kansas City, partied until midnight, and then boarded a night train for Detroit, their next port of call, with the regulars guaranteed a rest after the rigors of the race. There was some heavy drinking on the train. Finally, Ryne Duren, doing more than his share of imbibing, came across Ralph Houk, sitting quietly in his coach seat. Duren, a pugnacious drunk, needled Houk about his cigar, blowing slowly in the air. Houk laughed, attempted to defuse the situation with softness, and continued to blow smoke. Suddenly, Duren reached down and squashed the cigar in Houk's mouth. The first-base coach, knowing he was dealing with a drunken player, merely slapped at Duren's face with the back of his right hand. Unfortunately, Houk's 1947 World Series ring, symbolic of his first Series and his 1.000 Series average (one for one) caught Duren above the right eye. Several players, quickly sizing up the situation, pulled the pitcher away. Stengel was informed, came from the bar car where he was discussing his Series plans with the writers, saw that nobody was seriously hurt, and said, "Some guys get whiskey slick."

"Casey knew some players would drink," says Elston Howard, who almost never does, "but he tried to keep them from getting 'whiskey slick.' He didn't want guys drinking together. He felt that resulted in fights. One guy who was a fighter should never drink with another guy who was a fighter. He wanted the easygoing guys with the fighters."

Unlike some managers, Stengel never related heavy drinking with poor performance. He simply felt each man had to find his own level. He had a great skill of looking in a player's eyes and knowing how much drinking he had done the night before. He also had a way of protecting players from the press or themselves after heavy drinking. Many injuries of players like Mickey Mantle and Whitey Ford, described by Stengel to the press as problems of the legs or shoulders, were, in truth, old-fashioned hangovers. Casey understood a long night could sometimes get the better of a man. One day in spring training he didn't look so hot himself and when a sportswriter asked him what the problem was he said, "I've been up all night with a sick relative. Old Granddad."

The Yankees thought nothing of the Duren incident when they departed the train. Duren was feeling no pain, Houk had not been injured, and Stengel felt it was all good clean ballplayer fun—until the next day.

Leonard Shecter, a reporter for the *New York Post,* had been burned earlier on a story when George Weiss had dispatched detectives to trail the slumping Yankees. The information had leaked to Til Ferdenzi of the *New York Journal American,* who informed all of his colleagues except the rookie sportswriter from the *Post.* Shecter was awakened that night by his office, abused for blowing the story, and warned it better not happen again or he would be chained into a desk job, which he had just recently escaped. When he saw Duren's eye as he departed the train, he asked a few questions, wrote a quick story, and phoned his office. Newspaper rivalry being what it is, the story was expanded upon and screaming headlines in the *Post* said: YANKEES BRAWL ON PENNANT EXPRESS.

George Weiss had a fit when he saw the story and Stengel's stock with the image-concious Yankees fell again. If Stengel was so lacking in discipline, was the winning worth it?

It was the kind of question George Steinbrenner would ask himself over and over again twenty years later about Stengel's boy, Billy Martin. Martin had been drinking heavily, feuding with Reggie Jackson, sarcastic with many of his players, abrasive with the press, and falling further and further behind in the 1978 pennant race. Baseball owners tolerate almost anything in victory. They tolerate almost nothing in defeat. The Yankees fell fourteen games behind the Red Sox. Martin was an emotional wreck after suspending Jackson for bunting when he was instructed to hit away. On July 23, Jackson returned to the lineup without any lessening of the tension. Steinbrenner was torn between firing Martin and saving him from himself. A reporter cornered Martin in O'Hare airport in Chicago and when the manager volunteered his opinion of his two adversaries, Steinbrenner and Jackson, he was gone. "One's a born liar and the other's convicted," he said in reference to Jackson and owner Steinbrenner, who had pleaded guilty to a charge of illegal campaign contributions to the Nixon reelection fund. The personalities had changed from 1958 to 1978, but the tensions were much the same.

Topping, Webb, and Weiss were all edgy as the World Series opened October 1, 1958, at Milwaukee's County Stadium, again against the Braves. The Braves jumped off to a 3–1 Series lead after Warren Spahn pitched a brilliant two-hitter in the fourth game. Stengel's team was one game from elimination and only one team in baseball history, the 1925 Pirates, had ever come back from a 3–1 deficit to win. But Bob Turley pitched a five-hitter to shut out the Braves in the fifth game 7–0, the Yankees finally beat Spahn in extra innings 4–3 in the sixth game (Duren was brilliant in relief with eight strikeouts), and Turley, the clean-liver and hard-thrower, saved the seventh game win in relief.

It was Stengel's seventh World Series triumph, tying him with McCarthy again for world championships.

Now the Yankees were in a bind. They really didn't want a sixty-nine-year-old man to manage their team in 1959. But what could they do? Casey Stengel was a winner again, his stock had risen as the sportswriters applauded the team's dramatic Series comeback, his wizardry was now almost legendary, and the Yankees would have trouble, serious trouble from the press and public, if they eased Casey out.

Stengel had followed a steady pattern since the 1950 pennant. He would always sit down with Weiss and Topping before leaving New York for the winter, discuss the needs for next season, and sign a two-year contract. He did that in 1950, 1952, 1954, 1956, and. . . . He didn't do it in 1958. He wasn't sure he wanted to because he wasn't sure the Yankees wanted him to. His nerves had been frayed by the tough Series against the Braves. Now he rested in his Glendale home, talked to Weiss a few times by phone, agreed to come to spring training early, and spent a pleasant winter. He and Edna would dine with the Babe Hermans, the Dutch Zwillings, the Lawsons, and other friends in town. Casey debated his own future with Edna. As the winter passed, his stamina seemed to improve, color returned to his face, and he was motivated by the chance at catching his exalted manager, John McGraw, with ten pennants. He flew to St. Petersburg on February 24 and signed a new two-year contract calling for $85,000 in 1959 and $90,000 in 1960. Topping made it clear—without putting it in writing—that the 1960 season would be Casey's last as Yankee manager.

The Yankees, running away from Stengel now, laughed behind his back. They played cruel tricks on him, banging bats on the bench as he dozed, yelling in his ear, talking back to him more vociferously in arguments, bad-mouthing him to the press and opposing players. Ballplayers are gossips. Nothing entertains them as much as an embarrassing story about a teammate or manager. They can hardly wait to tell of a drunken teammate who fell down a flight of stairs, a paternity suit that a star was nailed with, a bad case of VD that a supposed clean-living player was discovered to have. Now their stories all humiliated Stengel. He was a sixty-nine-year-old man who had lost their respect. Why? Mostly because they were jealous of him. They became pawns in Casey's maneuverings. He had become bigger than the Yankees, and the players, Weiss, and Topping resented it.

The public was unaware of most of this, seeing only the bottom line, nine pennants in ten years, seven World Series wins. It was great to be young and a Yankee. It was greater to be young and a Yankee fan.

Now the Yankees of 1959 got off poorly. Bill Skowron pulled a back muscle. The pitching staff suffered from chronic sore arms. An attack of Asian flu leveled half the team. Mantle became more testy with the press and this was compounded by severe fan criticism. He was booed unmercifully on occasion. Stengel had protected and defended him as a young player, but now Mantle talked behind his back, blamed Casey for not keeping the press off his ass. The tension in the clubhouse could be cut with a knife.

The Yankees slipped into the American League cellar. By midsummer they were a dozen games out of first place and the rest of the 1959 season was an exercise in futility. Al Lopez led the Chicago White Sox to a stirring season with a 94–60 record. The Indians finished second and the Yankees limped home in third place, with a 79–75 mark, Casey's worst as Yankee boss.

With Casey back home in Glendale for the winter, Dan Topping, emerging more and more as an active power who liked the glow of Yankee success in the previous ten seasons before 1959, considered his next move. He could fire Stengel and pay him off (Stengel led the league in being paid off on unexpired managerial contracts) or he could stick it out for 1960, retire Casey with some grace, and bring in Houk to rebuild. Afraid to suffer the wrath of an aroused public, he decided to write off the 1960 season as a rebuilding year and then ease out both Stengel and Weiss, though neither was quite sure of the situation. Houk was now ready to manage and Roy Hamey, a Topping confidant, was being moved up rapidly within the organization.

Before the season opened Weiss was to complete his final big trade as Yankee boss. He was to obtain Roger Maris from Kansas City and it would turn the logy 1959 Yankees into the exciting winners of 1960.

Maris, who would hit 61 homers in 1961 to break Babe Ruth's 1927 mark of 60 ("Up your asterisk," began a rallying cry of fans supporting Maris in the great controversy caused by Commissioner Ford Frick who ruled Roger had to hit 61 in 154 games to beat the Babe), was always a direct, forthright man. He says now of Stengel, "I never had any trouble with him. If you played ball hard, kept your mouth shut, and hustled, he never said much to you."

Maris played ball hard in 1960, kept his mouth shut, and hustled like hell. He would hit 39 homers, bat .283, knock in 112 runs, and win the MVP title. Mantle, helped by the appearance of Maris and the softening pressure on him to carry the team, had another fine season with 40 homers and 94 RBIs. The Yankees won their last fifteen games in a row after a close race with a surprisingly good, young Baltimore team to capture the pennant by eight games.

Would a World Series victory change things for the seventy-year-old manager? On May 28, 1960, Stengel, suffering from a virus and high fever, had been hospitalized at Lenox Hill Hospital. Ralph Houk had run the club; it was a picture of things to come. Stengel returned on June 8 and sportswriters asked him how he felt. "I'll tell ya something. They examined all my organs. Some of them are quite remarkable, and others are not so good. A lot of museums are bidding for them."

Stengel, recovered now, enjoyed the victories of September, especially the big play against the Orioles when two young infielders named Ron Hansen and Brooks Robinson collided under a pop-up to help the Yankees sweep the Orioles. "My man used to catch those," he said, referring to Billy Martin, "and you could look it up."

Unknown to the Yankees and the press, Stengel had talked to Del Webb, the mostly silent West Coast partner-owner of the Yankees. Less abrasive than Topping, more kind, gentle, and considerate of the greatness of the man, Webb was allowed to ease Stengel out of the Yankee picture softly.

"We have this annuity," he began, "and it will pay you a great deal of money."

"Why did I need an annuity if I was working, so I got the hint I wasn't," Stengel said later.

Webb asked only one favor of Stengel: that he would announce to the press that he had "resigned." Image, image, image, that was the code word for the Yankees. Casey said he still thought he might want to manage. He told Webb they'd talk again after the Series.

In one of the most exciting World Series ever played, Bill Mazeroski of the Pittsburgh Pirates hit a home run off Ralph Terry in the bottom of the ninth inning of the seventh game to win it for Pittsburgh. Many people believed Casey's fate was settled in the home half of the eighth when Bill Virdon hit a hard ground ball that bounced off the concrete-like Pittsburgh infield and struck Tony Kubek in the throat. The Pirates rallied for five runs, and, after the Yankees scored two in the ninth to tie it, Mazeroski homered to win it.

Would Stengel's fate have changed if the Yankees had won?

"I don't think so," says Bob Fishel, who was the publicity director. "I think their minds were made up. You can feel change around a ball club. All of a sudden in the final weeks of that season, important people began ignoring him."

The players all awaited the change. They had subtly shifted their loyalty to Houk and away from Stengel.

"I think a lot of it had to do with the way Ralph took to the young players and Casey didn't," says Clete Boyer. "One day, I was on third, Kubek was on short, and Richardson was on second. We all made errors in the same game. Stengel called us an air-conditioned infield. The next year Houk called us his Million-Dollar Infield."

Boyer is a coach for the Atlanta Braves now and he speaks for many of the younger Yankee players when he says, "In 1960 I hated the man, I really did, I just hated the old bastard." And now? "Now I see why he made a lot of the moves he did, I guess all he was trying to do was win. Why didn't he explain it? I was young. I was sensitive."

Casey Stengel never explained his moves to his players. He treated them as professionals. He expected them simply to obey orders and do their work.

The final game of that 1960 Series was over and the press rushed into the Yankee clubhouse. Stengel was heaving a soaking-wet uniform shirt into his locker. Kubek lay unattended on a training table while trainer Gus Mauch conferred with the Pittsburgh team doctor. Mantle, drained by the defeat and shocked at the blood seeping out of a cloth on his teammate's neck, sat in the room weeping. Ralph Terry, the victim of the most dramatic World Series homer ever, sat immobile against a wall, his face buried in his hands, his shoulders bent with pain.

Soon Casey Stengel was surrounded by two dozen reporters. He flung one shoe on the floor. He called for a beer. He paraded around the locker in one shoe. He looked in on Kubek, had a whispered conversation with trainer Gus Mauch, and walked away. Sweat poured from his forehead in the small, steamy clubhouse under the stands at Forbes Field. He circled the room over and over again muttering unintelligibly to himself.

"What about next year?" screamed one reporter, intent on breaking the silence and hearing the rumors clearly.

"How do I know about next year? Some people my age are dead at the present time," he said.

"Will you be back?"

"Goddammit," he shouted, "I just told ya. I ain't gonna tell you anything about it because I didn't make my living here. Now go back and tell that to your editors."

He was crusty, nasty, intimidating. The reporters pressed in and he shouted that he would have nothing to say about the game, the Series, or his future.

"Go ask the players, they lost it," he said.

The bitterness began to spill out of him, the long seasons of rumor and innuendo, the criticisms from his players and his bosses, the failure to accede to some of his demands, the heartless way they allowed things to disintegrate, the constant conflict with Topping, mostly through intermediaries, the whispered gossip about his health, his supposed senility, his selfishness in not allowing the Yankees to ease him out quietly.

Again, with hardly any direct communication between Topping and Stengel the strain was overbearing. Topping liked to frequent the fashionable New York nightclubs, bask in the glory of his team, get his name in the columns, enjoy the fruits of his investment. The only difference between rich people and poor people, it is said, is money. The only difference between rich people and other rich people is fame, recognition, status, as measured in New York, by items in columns, by cabdrivers catching one's face, by fans stopping a man on a street and saying, "Hey, ain'tchoo . . . ?"

Topping was suddenly finding himself embarrassed by his team and uncomfortable with his manager. It would be a situation that would be repeated twenty years later when George Steinbrenner found Billy Martin an embarrassment among his peers. When enough of them began whispering in his ear at P.J. Clarke's or Elaine's or Joe's Pier 52 that Martin was an embarrassment to Steinbrenner and the Yankees, he was gone. (He would return, however, in another dramatic switch, on June 19, 1979.)

Topping had heard all he wanted to hear about Stengel from his players, his friends, and his sycophants. The manager's fate had been sealed earlier in 1960. Nothing would change it. Not the "accident" of the pennant or even— had it happened—the World Series victory.

By God, the man had won ten pennants in twelve seasons, had won seven World Series, had helped the Yankees draw more than twenty million fans, had kept baseball in the forefront of the sports pages. Didn't he deserve some kindness?

Casey Stengel was about to be relieved of his command of the Yankees. His crime? He had passed his seventieth birthday. Just around the bend another team awaited him. Why? He had just passed his seventieth birthday. Some people thought that was just the grandest age for the manager of an infant team.

12. Stengelese Spoken Here

A CLEAR, BRISK, early fall morning, 11:45 A.M. on October 18, 1960. Le Salon Bleu in New York's swank Savoy Hilton Hotel on Fifth Avenue is bustling with activity. Rows of metal chairs have been placed in the large room and reporters are filling up the chairs. "What do you think?" they ask each other. "They'll make him a vicepresident." Another says, "He'll manage in 1961 because he won the pennant." Another says, "I think he'll buy the club and fire Topping." Technicians fool with television cameras and lights. Radio reporters tie their microphones into the speaker on the lectern. The room is drenched in light. A bar has been set up in the corner of the room. Reporters drink Bloody Marys. At five minutes before noon, Dan Topping walks into the room. He is deeply tanned, his eyes focused on the ground, a sheet of white paper squeezed into his right hand. He heads for the lectern. George Weiss follows and moves off to one side. Bob Fishel moves to the microphone. Casey Stengel walks to the small bar. "Can I help you?" asks the bartender. "Bourbon, for crissakes," he says. "What about it, Casey?" He turns to the reporter. "What if I tell you why I'm here, what would you do, scoop the whole world? I commenced winning pennants when I came here, but I didn't commence getting any younger."

Fishel asked for quiet in the room. "Will everybody please sit down so we can begin," he said.

Stengel took his bourbon, walked to the front row of seats, and sat down.

Topping now stood in front of the lectern. He looked ill

and his voice was thin as he said, "Casey Stengel has been, and deservedly so, the highest paid manager in baseball history."

The reporters began scribbling furiously. Casey looked over the shoulder of a reporter next to him, scanned the notes, and examined the words. He was listening to his own obituary and wanted to make sure the boys had it right.

"Casey has been," Topping said, "and is"—and he paused—"a great manager. He is being well rewarded with $160,000 to do with as he pleases."

"Do you mean he's through—resigned?" screamed a reporter from the back of the room.

Stengel was standing now. He moved closer to the microphones. He was inching Topping out of the picture. This wasn't the way it was supposed to go. Topping was supposed to make the announcement and Stengel was to listen. The old manager was only supposed to talk about his career, reminisce, let the business details be handled by Topping. What was going wrong here? Why was this staged presentation going wrong?

"Now wait a minute, for crissakes," said Stengel, "and I'll tell ya."

His hair, glowing orange under the hot television lights, was plastered down on his head. His blue suit was neatly pressed. A blue silk tie, too large for the jacket, flapped under the coat. He looked like a seventy-year-old altar boy.

"Now I wasn't fired," he began, "I was paid up in full."

"The Associated Press has a bulletin, Casey," screamed a reporter. "It says you were fired. What about it?"

"What do I care what the AP says. Their opinion ain't gonna send me into any fainting spell. Anyway, what about the UP?"

The laughter ended all chances the Yankees thought they ever had of controlling this historic press conference. If Casey Stengel was going out, he would go out on his own terms. Like a great actor drawing strength from the audience, Stengel tightened his tie, tugged at his jacket, put his hands in his pockets, and took over the room.

"Mr. Webb and Mr. Topping have started a program for the Yankees. They needed a solution as to when to discharge a man on account of age. My services are no longer required by this club and I told them if this was their idea not to worry about me."

"Were you fired?" a reported yelled.

"Resigned, fired, quit, discharged, use whatever you damn please. I don't care. You don't see me crying about it."

"What will you do now?" he was asked.

"Have another drink, that's what," he answered.

Stengel walked from the lectern to the small bar. "Give me a bourbon with soda and not with water, just because I'm out of work and can't pay for it," he said.

Casey took a big gulp and then began explaining the situation further to a group of reporters that had encircled him like Indians at Little Big Horn. The bitterness of the moment ("I'll never make the mistake of being seventy again," he said) seemed to drain from his body as he began talking of his wonderful years with the Yankees, starting with the 1960 pennant winner, working backward through the Series of 1958, his last winner, and the great teams and the great players of his past. The names came in a rush, Mantle and Ford and Berra and then McGraw and Frisch and Ruth and Zach Wheat and Rube Marquard and Smokey Joe Wood, all in one torrential statement, as if the baseball games of 1910 and the baseball games of 1960 were somehow linked, as if Wheat and Daubert and Rucker were somehow teammates of Ford and Maris and Mantle. And somehow they were linked, through this leathery old face, each wrinkle an era, each season a part of the unbroken chain.

In another part of the room Topping, controlled now, trying to talk his way out of the cold firing, said, "I'm just sorry Casey isn't fifty years old, but all business comes to a point when it's best to make a change."

The rest of the afternoon was a muddle. Casey went from television interview to radio interview, from newspaper reporter to newspaper reporter, from media people to waitresses, busboys, and captains in the large dining room, telling stories ("What if Martin don't catch Rob-A-Son's fly ball, which he did splendidly . . ."), signing autographs, enjoying the attention and affection, talking about his Yankees, his time in the game, the ache in his heart now, the fun, the furor, the future.

A pretty middle-aged waitress came over, her starched uniform all white and neat, her face and hair all clean and shiny, carrying a small napkin. "Casey, for my nephew," she said. He held her pencil and carefully scratched out his name. "Who's it for?" he asked. "Me," she said, and blushed, caught now in a white lie. "Well, my nephew, too." "What's his name?" "Robert," she said, and he wrote that on the napkin. She leaned over and impulsively kissed him on the cheek, leaving a large blotch of lipstick on the side of his face. "Now you have to come home with me," he said, with twinkling eye, "and tell Edna you're the one who done it." She smiled and pulled away. "Thank you," she said. Then he said, "Thank you, three thousand thank yous."

Another knot of reporters had gathered near him and he began, without being asked anything, "What if the ball don't hit him in the throat, dontcha think we win it and I'm out with a championship even though I'm discharged?"

Reporters had finished their free lunch (George Weiss was right, a steak could turn them out anytime) and now the dining room was beginning to thin out. Waiters began pulling off the tablecloths and exposing the ugly, wooden tables.

"Damn ball park will be bare without the old man," a reporter said.

"Why don't they keep him and let him talk for the Yankees and sell tickets?" another reporter said.

"Who the hell will understand him?"

"Who the hell has understood him all these years?"

It was almost three o'clock in the afternoon now. The Yankee party had long left. Two young reporters, including this one, stood in the hotel lobby with him. His eyes were red now from tears and booze, his voice thin and cracking, the energies draining from his body. "I gotta go," he said, "Edna's waitin' for me."

Stengel walked out of the front door of the hotel and headed north up Fifth Avenue to the Essex House, where Edna waited for him. The brisk wind blew and his tie was thrown over his shoulder and his hair was loosened and his coat collar ruffled in the breeze. He stood at the corner waiting for the light, and when it changed to green, he started across the street. Halfway across, he jumped over the center line and broke into his stooping, shuffling trot and reached the opposite curve as the light turned red again. He hopped on the curb, first one foot and then the other, paused for a moment, waved his arm back at us, and was swallowed up by the crowd, this gnarled old man with floppy ears and deeply lined face.

I never knew until then how much I loved the old man.

The public reaction was one of incredible outrage. Newspaper editorials scorched the Yankees for the act. The *Toledo Blade,* where Stengel had managed the only championship in the city's history in 1927, ran a page of blistering letters from the town's old-timers. "You're as old as you feel," wrote Jesse Tucker, seventy-eight. "And if you ask me, Casey feels great. I was a tool and diemaker until I was seventy-two and the union retired me. I don't lie around. I paint pictures, make rugs, go fishing, work on my car. I seen Casey on TV. He looks pretty lively." Mrs. Charlotte Calhoun said, "I like to keep the old birds on because I'm one of them. I'm eighty-six and I'm not retiring from life." Robert Steward, seventy-four, said, "Hell, this makes me mad. It's a dirty trick. Is it a crime to get old?"

When a reported consoled Edna Stengel later by saying he thought it was unfair and that Casey had gotten a terrible deal, she smiled, patted his face gently, and said, "That's the world's opinion."

At that instant a few blocks south on Fifth Avenue, a man named Branch Rickey worked in an office marked "The Continental League." National League baseball was on its way back to New York. It would take a most circuitous route, through the founding of a new league after the old league refused to expand, through threats and law-

suits, through the efforts in New York of a successful lawyer with strong political connections named Bill Shea.
Mayor Robert F. Wagner had assigned Shea an insur-
mountable task after the Dodgers and Giants vacated the
city in 1957. He first attempted to get the Cincinnati Reds
to move to New York, then the Cleveland Indians, then
the Philadelphia Phillies. They all stayed put. Now a new
league, with franchises in such places as New York, Houston, Toronto, and Denver had been formed.

In some two months the American League would expand into Minnesota and Los Angeles, and, in 1961, the
Continental League was put to death with the expansion
back into New York of a new franchise as well as one in
Houston. The new National League teams would begin
play in 1962.

Some four weeks after the firing of Casey Stengel,
George Weiss, also receiving a large settlement, was ushered out of the Yankee organization. He was only sixty-
five and went quietly. A clause in his contract prevented
him from holding the title of "general manager" with
another baseball team for five years. In March of 1961,
Weiss was hired by the new New York franchise, the Mets,
as "president" of the club, a wonderful example of baseball finesse.

In Glendale, California, all of this was noted with
merely passing interest by Charles D. Stengel, retired
baseball person, bank vice-president, man-about-town,
senior citizen. When he got home from his firing, there
was a huge party of friends and relatives. A great deal of
mail had been forwarded to him from the Yankee offices.
They had received more than three thousand letters, telegrams, and phone calls protesting the firing of Stengel. A
one-hundred-year-old man in Florida, still working as a
clerk in a railroad station, fired off a one-word telegram to
Dan Topping. It read, "Nonsense." It was signed, "John
Randolph, age one hundred, railroad clerk." Old people
all across the country were outraged. America believed
now that quality of performance, not age, mattered in
holding a job. Torn tickets were sent to Yankee Stadium.
The press fanned the fire with critical evaluation of the

heartless Yankee move. In some ways, the Yankees would never recover. Attendance would increase in 1961 as a result of the home run race of Maris and Mantle but then would decline from a Casey Stengel era high of 2,281,676 in 1949 to a low of 966,328 in 1972. The heartless Yankee image would remain an albatross around Yankee necks until George Steinbrenner began turning the team and the image around in 1973.

Casey Stengel had become an elderly folk hero, more beloved, more comical, more renowned outside of baseball than he had ever been in baseball. Hardly a day passed without some reporter calling him for a story, his opinion on this or that, his ideas about the new teams or the new leagues, or just twenty minutes of rambling that could be turned into a column idea.

When he returned to Glendale, Casey Stengel's brother-in-law, Jack Lawson, was overseeing the finishing touches on the Toluca Lake branch of the Valley National Bank. Casey was given a second-floor office in the new bank, a huge mahogany desk, and two signs to be placed on opposite ends of his new office desk. One read: "Charles D. 'Casey' Stengel, Vice-President." The other simply said: "Stengelese Spoken Here."

"Casey was an important investor in the bank and a serious vice-president," says Jack Lawson. "He talked to customers, he worked with the staff, he interested business people in investment, he helped generate new income." The Toluca Lake branch was soon inundated with small investments of five-, ten-, and fifteen-dollar amounts from sportwriters, baseball players, and officials who wanted to brag about investing in "Casey's bank." Some investments were more serious.

"I wanted to open a studio, I didn't have a dime," says Los Angeles photographer Frank Worth. "I went to Casey. He asked me one question, 'How should I make the check out?' I needed ten thousand dollars. When I walked out of his office I had a check for twenty-five thousand dollars in my pocket."

Worth's collateral was his signature. It was all most people needed if Casey knew you.

"Everybody paid back loans made by Casey," says Worth. "If you didn't pay, he would blab it all over town."

Edna redecorated and repainted the house on Grandview Avenue. Casey plunged deeply into the work of the bank. Their social life was active with nightly dinner parties and long, downtown lunch dates with friends they had neglected for years because of the press of eastern business. Reporters continued to call Stengel at his office and he would say, "I'm outta baseball and I was in it for a long time and it don't have to be forever."

Did he mean he didn't have to stay out of the game forever or did he mean the opposite? "Stengelese Spoken Here" for good reason.

Letters and telegrams continued to pour in from elderly fans. When a reporter asked if he had heard from any other ball clubs he replied, "Just because your legs is dead don't mean your head is, too." Strangely, the seventy-one-year-old man received many calls from baseball people in the summer of 1961, from Bill Veeck in Chicago, from Horace Stoneham in San Francisco, from Walter O'Malley in Los Angeles, and from John Fetzer of the Detroit Tigers, who offered him a job managing the club. He was flattered but uninterested. He had crossed the line, so it seemed, never to run a team again.

As the 1961 baseball season began, Stengel would go off to games in Los Angeles as the guest of Walter O'Malley, and more frequently to American League games as the guest of Angels owner Gene Autry, the old cowboy star.

"I wanted him to join us," says Autry. "I thought he could be of much help with our young club."

Stengel refused to pin himself down, though he was free with his advice to Autry and his partner, Bob Reynolds. He enjoyed seeing baseball, and the Yankee players, now that he was no longer around them, seemed friendlier, warmer, and kinder to him than they had ever been. He went to almost every Yankee-Angels game, enjoying the game, renewing old friendships, kidding with "My writers."

Except for a bad back sustained after a fall near his Toluca Lake branch, he enjoyed excellent health. Under

Edna's careful handling, he was drinking less, resting more, and eating properly. The pressures of winning had disappeared and he was never crusty, unfriendly, or testy to anyone.

One morning in April, while he sat drinking a second cup of coffee and reading the sports pages of the *Los Angeles Times,* the telephone rang. Edna answered. Then she said, "It's George, Casey." Weiss was home with a cold and Hazel Weiss remembers the morning. "George said he was making a business call to Casey and would say hello for me," says Hazel Weiss. "I knew it was a business call because he picked up an envelope from his desk and began making notes."

Weiss, who, like Abraham Lincoln, always made his most important notations on the back of an envelope, wanted Casey's office phone number. Weiss said something about having a man named Don Grant call him later in the day.

M. Donald Grant, a New York stockbroker, handled the investment fortunes of Joan Whitney Payson. Mrs. Payson, a sports fan of note with a share of the New York Giants and large holdings in race horses, had put up most of the money and become the majority stockholder in the new franchise in New York. Grant, who represented her on all her investments, was named the chief operating officer of the team. Weiss, who had considered Stengel from his first day on the job as president, now wanted Grant to talk with Casey. They chatted about the possibility and Casey thanked Grant for the call. He said he was happy in retirement, wasn't interested in managing again, and wished Grant and his team well.

Two months passed. The team held a contest and Mrs. Payson decided she liked the name Mets for her new club. Leases were signed for the use of the Polo Grounds, the old home of the Giants until a new stadium, to be built by the city on the sight of the 1939 World's Fair and in conjunction with a new proposed World's Fair in 1964, could be completed. More office people were hired. Baseball was enthralled by the excitement of Roger Maris' pursuit of Babe Ruth's home run record. Weiss called Stengel again in July. Stengel said he was still retired. The press questioned Weiss about his manager. Weiss said, "There's no rush. We'll have a manager, I'm sure." October 10, 1961, was set as the date of the expansion draft. The Mets would get twenty-two players for $2,800,000 and the right to play in the National League.

Weiss knew he had to have Casey. The Yankees were having a marvelous year under new manager Ralph Houk. The new Mets could not compete with them for the ticket dollar in New York with talent. They needed an attraction. There was only one attraction, only one man who could handle the press and win the public, Casey Stengel. Weiss called Casey in late September and formally offered him the job. He weakened, said he would consider it, and told Weiss to call him again in forty-eight hours.

Casey weighed the decision. Did he want to return to managing at the age of almost seventy-two? Did he want those long trips and sleepless nights again? Would Edna be willing to go east again?

"I don't think she was terribly excited about getting back into baseball again at that stage," says Jack Lawson. "I think she would have preferred it if Casey stayed away. I can tell you this. Casey would not have gone back if she had made a strong stand against it. They always made decisions together. Casey knew baseball. Edna knew business and she knew Casey."

Edna could see that Stengel, as happy as he was in Glendale, missed the action. There was another major selling point: loyalty. Stengel felt deeply that George Weiss, as cold and hard and budget-minded as he appeared to the public, was a friend in need. Casey understood that Weiss had stuck his neck out to take this job with the new franchise and a complete failure, like that of the new franchise in Washington, would hurt George badly. Now Weiss, with time running out and the press clamoring for a name of a manager before the expansion draft meetings, made two moves. He called Cookie Lavagetto and Solly Hemus, promised each of them they would be considered for the managerial post if Casey refused, and got them to agree to be coaches if he did accept. It was the same fail-safe method he used in 1948 with Jim Turner and Casey. Then he played his trump card. He asked Mrs. Payson to call Casey directly. While Leo Durocher and Charlie Dressen campaigned hard for the job through friends in the press, Mrs. Payson, from her Manhasset, Long Island, estate, called CIrcle 1-4041 in Los Angeles. It was shortly after 8 A.M. Thursday morning in California.

"Casey," she said, "this is Joan Payson."

She told Casey the New York Mets needed him badly. He said, "I think it would be splendid working for you."

Casey could understand what effort it took for Joan Payson to make that call. After all, millionaires don't ask people to work for them. They tell people to work for them. Casey understood millionaires, having worked for them most of his life, and besides, he now was one himself. She was wealthy and wanted to have some fun. That was the kind of boss he liked.

Weiss later called Stengel and the deal was completed. Casey would have a one-year contract for $100,000 and the Mets would have themselves a name manager.

On October 2, 1961, Casey Stengel blew the Yankees and Reds right off the front pages. The World Series would start in two days, but for now, nobody cared. The Old Professor was back in town. Life was beginning again for him just short of his seventy-second birthday. In another of a long series of digging notes at the Yankees, Weiss decided to hold the crowning of Casey Stengel in the same Le Salon Bleu in the Savoy Hilton where Stengel had been "resigned, fired, quit, discharged" less than a year earlier. This was the most riotous press conference most reporters ever experienced. All questions were shouted and all answered with shouts. Nobody sat down. Everybody laughed throughout the short interviews. "What about your health?" someone screamed. "What about yours?" screamed Casey. "I didn't say I'd stay fifty years or five and my health is good enough above the shoulders." Then somebody said, "Do the Yankees still have to pay you?" Said Casey, "I worked there for twelve years, didn't I?"

Soon Casey was introducing his new coaches, Solly Hemus and Cookie Lavagetto, each certain in his own mind that George Weiss had promised him the managerial job after Casey left in a year. A broom was on the side wall and Stengel picked it up while Hemus and Lavagetto, looking chagrined, held it high in a clean sweep photo. "Casey, Casey, over here," screamed a photographer. "Wait a minute, will ya, until I put down my bourbon."

When the last question was asked, the last interview given, the last photograph taken, Stengel stood at the door of the hotel, as he had a year earlier, this time with a huge grin on his face. He straightened a new felt hat on his head, pulled the belt of his topcoat tight, and started for the exit. His eyes were bright and clear, his facial lines a little deeper but more picturesque, his step a little quicker. A cab turned a corner and he almost stepped off the curb near it as he talked to a couple of reporters. "Whoops," he said, as he saw the cab spin close by, "I already done that." Another cab stopped at the light, the driver spotted Casey, he leaned out of window, and yelled, "Hey, Casey, welcome back. We missed ya."

"I missed ya, too," Casey said. "Now come out and see this new ball club which is here."

Casey's step was lively as he walked back to the Essex House again. Why not? He had a ball club to boss again, there would be no pressure to win, and he didn't have to stay fifty years or five if he didn't like it.

In some few days he actually had some ballplayers. The first player drafted was a journeyman catcher named Hobie Landrith. Why was Landrith picked first? "If you don't have a catcher," Casey explained, "you have a lotta passed balls." Then the Mets picked up four premium picks in Jay Hook, Bob Miller, Don Zimmer, and Lee Walls, each for $125,000, paid $75,000 for Craig Anderson, Roger Craig, Ray Daviault, Alvin Jackson, Chris Cannizzaro, Choo Choo Coleman, Ed Bouchee, Gil Hodges, Elio Chacon, Felix Mantilla, Sammy Drake, Gus Bell, Joe

Christopher, John DeMerit, and Bobby Gene Smith. For $50,000 they acquired Jim Hickman and Sherman Jones. These were the original Mets.

Stengel returned to Glendale after the draft and came back to New York again for a Thanksgiving Day ceremony. The annual Macy's parade was being held and the Mets had a float, manned by Stengel, Gil Hodges, who made his home in Brooklyn, Billy Loes, who signed a contract as a free agent and then never reported, and Monte Irvin, who worked for the team's beer sponsor, Rheingold.

It was a bitter cold day. The vicious November winds lashed at the parade participants and the spectators with equal anger. Everyone was bundled up tight against the cold and the wind. The temperature dropped to twenty-nine degrees, and under a cloud cover and with strong winds, it felt much worse than that. Hodges had his topcoat pulled tight. He waved those huge hands of his weakly to the cheering crowd. Loes, wearing a thin raincoat, stood glumly in the corner of the float wondering what the hell he was doing there anyway. Irvin stood and shivered.

Only Casey Stengel, who had just flown in from sunny California, stood on the float without a topcoat, without a hat, with his hands, his eyes, and his mouth moving constantly, yelling back at the fans, imploring people to come out to see his new team, patting the heads of small children, shaking hands with adults, signing autographs as the float moved, telling people how many home runs Hodges would hit next season and how good Loes would pitch and how he remembered Irvin from his steal of home in the 1951 World Series against the Yankees. His voice could be heard above the brass bands as he shouted greetings to people along the way.

"Have a nice day," one young man said to Stengel.

"Yeah, yeah, the same to yourself, it is a splendid day and I'm glad everybody came out to see the amazin' Mets ride in this here parade."

What did the man say? "Amazin' Mets."

They had not collected yet for spring training, they had

only untried kids or used-up veterans and Stengel called them amazing. Hell, he was right again. They would be amazing because they would be on the same fields with the Giants and the Dodgers, they would be amazing because they had been put together so soon, they would be amazing because they had the unenviable chore of bucking the Yankees in New York after Roger Maris had set a new home run record, they would be amazing because they would never fail to entertain, they would be amazing because they became the most down-trodden and most loved team in baseball history.

They would be amazing most of all because their grizzly old manager was amazing. He would be nearing seventy-two years of age when he first met up with them in the spring of 1962 in the old Yankee camp at St. Petersburg. No Met would be more enthusiastic. His energies would prove boundless, his performance perfect, his optimism enviable. Charles Dillon "Casey" Stengel, the Kankakee Kid of 1910, would be back in baseball, back where he belonged, back with a new team in one of the most joyous experiences of his life.

13. Can't Anybody Play This Here Game?

IN THE STANDS at Miller Huggins Field on March 1, 1962, more than two hundred people, mostly elderly winter vacationers from the snows of the North, sat bundled up against the early morning chill. St. Petersburg, Florida, is a resort town built between Tampa Bay and the Gulf of Mexico on Florida's west coast. So many retirees and older vactioners come there each winter, it has acquired the cruel nickname of the Land of the Living Dead. An old St. Petersburg gag goes, "Somebody got a heart attack and died right on a bench downtown." Pause. "How could anybody tell?"

Into this aged population came a frisky old warhorse named Casey Stengel. On that March morning, while his new team assembled and dressed shortly before 10 A.M., Stengel, his new Mets jacket zipped tight against the cold and his hands stuffed into the back pocket of his uniform trousers, jogged on to the field from the clubhouse. The fans stood up when they saw him and began applauding. He tipped his hat, came near the fence, and began chatting with them. Most of their conversation was not about the weather or the team or even their vacation. Mostly, these old people wanted to know, how did Casey like working again at his age. "Well, a lot of people my age are dead at the present time and if you ain't, it ain't bad." They laughed at him, hardly understanding him, but enjoyed seeing him. As the sun grew a little warmer, they began taking off their topcoats, removing their gloves, taking off their caps. If Casey was warm enough in a jacket, they would be, too.

Clubhouse man Herb Norman walked around the large room adjusting uniforms, checking equipment, reminding players the old man was already on the field. Before 10 A.M. they were all on the practice field—Gil Hodges and Richie Ashburn and Charlie Neal and Clem Labine, skilled veterans in the final days of their career; untried kids named Ray Apple, Bruce Fitzpatrick, and Dawes Hamilt, all thinking they could be major-league players. Two benches were outside the clubhouse entrance, one marked GEORGE WEISS and one marked CASEY STENGEL and Stengel brought the players to him and stood on his bench.

"Now you can make a livin' here," he began, "because this is a new team and nobody has a job yet. The owners put a lot of money into this team and they wanna see how fast you can get better."

He began walking down the length of the field, as the fans applauded the Mets, toward home plate. The players, many with silly grins on their faces, followed. "Now this here is where the game starts when the pitcher lets go of the ball." Then he walked toward first base, his players followed and he continued his monologue, about how good Babe Ruth was hitting and pitching if any of them could do that, about why the fans wanted them to be good because the Dodgers and Giants left, how he would hope they would all enjoy New York, and then he said, "I'll rent you my room in the Essex House cheap for the winter because me and my wife go back to Glendale because she don't like the cold and why should ya?"

Now he was turning toward second base and explaining how he had first come to New York in 1910 and said, "A lotta good things can happen there, which is the biggest city, if you play good," and moved on to third. He paused for the first time until all the players could hear him again and said, "This is third base, which is only ninety feet from home, which is the same as the distance from first to second, but a lot of them think it's all uphill, which it isn't if you can hit because you can't bunt the lively ball so good." He marched toward home, put the front part of the left toe on the plate, and said in a loud voice, "All right, Mets, let's commence playin'.'"

"It was a brilliant speech," says Rod Kanehl. "When it was over and we started working out, I had to translate for a few guys, but they all appreciated the part about making a lot of money."

Kanehl, a twenty-eight-year-old rookie that spring, had been a Yankee farmhand since 1954. He had endeared himself to Stengel by leaping over a low outside fence and retrieving a baseball that had bounced away before a fan could get it, thereby proving his business sense and loyalty to the organization. He had never made the Yankees because he couldn't hit, but he was a very bright, hustling, aggressive minor-league player and the Mets weren't the Yankees. Kanehl would become "Casey's boy," a focus of many of the battles over personnel with George Weiss, a tremendous favorite of the fans, a representation of what the Mets were—short of talent, long on desire. The first player banner to fly over the Polo Grounds would read simply "Hot Rod."

"From the first day in the Mets camp," says Kanehl, now in private business in Los Angeles, "what struck me was his energy and enthusiasm. He seemed an old man with the Yankees, tired, crotchety, aloof from the players. With the Mets he was incredibly energetic, warm, involved, a great teacher. He always used me as one of his instructors. He knew I was well trained with the Yankees. We would be having a bunting drill and he would say, 'Now let Kanehl show ya the rest.' He made me feel important."

The elderly rookie made the club and he was the first Met to collect on one of Stengel's standing offers.

"He told us the first day that if any player got hit with a pitch with the bases loaded," says Kanehl, "it would be fifty bucks. I did it in the first week and he went right to his checkbook and gave me a personal check for fifty. I have it still."

In those early days of the first Mets spring training the personality of the club was slowly being formed. The veteran Dodgers—Hodges, Craig, Zimmer, Labine—got the early attention. Ashburn supplied the humor (he always managed to park his antique automobile in the parking lot spot marked GEORGE WEISS) and Kanehl supplied the ham. After each exhibition game Stengel would discuss the team's performance with the press. Then the reporters would move to the players for more lucid explanation. When they came to Kanehl he would greet them with a crusty, "You saw it, write it," doing a splendid imitation of an earlier generation Casey Stengel.

On the evening of the first day the players rested. Casey Stengel did not. He stood at the bar of the pressroom in the team's hotel headquarters at the Colonial Inn on St. Petersburg Beach and talked nonstop for more than three hours. Lou Niss, the traveling secretary and a former sports editor of the *Brooklyn Eagle,* reminded him that Edna awaited his appearance for dinner.

"Casey, we have to go now," Niss said.

"For crissakes, don't ya see I'm trying to tell my writers about this here team," he shouted.

Forty-five minutes later there was a gentle knock on the door of the pressroom. Edna Stengel, tanned, lovely, and sleek in a new powder-blue dress, appeared. "Casey," she said, stretching out his name.

"Gotta go, gotta go," he said, bouncing out of the door.

In the hotel lobby Edna, Lou Niss, Solly Hemus, and Cookie Lavagetto stood waiting as Casey signed autographs. He asked for names of all the people who requested his. He signed each autograph carefully. He never stopped talking about the Mets, the Mets, the Mets.

"He was the world's greatest salesman," says Lou Niss.

Niss, about fifteen years younger than Stengel, smoked nonstop. Stengel, who had cut down from a Yankee high of some three packs a day to ten cigarettes a day, was working on Niss to cut down. All the talk in the world didn't move Niss. What got him to quit was Stengel doing an imitation of Niss walking and smoking with his right elbow cradled in his left palm, the cigarette dangling from his mouth and the ashes falling on his suit. Hardly a day in the pressroom was complete without some writer begging Stengel to do the "Niss walk."

The World Champion Yankees were being pushed off

the sports pages as the doings of the Mets gained more and more attention. Stengel, knowing full well the value of publicity, had time for any sportswriter, any columnist from any paper, or any television or radio interviewer. His energy was boundless and his enthusiasm was contagious. The press, a talented, creative group, led by Dick Young of the *Daily News,* Jack Lang of the *Long Island Press,* Leonard Shecter of the *Post,* and Stan Isaacs of *Newsday,* had independently decided the emphasis would be on the lighter aspects of the team. Baseball people understood this would be a losing team. It was also a funny team, with their inadequacies pointed out repeatedly by these sportswriters and a following group of younger reporters. Before the team broke camp in April, it had a group personality. They were Stengel's creation, lacking talent to be sure, but enthusiastic, energetic, and filled with the mission of the moment: to build a National League franchise in New York. Broadcaster Lindsey Nelson moved to Stengel for the final preseason interview. It was time now for Casey to reveal his starting lineup.

"At first base I have the noted Mr. Hodges of the Dodgers," he began, his eyes twinkling, his voice strong, his feet slightly elevated on his toes, "at second base, there is Mr. Neal, also of the Dodgers and at shortstop. . . ." He moved from position to position naming all his starters, recalling their names remarkably well until he came to the right fielder. Here he stopped as he struggled for the name, seeing the player in his eye, describing his ability as a left-handed power hitter from Cincinnati, his throwing arm, his handsome face, everything about him but his name. Then he said . . . "and when he hits the ball he will ring a bell and. . . ." Now he had it . . . "that's his name, Bell." Gus Bell was the right fielder. Bell had eight children, left-fielder Frank Thomas had six children, and center-fielder Richie Ashburn had six children. Stengel turned to a reporter as the interview ended and said, "If they produce as well on the field as off, we'll win the pennant."

On April 9, 1962, the new New York Mets flew from St. Petersburg, Florida, to St. Louis to open their first season.

They arrived at the Chase Hotel, were assigned rooms, and immediately walked to the elevator. Sixteen players jammed into a small elevator. It went up half a floor, coughed, and was stuck. It was more than half an hour before they could be freed. "I finally get a chance to open a season," said tall, slim Roger Craig, who was always behind Sandy Koufax, Don Drysdale, and Johnny Podres with the Dodgers, "and I spend it in an elevator."

It rained the next night and the game against the Cardinals was postponed. Naturally, sportswriters pointed out the Mets were undefeated, untied, and untried in National League play. It all ended the next night. Under clear, cool skies, Larry Jackson beat Craig; Gus Bell had a single for the first hit, Hodges had the first homer, and the Mets had their first of 120 losses in 1962, by a score of 11–4. The key play was a fly ball that fell between Ashburn and Bell, opening up a five-run inning for St. Louis. "My head knew I had it," said Ashburn, "but my legs forgot to get it." Stengel took the defeat as well as could be expected from a man who had gained the reputation of being a sore winner and an inconsolable loser. He rolled down his socks, threw them on the floor, took a large swallow of beer from a paper cup, lit a cigarette, and announced, "When you're losin' everybody commences playin' stupid." Then he continued to talk for thirty minutes. It was a pattern he would follow as long as he led the Mets. The worse the team played, the more he talked. He would do the entertaining after defeats. After rare victories, he would excuse himself quickly, move to the shower, and send the press to the players.

The players dressed quickly, boarded a bus, and soon were on their way to New York for the first time as a team. They were off the next afternoon and they were paraded in open convertibles down Wall Street to City Hall. There, Mayor Wagner greeted them with warm words. Stengel was presented with a huge, gold key. "I got a lotta keys to a lotta cities," he said, "but this is the first one I'm using to open a team."

The next afternoon, Friday, April 13, 1962, the Mets opened their home season at the Polo Grounds. It was a gloomy afternoon with leaden skies, a chilling rain, and some snowflakes falling as temperatures dropped below the thirties. Bob Friend started for the Pirates and Al Jackson, a small black pitcher from the Pittsburgh organization, started for the Mets. The first banner appeared and the first "Let's Go Mets" cheer began about the fifth inning. The Pirates won 4–3, but a good time was had by all. The bedsheet banners would soon become a staple of Polo Grounds attendance, kids lettering their torn sheets with such immortal words as "Good Grief, Mets," or "What Me Worry? I'm a Mets Fan," or "Welcome to Grant's Tomb," in honor of board chairman M. Donald Grant. Dick Young would soon label the enthusiastic rooters, "The New Breed," a badge of honor all fans would wear proudly. Mets fans, some as young as eight, nine, or ten, would often say of their embryo team, "I've been a Mets fan all my life."

The Mets lost nine in a row before Jay Hook beat the Pirates 9–1 in Pittsburgh. Backup catcher Joe Ginsberg roared through the clubhouse shouting, "Break up the Mets," and back in New York, candles were lit for the deliverance. "I'm gonna let Hook pitch every day," shouted Stengel, as he floated through the dressing room. "He'll go in the next hundred games so I can win the pennant. We shouldna lost the first nine and I don't see how we lost a game. The damn streak cost us the pennant. We might win the next twenty straight."

By early May the Mets, 5–16 on the season and nine games out of first place, had become a major attraction around the league. Everybody wanted to see just how bad this team was. Ralph Kiner, one of the team broadcasters, who had played on the 1952 Pirates (42–112), argued that his former team was worse. Purists said it was too early to tell. A move in the wrong direction—or the right depending on one's point of view about the Mets—was made on May 9.

"We've tried to make the Mets look better with distance hitting," explained Casey, "so we brought in this here new fella."

His name was Marv Throneberry, labeled Marvelous

Marv by Leonard Shecter because he wasn't. Throneberry was a moon-faced, balding redhead with a large
chaw of tobacco stuck in his cheek on the field, and black,
well-chewed cigars hanging from his lips off the field. He
became teacher's pet, Stengel, Ashburn, and Kanehl making fun of him every chance they got, which was most
every day. Throneberry was a journeyman player, but he
had some magical propensity toward making errors only
when it counted. Other players made errors anytime.
Marvelous Marv did it with two out in the ninth inning.
Ashburn, who dressed next to Marv, reminded the press
of his teammate's bad hands any chance he got. "Go ask
Marv if he has oiled his hooks," Ashburn would advise
young, bewildered sportswriters. Throneberry would
personify the incompetance of the Mets with his poor
play, his gift for failure at dramatic moments, and his
drawling, ungrammatical use of the language. When he
was finally sent back to the minor leagues he announced
to the press, "I ain't gave up yet." Through the efforts of
the press he became a folk figure and was able to gain the
kind of identification that years later would make him a
popular figure on beer commercials.

On May 21 the Mets lost 3–2 to the Houston Colt 45s.
Then they lost the next day by the same score and took
off on a flight to Los Angeles for their first trip to the West
Coast. The plane was delayed leaving Houston. There was
an interminable layover in Dallas. There was a fuel stop
in Nevada. The meal was cold and the coffee was worse
on the commercial flight. The sun was coming up when
the Mets trudged into their hotel in Los Angeles. Stengel,
looking to be about three hundred years old, labored to
walk to the elevator. Traveling secretary Lou Niss followed close by. Stengel turned to him just before the
elevator doors closed and announced, "If any of my writers are looking for me," he said, "tell them I'm being
embalmed."

Three hours later, refreshed from a bit of sleep, he sat
in the hotel coffee shop, read the sports pages of the *Los
Angeles Times,* and enjoyed a breakfast of eggs, bacon,
and coffee. He then spent the next five hours sitting in the

lobby of the hotel, talking with the sportswriters, entertaining the fans, addressing the hotel bellboys, and selling the Mets. "Are you from New York?" he would ask autograph collectors. "Come out and see my amazin' Mets."

The Mets lost all six games in Los Angeles and San Francisco and had the misfortune of facing the same quality teams back in the Polo Grounds the following week. Even with fans booing the Dodgers and Giants for leaving town and cheering every move of the Mets, the results were the same, six straight losses. Now the losing streak was at twelve and counting. It reached seventeen straight losses on June 6 before the Mets beat the Cubs.

"Whew," whistled a relieved Casey Stengel, "I thought we would have to call in the fire department, my team's so hot."

Marvelous Marv came off the coaching lines (Solly Hemus had been excused for arguing) to hit a home run and win a game in July. He was forced out of the clubhouse door in his torn underwear by his teammates to answer the pleas of cheering fans. Kanehl was hit with a pitch to win a game in early August. Ashburn, after fouling off ten straight pitches, singled through the middle to win a game in September. The Mets continued trying.

"There was never a game that Casey didn't think we could win," says Ashburn, now a Philadelphia broadcaster. "He never gave up, he never lost his enthusiasm. I learned more baseball and had more fun playing one year under Casey with the Mets than in any other season in my entire career."

When the season began Casey had been asked where he thought the Mets would finish. "We'll finish," he said, "in Chicago."

He was right. On September 30 the Cubs beat the Mets 5–1 at Wrigley Field and it was over. They had won 40 games, lost 120, and finished 60 1/2 games out of first. They had drawn 922,530 to the Polo Grounds.

Ashburn won a boat as the Most Valuable Met in a vote of the fans. Throneberry won another for hitting a Polo Grounds sign. The income tax people ruled Ashburn's gift was not income, but Throneberry had to pay tax on his since on-field play earned the award. He was also given the Good Guy Award by New York baseball writers. He accepted the silver tray with humility. "I don't know if I should take this," he said. "I might drop it." Years later home run king Hank Aaron was given the same award. "I guess this is a real important award," he laughed. "I see Marv Throneberry earned it."

In some few days the press was speculating on Stengel's future with the Mets. It would be an annual ritual. An Associated Press reporter, humorless and pompous, unable to get along with Stengel around the Yankees, wrote that Casey would be gone in a few days. The announcement would be made after the World Series. He would write the same story every year of Casey's Met career. When asked what his future was, Casey would say, "A lot a people my age are dead at the present time and I didn't say I would stay five years or fifty." Another week or two would pass and then the announcement would be made, "Casey Stengel has agreed to manage the Mets in 1963."

There were three major additions to the team in 1963. A longtime Dodger favorite named Duke Snider had been traded over to the Mets, a youngster named Ron Hunt would make the club as the second baseman, and a first baseman out of James Monroe High School in the Bronx was ready now at eighteen to open the season in right field. His name was Ed Kranepool.

"I hadn't played much outfield and Casey started working with me in the spring," Kranepool says. "He knew I hadn't thrown long. One day he stood with me in the outfield and began showing me how to throw. 'Keep it low, keep it low,' he kept saying. He was holding the ball over his head now, looking toward home plate and saying, 'Keep it low.' Then he let the ball fly, banged it off his toe, jumped in the air, and shouted, 'Now that's how you keep it low.'"

Kranepool, who would cry when he saw a banner when he was nineteen in the first season at Shea in 1964 asking, "Is Ed Kranepool over the hill?" made the opening day lineup in 1963 in right field.

"There were some long days on that team. People said

Casey fell asleep on the bench. Sure he did. I did too and I was a hell of a lot younger. I always knew what he was saying. When he double-talked he was simply taking the pressure off the players," says Kranepool.

When Kranepool was twenty years old another twenty-year-old player, a catcher named Greg Goossen joined the Mets. Stengel was describing both youngsters to the press. "Now here's Mr. Kranepool," he began, "he can hit left-handed with power and he can field and he can th'o. In ten years he has a chance to be a star. Now here's Mr. Goossen. In ten years, he's got a chance to be thirty."

"Casey spent most of his time with the younger players, quizzing them about the game, teaching them, observing them. He knew what you were doing on and off the field. One time he saw me and Larry Bearnarth [a young relief pitcher] out one night. I was in the starting lineup the next day and ten minutes before the game I was scratched. He suddenly remembered he had seen me out late. He had this way of checking up on guys by asking them for a match. They would pull out a book of matches, he would read the name of some bar on the matches and the guy would be out of the lineup," says Kranepool.

Kranepool was sent to the minors early in 1963. It was his eighty-ninth day in the major leagues.

"I had a bonus agreement that called for seventy-five hundred dollars after I stayed ninety days in the bigs," Kranepool says. "I told Casey about that and he said he would get me my money. It didn't come and when I asked him about it when I was recalled he called George Weiss up in front of me and said, 'For crissakes, where's the kid's bonus money?' The next day I had a check."

Besides learning how to run, hit, and throw, Kranepool also learned how to drink from Casey Stengel.

"Alone or with one guy," he laughs. "Casey explained that to me early in my career. He said when you go out with six or eight guys everybody wants to buy a round. Pretty soon you've had fifteen drinks. With one guy you won't have more than four or five."

The second season began in the Polo Grounds in 1963 against the Cardinals. Curt Flood hit a ground ball leading off the first inning to Charlie Neal at third. Neal picked it up, threw wild at first, Flood raced to third, and the Mets were beaten 7–0. Stengel looked at the approaching sportswriters, took a huge swallow on his beer, and announced, "We're a fraud again. The attendance got trimmed."

The Mets had lost, of course, but the attendance really hadn't been trimmed. Losing was as much fun as winning for Mets fans, and as Casey struggled to make the team better, the people of New York grew fonder and fonder of the Mets and of Stengel. There was developing an incredible bond between the fans and Stengel, he the all-knowing father, and the fans, mostly young and happy with their own new team, learning baseball at his knee. Stengel had become a folk figure around the league, describing the unfinished bridge to nowhere in Pittsburgh to Pittsburgh sportswriters, telling how he once hid under a rolled-up canvas in Crosley Field to Cincinnati writers, describing his contract battles in Philadelphia to Philadelphia writers, showing the spot in Wrigley Field where he banged his heel in 1923 to Chicago sportswriters. In each town the coming of the Mets was heralded with long Casey Stengel stories about birds in the hat, World Series heroics, or great Yankee teams. In Chicago, a thirty-three-year-old player-manager named Elvin Tappe announced he would catch one day and Stengel, near seventy-three, announced he would also. A front-page picture of a grouchy-looking young Stengel and a smiling old man ran side by side in the *New York Post*.

Stengel seemed to be able to tolerate defeats better than he had ever done before, knowing full well improvement would be slow with an expansion team. Once in a while he would lose patience, blow up in the clubhouse, and drink loud and long with the writers after a tough game. He did it after a game was blown in St. Louis with the Mets ahead by three runs, nobody on, and two out in the ninth. The Cards rallied for four runs to win and Stengel stormed, "Can't anybody play this here game?" Writer Jimmy Breslin, unused to Stengelese, confused it in his popular book on the Mets and it came out, "Can't anybody here play this game?" The 1963 season began as 1962 had, with eight straight defeats. Then, a rookie second baseman named Ron Hunt hit a ninth-inning double and the Mets beat Milwaukee 5–4 for their first win of the year. Owner Joan Payson, so overjoyed at the triumph she couldn't stop celebrating, sent flowers to Hunt's room for his wife, Jackie. They were lovely. There was only one problem. Hunt, allergic to the flowers, was up all night sneezing.

"I was at home in Overland, Missouri, shortly after the Mets bought me from the Braves organization. The phone rings and a guy says, 'This is Mickey Mantle.' I thought some friend of mine was pulling my leg. I listened and he says, 'We know you are going to be in New York with Casey and I'm opening a motel down here in Joplin, Missouri, and since you'll be playing for Casey, I thought I could tell you a few things.' I went down there, thrilled out of my mind, and met Mickey and Whitey. They taught me a few things, all right. They taught me how to get drunk," says Hunt.

A scrappy player, who would become know as an expert in getting hit with a pitch, Hunt sat on the Mets bench for a week after hustling to the club in spring training.

"I was sick and tired of sitting. I went to Casey and said, 'I'm twenty-two years old and I wanna play. What about it?' He said, 'You'll play tomorrow, I ain't got any old ones doin' any better.' I played and got four hits and we won," says Hunt.

Hunt had broken in against the Braves and was immediately a Mets hero because he was the first home-grown star they had.

"A couple of weeks into the season I'm playing regular now and Casey asks me how much I'm making. I tell him I'm making the minimum. He says, 'Wait a minute now, for crissakes, you're a regular,' and goes to the phone. He comes back and says, 'Go up stairs and get a raise.' I went up later and I had a new contract calling for a thousand dollars more."

The Mets were playing good ball in mid-May with a 15–19 mark when they ran into the tough part of the schedule again with the Dodgers and the Giants and fell out of contention, to ninth place. They weren't much better than they had been in 1962, even though they had added some better players in Hunt, Kranepool, and Duke Snider, the great center fielder of the powerful Brooklyn Dodger teams of the 1950s.

"I had always been on a contender," says Snider, now a Montreal broadcaster. "If it wasn't for Casey I would have gone nuts with the Mets. He made it fun. He used to call me kid and at my age [thirty-seven] that was nice to hear. One day he called me over to him on the bench and said he wanted to talk about the 1952 Series [Billy Martin makes his catch] and I said, 'Why do we always have to talk about '52, Case? Let's talk about '55.'"

The Mets lost that day, of course, and Casey, wearing his red, silk undershorts with the Yankee "NY" emblem, came over to Snider after the game and said, "Tomorrow you'll sit on the bench and talk about '55. Maybe it will bring us luck."

"We were playing the Dodgers one day and we're losing 3–0. I'm mad because I'm not playing, but I'm sitting next to him and he says, 'They're mahogany over there and we're driftwood.' His head starts falling a little and he says, 'Look kid, I'm tired. You know the signs. You run the club.' I did and he dozed off. When he wakes up a couple of innings later the score is 9–0 against us. 'I'm sorry, Casey.' He says, 'That's all right, I told you they were mahogany and we're driftwood.'"

On July 30, 1963, the Mets broke a losing streak of twenty-two straight road losses. Tracy Stallard, who had allowed the famous sixty-first homer for Roger Maris in 1961, breaking the Ruth record, beat Los Angeles 5–1. Casey was in a marvelous mood as he pranced through the door at his Glendale home. A huge birthday cake sat on the dining room table. It was a gift from the Los Angeles Dodgers.

"The Dodgers gave me that," said Stengel, "and I commenced giving them the bird."

Edna Stengel had decided to throw a surprise birthday party for Casey's seventy-third (she insisted it was his seventy-fourth) birthday and asked Lou Niss to invite all the writers with the club out to the house on Grandview Avenue in Glendale. They were told to arrive at seven while Casey was engaged out back with members of the board of directors of the Valley National Bank. The writers had assembled, there were television cameras in place, and the moment arrived. Edna walked out back.

"Casey, George Weiss is on the phone," she said.

"Put it on the phone out here," he said. "Can't ya see I'm in a meeting?"

"He said he only wanted to ask you one quick thing," said Edna.

"That's all right, Casey, go ahead," said one of the board members, in on the plot. "We'll wait."

He walked out of the garden into the house. The writers had assembled near a side door, and as he walked into the living room, he spotted them. "Now wait a minute, what is all this? My writers are here. Everybody's here."

Everybody was there, his writers from New York, his writers from Los Angeles, his coaches, his bank board members, local friends, and the mayor of Glendale, who hung a key to the city around his neck. He stood motionless in the first burst of this surprise party, recovered, and announced, "Edna, these here are my friends, show 'em the place." In some few moments he was talking and drinking and walking around the house, pointing out the trophies and the pictures, the autographed baseballs and the crossed bats, the plaques and the awards of a lifetime in the game. "Now I have had a number of birthdays as you can see if you was to look it up and I have to say the house has been cleaned up so all you lovely gentlemen can see I wasn't born in a dugout and I have worn shoes for quite a few number of years now."

Then it was out to the garden with lights blazing down on huge roasts of beef, heaping tables of salads, cold cuts, hors d'oeuvres, and creamy cakes. Two separate tables were filled with booze and were steadily unfilled as the night went into morning. At 4 in the morning the last guests left and Stengel shouted, "And if you don't think he would be a better pitcher if he didn't chase those damn women at every corner, you don't know what it can do to you if you are not serious about baseball you should get out."

On August 20 the Mets won game number forty and tied their 1962 total of victories. The winning pitcher was a handsome left-hander named Grover Powell. He was twenty-one and writers gathered around him after the game for his first mass interview. While they asked their questions, Stengel pushed through the crowd around the rookie, nudged forward with a pencil in his hand, and asked, "Wuz you born in Poland?" For several years afterward, any writer interviewing a new player on the Mets, would ask, "Wuz you born in Poland?" while the player looked stunned and the writers enjoyed their inside joke.

On September 18 the Mets played the final baseball game ever at the Polo Grounds, ticketed for demolition as Shea Stadium was being finished in Flushing, New York.

"I'm sad about it closing," said Larry Bearnarth, a native New Yorker. "It has meant so much to baseball."

"I closed it last night," said Powell, already a losing Met, "when the Phillies bombed me."

Stengel undressed and talked about playing there under McGraw, hung up his uniform shirt number thirty-seven carefully, and said, "Why wouldn't you think it was a good park if you made a living here and they could." Then he looked out at the players in the clubhouse and said, "You hope they get better and some did."

Was he issuing his farewell address? Stengel had never said much very directly but had always dropped hints for those who understood Stengelese. In some few days, with the season ending, the annual Associated Press bulletin moved on the wire: Stengel fired.

"Don't you think they'd tell you if you was and they haven't," he said. Then he smiled and said, "I heared they're gonna have fifty-six bathrooms in the new stadium."

The Associated Press would have to wait a little while longer. So would the United Press. Casey Stengel was only nearing seventy-four years old. Certainly that was too young to retire.

Casey and Edna say
goodbye to the Polo
Grounds. *(Photo courtesy
of Louis Requena.)*

Casey says goodbye to
his Polo Grounds
"writers" for the last
time in 1963. Author,
young at that present
time, is at the far right.
*(Photo courtesy of Louis
Requena.)*

14. The Youth of America

ABOUT A DOZEN LITTLE OLD LADIES, squashed into flowered bathing suits, all manicured and made up, stood in the alcove outside the main lobby of the Colonial Inn in St. Petersburg, Florida, on February 6, 1964. One looked at her gold watch.

"When will he be here?" one lady asked.

"Soon, soon," said the inn's social director, his chubby belly shaking like a bowl full of jelly as he talked. Then he nervously stage-whispered to his young assistant, "Where is that man? He's driving me nuts."

A station wagon pulled up in front of the hotel. A *St. Petersburg Times* photographer, who had spent a good part of the afternoon asleep in the lobby, leaped to his feet. He rushed outside. Two handsome young men, pitcher Tracy Stallard and outfielder Duke Carmel of the Mets, walked out of the back seat of the car. Out of the front seat came a bowlegged man with floppy ears, a green shirt, an orange tie, and a cute grin. Casey Stengel was back in town.

"Casey, Casey, how about a picture?"

"Sure, sure, just as soon as I unload myself," said Stengel.

"Good to see ya, doctor," I said. Casey, never one for names, began calling all of his regular writers "doctor" and soon they were all calling him "doctor."

"Yeah, me too," he said. "Amazin' trip. All of Stallard's fans came to the airport to see him off."

"They weren't seeing me off, they were seeing you off,"

236

said the handsome pitcher. "They were just running me out of town."

By now the little old ladies had heard about his arrival and—violating the house rule—marched into the lobby in their bathing suits. They squealed like teen-agers, screamed for paper and pencil from the front desk, and began attacking the old man for autographs.

"Now is this for you or your grandchild? Let me see, his name is David, right? Is he gonna join the Mets? Only six years old, well, I got some teen-age players myself and why wouldn't ya make them better if they ain't failed yet?"

Now he was in high gear, licking the pencil every so often, signing autographs, bragging about the Mets, advising the ladies to have their grandsons sign with the Mets, talking, selling, charming, working at his job.

His bags were carried to his room, he peeled off a five-dollar bill, and said, "If you don't tip them, you won't see them from one week to the tenth." Then he gave the bellboy the bill and continued, "I wanna see these young fellas myself."

As he had with the Yankees, Stengel pushed for extra instructional time for young players. The Mets had decided to go along by opening the training camp early, bringing in their best prospects, and hopefully accelerating development in Casey Stengel's first "instructural school" with the Mets.

"We got Gardner and we got Wilson and we got Selma," he said, reciting the names of some young prospects, "and why wouldn't you get better if they're the Youth of America."

They would be there that spring, the youngsters the Mets felt might become important major leaguers, Casey's Youth of America, Rob Gardner, Bruce Wilson, Dick Selma, Bud Harrelson, Cleon Jones, Tug McGraw, and Ron Swoboda. One way or another, they would all contribute to the legend. Harrelson, Jones, McGraw, and Swoboda would actually play on a World Series winner in five years.

Traveling secretary Lou Niss, doing the Niss walk, came into Casey's room. He wanted to know if Casey would talk on the phone to a reporter from the *Herald Tribune* in New York. The caller was doing a survey on famous people who smoked and what their reactions were to the Surgeon General's report on smoking and cancer.

"No, I don't smoke all the time," growled Casey, who had different manners for nonsports reporters. "I stop when I go to sleep." Then he hung up the phone and resumed the conversation with the sportswriters about the Youth of America. "What if Gardner, Wilson, and Selma strike out two hundred men, don't you think we'll do better?"

"But the big leagues aren't the bushes," one reporter said.

"Now wait a minute, will ya, for crissakes, don't ya think I know that?"

Casey slid off the Youth of America and into Edna's battles with an insurance company over fire damage that blew some smoke into the house (it would delay her spring training arrival for a week), about other teams and other players, about the Baseball Writers' Dinner (the hit song that year was entitled "Glory, Glory, Casey Stengel"), about the cancer scare and smoking, about the size of his room and the color of the bedspread. "Pink," he said, "so Edna will feel at home when she gets here."

Several days later, with the Youth of America practicing faithfully on the field now renamed Huggins-Stengel Field, Casey sat in his office working over lineup cards for the first squad game. Several sportswriters sat on the Casey Stengel bench outside and one dared to sit on GEORGE WEISS. Suddenly, somebody spotted a baseball flying madly toward the clubhouse and yelled "watch it" as reporters ducked and the ball crashed through the window of the manager's office. It was in foul territory, but it was a long way from home plate. Casey, his pants unbuttoned and wearing an undershirt and slippers, jumped outside.

"Who done it?" he asked.

Casey addresses his "writers" and announces, "Now that fella here, he done splendid for me but that one there is a fraud and a road apple and I gotta fire him before he tears down the building." *(Photo courtesy of Louis Requena.)*

The hitter in the batting cage was a husky youngster from Baltimore named Ron Swoboda. "If he commences hitting balls over buildings," said Casey, "we'll keep him."

Swoboda hit .300 in spring training that year, was farmed out to Williamsport, and was brought back in 1965. He became one of the most popular players to ever wear a Mets uniform, as much for his hustling play as his brilliant quips. After striking out five times in a doubleheader the Mets split, he said, "It's a good thing we won a game. If we didn't, I'd be eating my heart out. As it is I'm only eating out my right ventricle."

He was big and strong, appeared to be another Mickey Mantle in Stengel's hopeful eyes, and was soon treated as a pet.

"The old man would get angry at me, but he knew I loved him," says Swoboda, now a television sportscaster. "One time I blew a game when I missed a fly ball and then struck out the next inning. I was so damn mad I came into the dugout and began jumping on my helmet. Casey said, 'I'm gonna go inside and throw your watch on the floor and jump on that.' The man did have a way with words."

The Youth of America were all swell kids, but not many of them were ready for the big leagues. The motto was "We'll win more in '64," but Stengel worried about it. He pushed the team hard, worked on fundamentals, encouraged his coaches to spend more time with the players, and prepared for the coming season. The Mets journeyed to Mexico for a series of exhibitions. They lost the first game and won the next two. Casey talked Stengelese in all his press conferences there and several of the Spanish-speaking players on the team said the newspaper reports of his talk were more confusing than in English. Edna made the trip with him and Casey became angry at her when she lost her identification papers. It had held up the entire team and it embarrassed him.

Stengel cut the squad and prepared for the trip back to New York. One of the original Mets, catcher Chris Cannizzaro, who had been sent out for seasoning, was back with the team.

"He always called me Canzoneri and I resented it," says

Cannizzaro, now a coach for Atlanta. "I thought the least he could do was learn my name."

Casey didn't have to learn names because he knew faces, character, and skills.

"Canzoneri can th'o," he would tell the writers, "and a lot of them can't."

Cannizzaro had seen Casey Stengel for the first time in 1948 when Stengel managed the Oakland Acorns and Cannizzaro was a ten-year-old fan.

"I remember getting his autograph and saving it because he was somebody famous, somebody who had been in the big leagues," says Cannizzaro. "Then I joined the Mets in 1962. I was young, immature, intense. I wanted to play. He didn't play me a lot and he pinch-hit for me. I guess I had a lot of resentment for him."

Cannizzaro developed into a fine defensive catcher and was the Most Valuable Player for the San Diego Padres in 1970.

"We had about ten thousand people there that day, a big crowd for us," says Cannizzaro, "and Casey Stengel, old and bent over now, traveled to San Diego to be with me. He got on the microphones and heaped praise on me, said I was one of the greatest catchers he ever had and was proud to see me do so well. Tears came to my eyes."

Cannizzaro stood on the field at Atlanta Stadium and told the story some eight years later. Tears came to his eyes again.

"I have a soft spot for him, always," he said. "My son out there"—he pointed to a sixteen-year-old working out on the field—"was the first Met baby. He was born two weeks after we went to camp. When he sent me out the first year I told him I hadn't yet seen my new baby and my wife. He said, 'I'll bring you back in two weeks.' He did and we were able to spend the summer together."

The Mets opened the 1964 season in Philadelphia. Fine fielding by second-baseman Tony Taylor, left-fielder Danny Cater, and first-baseman Ruben Amaro won the game. "We woulda beat them," said Casey, "if they hadn't commenced being wonderful."

The Mets lost again the next day and now boarded a bus

from Connie Mack Stadium for the short ride to New York. They would open at Shea Stadium for the first time the next day.

On the bus home Stengel squeezed next to four of his younger players, Bill Wakefield, Ron Locke, Steve Dillon, and Jerry Hinsley. He would always be rejuvenated when he was around young players, more determined to teach, more concerned with the happy future instead of the unhappy past. He began a monologue on the bus that covered every park he played in, every uniform he wore, almost every manager he played under, and a lot of players he played with. As the bus rolled over the George Washington Bridge into New York he said, "Now this new stadium, it's in Queens. It's Shea Stadium. Don't go to Ebbets Field by mistake. It's tore down." As the bus reached New York and unloaded the players, he looked off into the night and said, "You'd wanna play these young players because some of them are eighteen and how do you know they won't be good when they're twenty-six, since I got fellas who are twenty-six and they're not winning. You try to improve them and when you go, you leave something behind in this town for ten or twelve years."

He seemed to sense that his place in history, solid as a result of his performance with the Yankees, would have another dimension. The Youth of America, players like McGraw, Harrelson, Swoboda, Kranepool, Jones, youngsters he had taken hold of as babies, would carry his mark for the rest of their playing days. And beyond.

"What I first remember about Casey Stengel," says Ed Kranepool, "is how much he wanted to win."

Casey Stengel arrived at the new Shea Stadium the following morning at 9 A.M. Construction workers were everywhere. The park was to be opened to the public in three hours, but it would not be completed for many weeks. There were problems, but the game would be played and the Mets would have a new home at Flushing Meadow, across from the 1964 World's Fair. The Pirates beat the Mets 4–3 in the first Shea game, but 50,312 people

The women in his life, boss Joan Whitney Payson and wife (partner, not boss) Edna Lawson Stengel at 1964 Shea opening.

were thrilled to be in on this historic event.

When it was over Stengel sat in his new office, a huge bouquet of roses, a gift from Mrs. Payson along the wall, his eyes filled with excitement, his manner bouncy and joyous. "What do you think of the new park?" He stuck out his chest and bellowed. "Lovely, lovely," he said, "lovelier than my team."

The Mets lost again the next day. On Sunday, Alvin Jackson pitched a shutout beating the Pirates 6–0. Rod Kanehl was the first to shout, "Break up the Mets."

Jackson had been able to pitch a strong game despite a steady rain all afternoon. Casey was ecstatic. "It was amazin' and the rain poured in through the roof [the park had no roof] and rained all over my little pitcher, but he won. He's my greatest living pitcher."

The Mets flew to Pittsburgh the next day to open a long road trip. Dozens of helmeted police officers stood outside the Pittsburgh Hilton Hotel as the team bus pulled up. "Whatta we done now?" asked Casey. The players got off the bus and traveling secretary Lou Niss walked up to one of the cops. "What's going on?" The policeman said, "We just had President Johnson here. He gave a speech on poverty."

When the information was relayed to Stengel he said, "He picked the right team."

Lyndon Johnson and Barry Goldwater were engaged in a heated battle for the presidency that season. Casey was asked if he had a preference. "I'm in baseball," he said. There is no indication that Stengel ever voted in any election. He had met every American president from Woodrow Wilson and spent some drinking time with Truman in Kansas City and Nixon in New York, when each was out of office, but never publicly identified himself with any candidate. He had turned down constant requests for political endorsements. Casey was a voracious reader of newspapers, starting with the sports pages, but moving steadily through every page of the paper. He had opinions on everything, including politicians, but never pushed for any candidate.

One thing he read carefully every morning were the baseball box scores. He studied the doings of his future opponents, storing information on what batters were hot, what pitchers were not, what pinch hitters the opposing managers were using in tough game situations, always ready to take any little edge he could get.

In 1964 Yogi Berra had been named manager of the Yankees and Stengel followed his old team's progress carefully. He knew the Yankees had better players than he did, but he could show them up in other ways. He was thrilled when the Mets would outdraw the Yankees, and when the total attendance for the year showed the Mets some 400,000 in attendance higher than the Yankees, it was quite an event. One day a fan came up to Stengel in the lobby of the Hilton Hotel in Pittsburgh and asked for his autograph. Stengel scribbled his name carefully in large letters and was almost finished when the fan said, "I'm a Yankee fan. I loved it when you managed the Yankees." Stengel's jaw stiffened and his face tightened. "I work for the Mets," he said and stormed away. The rivalry between the Mets and Yankees had become bitter. Stengel could reminisce about his players, Mantle, Berra, Ford, Maris, but he wouldn't talk of the organization. The wound in his heart over the firing ran deep. It would be manifested strongly in exhibition games when the Mets beat the Yankees. "I'm gonna have a drink or ten," he announced after one spring win, "because I just won the city World Series."

The Mets continued to lose regular season games but a good time was had by all. Stengel had this marvelous capacity for shaking off defeats and soon would be looking forward to the next day's game as if it were the most important his team had ever played. One night the Mets decided to take the sportswriters, the coaches, the broadcasters, and Lou Niss to dinner at Stan Musial's restaurant in St. Louis called Stan and Biggie's. The night was loud and long. Casey did the Niss walk. Niss imitated Casey. The writers all talked Stengelese. The drinks continued to arrive on schedule. When it was last call for drinking, Casey was saying, "That's what I'm telling ya, will ya listen? . . ." Then he paused. "Sure, a double, why wouldn't ya?" Then he continued, "What about [Bill] Veeck. I worked for him in Milwaukee and he went away to the war and came back with the jungle rot on his leg. I took myself and my wife up to see him and she like to die when he started taking off that wooden leg and washing that stump right in front of her."

Just then Stan Musial came over. The recently retired star of the Cardinals asked Casey, "Can you use an old pinch hitter?"

"It's a good thing you retired," said Stengel, "because I can't afford to have you breaking up the seats in our new stadium."

After Musial left the table, Stengel got up to go to the bathroom, stopped on his way to sign autographs, talked for fifteen minutes, and sat back down without making it to the men's room. Now the check came. Casey said, "Sign George's name and tell him I bought Mays." Lou Niss pulled out a Mets check, signed the bill, and laughed the loudest when Stengel said, "You could lose more money

Casey leading his troops to another Shea victory. Hands in the pocket was the sign for stealing or run, sheep, run and they did. *(Photo courtesy of Louis Requena.)*

Casey admired great
skills and was a Stan
Musial fan for years.
Musial volunteered to
come back at fifty to play
for Casey. Here he is
presented an award by
the Mets. *(Photo courtesy
of Louis Requena.)*

than that in a panic. I lost my money three times in three
panics. You ever try and go to a bank on Saturday night
and get out your money if it's closed."

The Mets had become an institution by now. In each
town New York fans, on vacation or in school or just visiting, would sit together in ball parks yelling, "Let's Go
Mets." One afternoon the Mets played in Milwaukee.
There were 7,369 fans in the park, a good many of them
New Yorkers rooting for the team. The crowd was loud
and the game was heated. It ended when Ron Hunt tried
to score from second base on an infield force at second.
Second-baseman Frank Bolling had thrown home to get
the hard-sliding Hunt. The pugnacious Mets second baseman had crashed into catcher Ed Bailey and now a fight
ensued. Soon the field was swarming with players and
coaches. In the way of baseball fights, Hunt and Bailey
were swinging, but most of the others were pulling and
tugging with very little damage being done. Casey Stengel, some six weeks short of his seventy-fourth birthday,
was on the field. His strong arms grabbed Milwaukee

shortstop Denis Menke around the waist. Menke pulled away, heaved the man on his back to the ground, turned to see who it was, spotted a gnomelike figure with number thirty-seven on his uniform hitting the ground, and screamed, "Oh my God, I've killed Casey Stengel."

On a bright, sunshiny afternoon, May 26, 1964, the Mets played the Chicago Cubs in Wrigley Field. For some strange reason they crushed the Cubs that day. As the score mounted Rod Kanehl, who sat in the bullpen near the stands, was asked by two sunbathing reporters, "Is this a laugher?" Kanehl shook his head, "I'll tell you when it's a laugher." With two out in the bottom of the ninth and the Mets ahead 19–1 Kanehl turned to the reporters and announced, "Now it's a laugher."

The large score—the biggest ever for the Mets—shocked the fans and the press. The biggest shock came that night when a caller reached the sports desk of the *Waterbury Times* and asked, "How many runs did the Mets make today?" The answer was, "Nineteen." The caller paused and then asked, "Did they win or lose?" Mets fans had no faith. In Stengel's words "They had seen what they done."

Each incident, each amusing anecdote about the Mets, helped sell tickets, bring more attention to Stengel, and buy time while the Mets attempted to build a team. While the Mets floundered in the summer of 1964, there was another more-heated contest going on in the country. The Republicans were about to nominate a candidate for president to face Lyndon Johnson. Goldwater's forces were on the right and the forces of New York Governor Nelson Rockefeller were on the left. Rockefeller called in all his big guns as he fought for the nomination. One of his supporters was Jackie Robinson, baseball's first Negro player.

Robinson toured the country for Rockefeller, addressed political groups, carried his message to civil rights groups, worked hard to reach students. Question and answer periods would invariably sway from Rockefeller and politics to baseball. At Concordia College in Moorhead, Minnesota, Robinson was asked about Casey Stengel and the Mets. Still vivid in his mind were his battles across the

Hall of Famer Ralph Kiner interviews Stengel at Shea. The manager is giving him the starting lineup ahead of time. The interview only took thirty minutes. *(Photo courtesy of Louis Requena.)*

field with Stengel and the Yankees. He had always been certain in his own heart that Stengel was a raging bigot. He attacked him every chance he got. He never particularly accused Stengel of being a bigot publicly, leaving that to the questioner. When asked about Stengel that day at Concordia, Robinson said, "Casey Stengel is too old to manage. He should quit. He's asleep on the bench."

No one denied—least of all Stengel—that he took occasional naps on the bench. Too old to manage? That was another question. The story made the wire services and soon sportswriters were questioning Stengel and his players. Jerry Hinsley, nineteen, said, "How could he be too old? He knows so much about baseball." Larry Bearnarth, twenty-two, said, "How about Charles de Gaulle? He's older than Casey and he's running a whole country." Some of the players suggested Casey's advanced age did not diminish his energies or decrease his enthusiasm. Tracy Stallard suggested Stengel was probably in better shape than the former Dodger, now grown heavy and gray. Said Robinson, "Tracy Stallard is right. Casey is in

Old pals get together at 1964 Shea reunion (from left) Bill
McKechnie, the last known living man to call Stengel by his given
name of Charles, old KC and Dodger pal, Zack Wheat, and slugger
Edd Roush. *(Photo courtesy of Louis Requena.)*

better shape than I am. That's why I retired."

Fanned by Howard Cosell's comments on the air, Robinson continued to attack Casey every chance he got. Casey refused to be dragged into the battle. He figured his record would stand any examination. Robinson, who had left baseball in 1956 to join the Chock Full O'Nuts Company, knew he could use this argument to further Rockefeller's political ends. For Casey's part he had a short answer when anyone inquired about Jackie. "Rob-A-Son," he would say, "he's chock full o'nuts."

On May 31, 1964, the Mets lost a doubleheader to the San Francisco Giants. It only took nine hours and fifty minutes to do it and the *New York Post* headlined: WELL, YOU DON'T BEAT OUR GUYS IN A HURRY. Casey Stengel, who had gotten out of a cab at Shea Stadium at 9:30 Sunday morning, got into another heading home to the Essex House at 12:10 Monday morning. The first game was nine innings and the second game was twenty-three innings.

"Casey stood up all the way," said pitcher Jack Fisher,

who had been on the bench next to him all afternoon. "He stood up a lot better than the rest of us. In the twenty-third inning of the second game he stood up on the bench and yelled to John Stephenson to watch out for a curve ball."

On Father's Day, Jim Bunning pitched a perfect game at Shea against the Mets. Now Casey knew how the Dodgers felt in 1956.

The Mets continued to lose at their regular rate. The fans were breaking down the doors at Shea and Stengel studied his roster. On the morning after Barry Goldwater had been nominated for president by the Republican party, Casey was asked by a reporter, "Who are you for?"

"I'm not in politics," he said. "I'm in baseball."

"Do you like Goldwater?"

"I'll tell you something if you just wait a minute, will ya. I stayed up last night and watched the convention all night long. I watched all of them talk, and listened to them and seen them and I'm not interested in politics. If you watch them and listen to them you can find out why you're not."

Goldwater was no longer important the next night as the Mets lost again. The team seemed on a treadmill to nowhere. The faces were different, but the results were the same, losing, losing, losing. The fans showed some signs of restlessness and the press began attacking the team instead of coddling it. Some of the players, repeating the Yankee cycle, were jealous of Stengel and began talking behind his back to reporters.

One of his coaches, Wes Westrum, pointed out one of Casey's major shortcomings. He didn't press discipline. "These players don't care," said Westrum. "They're just happy being in the big leagues."

Westrum wanted Casey to get tougher with the players, impose a curfew, control their late-night barhopping, stress discipline. Casey, who had bristled under discipline as a player, thought it wasn't very important with major leaguers. "If a player doesn't go to sleep," he said, "you'll see it on the field the next day."

Despite his proclivity to take a drink or ten, and despite

the warm spot he always had for others who did throughout their careers, Stengel also admired the clean-living player and the family man. When he sent away Jay Hook, a bright, handsome, personable family man, Stengel said, "He was a lovely fella who busted his butt for you and lived nice. You wish he coulda done better." Stengel had nothing against players who drank and played well or players who didn't drink and played well. He didn't worry about personal habits or lack of discipline, he worried about performance. All Casey Stengel demanded of a player was total commitment and excellence.

There was a hard-drinking, tough-talking manager of the Cincinnati Reds, a former pitcher by the name of Fred Hutchinson, who was dying of cancer in 1964. While some members of the press and some fans questioned Stengel's age and stamina, Hutchinson was disintegrating before everyone's eyes, a bull of a man, now turned into a whisp by the heinous disease. It touched Stengel, who admired physical courage, to a great degree. "Why would a nice man like that get the disease?" When a reporter suggested that smoking and drinking may have had something to do with it Casey bristled. "A lot of them live good and cheat on their wives, too."

In Casey Stengel's world there was room for every man, every human trait, every strength, every weakness. All a man had to do to earn his respect was prove something on the field.

On July 29, one day before his seventy-fourth birthday, a six-hundred-pound cake was wheeled into Shea as a gift from the Master Bakers of Metropolitan New York. It measured eight feet, was made with one hundred twenty pounds of flour, seven hundred eggs, seventy-two pounds of butter, and one hundred pounds of sugar. The word "Casey" on the cake had been smudged and all that could be read was "Case," truly a Mets cake. "We had to give it to you tonight," explained the bakery man, "because it couldn't stand any longer." Said Casey, "Why didn't you just put it into a box?"

The National League season was coming to a close. The Philadelphia Phillies, who hadn't won since 1950, were six and a half games ahead of the Cardinals with ten games to go. Cincinnati and San Francisco were also within range. The Phillies began losing every day and the Cardinals won.

On the final Friday night of the 1964 season the Cardinals had moved into first place. One win over the Mets in three games would give them the pennant. On Friday night, with Stengel standing in the St. Louis chill imploring his legions onward, Al Jackson, the doughty little left-hander, beat Bob Gibson 1–0. The Mets won again 15–5 on Saturday. Stengel was ecstatic Saturday night in the bar at the Chase-Park Plaza. "If the season goes to Christmas," he said, "we'll win the pennant. My team is playing splendid ball and why wouldn't ya if ya was in a pennant race?"

The Cardinals, using Bob Gibson again in relief Sunday, finally beat the Mets for the pennant. St. Louis Catcher Bob Uecker, dancing barefoot in a bucket of ice, said, "I never felt so warm."

The Yankees had come from behind to win the American League pennant under Berra, whose fate had already been sealed in August. He had been fired with the announcement to be made after the Series. Stengel watched the first two World Series games between the Yankees and the Cardinals in St. Louis.

Casey, wearing a light topcoat and a blue felt hat against the early fall chill, left the stadium after the second Series game. He seemed terribly old, tired, his face a rubbery flow of peaks and valleys. The Mets had finished last for the third straight time, won fifty-one games, and drawn 1,732,597 fans to Shea Stadium. Would Casey return in 1965?

Ritualistically, the Associated Press reported that Casey was finished and his retirement would soon be announced. At that very instant he was sitting in his Glendale home, talking to Babe Herman and saying, "He can run." A puzzled Herman asked, "Who can run, Casey?" Said Stengel, "Suh-boda."

Casey had seen young Ron Swoboda hit some home runs in the spring, thought he might be ready, and was soon to discover some more interesting people with him around the Mets. Quitting? Not now, he wasn't. The only reason he looked old was because he was sitting without a baseball uniform. Quitting? Nonsense. Edna had already purchased three new bathing suits for Florida.

15. You Expect Me to Pull 'Em out with a Cane?

SOME FIFTY-FIVE YEARS after he first set out for Kankakee, Casey Stengel journeyed to St. Petersburg for the fourth spring training of the Mets with boyish enthusiasm. An expression that would soon grow popular in military-political circles summed up the situation: Casey Stengel could certainly see "light at the end of the tunnel." The 1965 Mets were more than has-beens and never-will-bes. They were starting to include some talented young players and some class veterans.

There were two people in the cast of characters in 1965 that had been—and would be again—important people in the team picture. One was Casey's favorite player with the Yankees—save for Billy Martin—and the other was his worst mistake in Boston. Yogi Berra, recently deposed as Yankee manager in a bloodless coup led by Dan Topping with assistance from Ralph Houk, would be a coach under Casey, along with Warren Spahn, the geriatric wonder of a left-handed pitcher.

"I got 'em because they add brains to the team," Casey said, as spring training opened.

Spahn still wanted to pitch and Yogi no longer wanted to catch, but things didn't quite work out that way. As pitcher-coach, Spahn was more concerned with his starts than any other pitcher's. As catcher-coach, Yogi had to be pushed into his catching gear. After one memorable pitching victory by Spahn with Yogi squatting in pain for nine innings, Yogi was retired. Spahn would drag it out until the All-Star break, fight with George Weiss, who wanted to release him as a player and cut his salary, and finally leave in a huff. In the spring it was all upbeat.

"I came there to coach," says Yogi. "Casey asked me to catch a couple of games. I tried, but my legs wouldn't take it anymore."

Yogi was forty years old that May and Spahn had passed his forty-fourth birthday and not even eighty-four years of baseball savvy could halt the relentless clock.

"At the All-Star break George Weiss said he wanted to release me," recalls Spahn. "They offered me two months severance pay. I still thought I could pitch. That's why I took Chub Feeney's offer and went over to the Giants."

Spahn came to the Mets to pitch and Casey thought he came to teach other people to pitch. That misunderstanding hurt the Mets severely. Stengel was interested in using Spahn's knowledge.

"I really respected Casey," Spahn says. "He was an intelligent son of a gun. He knew the breath and pulse of an organization. He knew every kid in it."

Yogi and Spahnie, two Hall of Famers now, were roommates early that year and Spahn asked Yogi how to handle a job under Casey.

"Just keep your mouth shut and laugh at his jokes," said Berra, wise in the ways of the wise old man.

There was one meeting early in the season that Spahn recalls now with much clarity.

"Casey called us up to his hotel room, Yogi and I. He said we were his two most experienced coaches and he wanted to have a coach's meeting with us. It was about five o'clock and it was an open date and we all had planned dinner. Then he began talking. I just listened and kept my mouth shut the way Yogi said. Before I know it, it was midnight. By now he's gone through most every player on the Yankees in all his pennant-winning years. I think he was on Woodling and Bauer and he couldn't make up his mind. Then he calls Gus Mauch, the trainer, wakes him up, and tells him to get to his room right away. He walks in, figuring somebody is dying, and Casey says, 'Who's the greatest, Woodling or Bauer?' Mauch looks at him, says, 'Woodling from the left side and Bauer from the right side,' and he leaves."

Spahn had been cut by Stengel on the Braves in 1942 and was a half-season pitcher (4–12) for the Mets in 1965 before being asked to leave. He is fond of saying, "I played for Casey Stengel before and after he was a genuis," but he also says, "Nobody knew more baseball or cared more passionately about the game than Casey Stengel."

With Spahn and Berra soon showing their age and the youngsters not quite ready, the Mets quickly fell into their accustomed spot in last place. Swoboda showed much promise with long home runs but soon curve balls would level him. Ron Hunt was becoming a star and Tug McGraw, one of Spahn's pet projects, was a promising youngster. Through it all, Stengel lost none of his enthusiasm.

On May 10, 1965, the Mets journeyed up the Hudson River by bus for an exhibition game at the United States Military Academy at West Point. The Mets were following a tradition that began some forty years earlier when John McGraw led his Giants, including a platooned left-handed hitting outfielder named Stengel, to West Point. The bus deposited Stengel and the players at the gymnasium where they were greeted by the cadets, shown around, and taken to lunch. There, in front of the cadets corps, Casey Stengel read the orders of the day unlike General MacArthur. Those cadets on walking tours because of demerits weren't quite sure why they had been excused.

Shortly before 3 o'clock, Stengel pushed his way past a group of adoring cadets and instructors in the gymnasium, walked out of the door, and went into a jog toward the bus. It had rained early in the day and the cement walks were still slick. Casey burst through the door, took a couple of small running steps, and slipped on the pavement. He fell hard on his wrist. In much pain, he was taken to the post hospital. The broken bone was set in a cast as the game began without him while Edna, the wives of other Mets officials, and many of the players' wives sat for tea in the living room of the commandant of the corps.

He looked groggy as he walked through the entrance of the Essex House shortly before midnight, his right arm in a bandanna sling, his hair disheveled, his eyes weary, his face so tired, worn, and aged. This would certainly be the end of Casey Stengel in baseball.

"Whatta ya mean, can I still manage?" he bellowed to a group of waiting reporters. "If I wanna take a pitcher out I can hit him over the head with my cast to convince him."

Then, taking a deep breath, he continued, "I didn't fall on my head, so I don't think I'll handicap the club if I manage with one arm. It's not the first time I had a broken bone or two or six in my arms or legs and ya would if ya played the game hard the way ya should. I been up there before with McGraw so I know they'd do somethin' to me because they always wanted to show up the big leaguers, those very smart college army boys and I expected it but not the fallin', which was my own fault 'cause I didn't look."

"How long will you have to wear the cast?" a reporter asked.

"I'm glad you asked me that one because if ya listen, I'll tell ya. The doctors say it don't hurt none if I shake my arm once in a while and wear the cast to bed, but to watch out I don't drop it on Edna so maybe this should be the time she sits up watching me sleep all night like she does when I'm sick cause she cares about me which some of you gentlemen, if you listen to the Yankees some years back, would hardly believe.

By some miracle of constitution or determination he was in the dugout the next day leading his troops. And when he had to take out a pitcher, he would slip his fractured arm out of the sling and walk to the mound. Then he would slip his arm back into the sling as he disappeared into the sanctity of the dugout. At seventy-five, with a broken arm, he was as vain as ever.

The season continued on its merry way, the Mets showing no improvement in their won-loss record, but the manager stressed the development of the younger players, McGraw, Swoboda, and a pitcher from Kansas City named Jim Bethke. The young right-hander had come to the attention of the Mets through a letter sent by a friend of his father to Casey Stengel. The friend knew Stengel

"Spahn and Sain and Casey's in pain." Warren Spahn and Yogi
Berra, his aged coaches in 1965, are all smiles after Stengel returns
to dugout after breaking his wrist in West Point fall.
(Photo courtesy of Louis Requena.)

from Kansas City, recommended young Bethke, and was
in the stands on the third day of the season when Bethke
was credited with the first Mets win of 1965. Bethke was
eighteen years old when he won his first major-league
game. Unfortunately, he was to win only one more game
before drifting out of baseball.

As he approached his seventy-fifth birthday, Stengel
still was driving his team hard. He had lost none of his
enthusiasm, none of his devotion, showed no signs of slowing down, gave no indication that the end was near. He
seemed healthier and more alert than he had been in his
final days with the Yankees. There was color in his face,
a light step in his moves, and warmth in his heart. His
wrist had healed cleanly and his staying power with his
friends and the press continued to amaze all. In the final
week of July, he grew even more animated as Old-Timer's
Day approached, this year a celebration of some of the
great names of the New York Giants and Brooklyn Dodgers.

On Friday night, with some of his old pals, Stengel sat

at the bar in the pressroom at Shea Stadium and entertained until four o'clock in the morning. He let the names of the old guys fall off his tongue with stories about each of them. Some of the names were not household words like Ruth and Frisch and McGraw.

"See," he was saying, "I played with these guys, the Grimes brothers and you could win a lot of bets with them. I would go with them to a bar and clean up. 'How many balls you got?' I would ask guys and they would say, 'Two, ain't you?' and I would say, 'How many you think those two guys, the Grimes brothers got?' and when they all said four, I would bet them and you'd have them because the Grimes brothers had five and which one had the most I wouldn't know, but you could make a lot of money betting it."

His other story that night concerned an old pitching pal in Brooklyn in 1915 named Wheezer Dell.

"He would get on the mound, get into a jam, and all of a sudden you would start hearin' this whoop, whoop, this wheezin' you know, which is why they wuz calling him Wheezer then and now," said Stengel. "This one time Wagner was the hitter and he complained to the umpire he couldn't concentrate on the ball what with Wheezer giving him that whoops, whoops from his wheezin' and damned if the umpire didn't go to the mound and tell him to quit it. Wheezer said he couldn't help it and the umpire asked him not to do it on this one hitter, Wagner, because he was a big star and he didn't want to hold up the game none. Wheezer held his breath and pitched and Wagner hit it off the wall. He commenced wheezin' in the shower after that."

Stengel was chipper the following day as the Mets played the Phillies and the old-timers took their bows on the field. The game was over and now the old-timers adjourned to Toots Shor's restaurant for a celebration. It was one of Casey's favorite rituals.

The weekend schedule included the old-timers game on Saturday, the party at Shor's Saturday night, and a huge celebration for Stengel's seventy-fifth birthday the next day between games of a doubleheader. The Mets would be on the road on Stengel's birthday, July 30, in Philadelphia.

The party at Shor's was splendid. The food was magnificent, the drinks were endless, and the laughs were enormous. Shortly before midnight Casey, weary and slightly inundated with booze, walked into the men's room. He slipped on the wet floor, felt some twisting pain in his side, struggled to his feet, and said nothing about it. He continued to drink with Shor, the bombastic owner of the best sports joint in town, with Frankie Frisch, his old pal and teammate, and with a half-dozen sportswriters. Shor was forced to close by 2 A.M. and Joe DeGregorio, the Mets controller, offered to take Casey to his home in Queens, just a short hop from Shea Stadium, instead of sending him off to the Essex House. Stengel agreed and they drove home with Stengel sleeping most of the way. When they arrived at DeGregorio's home and he opened the door for Casey, the manager took an awkward step out of the car and said, "I musta hit a curved street."

Stengel was restless and couldn't sleep. Shortly before 8 A.M. the pain had grown so severe in his left hip that he moved from the guest bedroom to inform DeGregorio. "Call Doc," he said. Trainer Gus Mauch was summoned from his home near the ball park, took one look at the agony on the old man's face, and called the team physician, Dr. Peter LaMotte, an orthopedic surgeon.

While fans were pouring into Shea Stadium—there would be nearly forty thousand on hand—Stengel was on the operating table at Roosevelt Hospital. Dr. LaMotte placed a metal ball in his hip in an operation that had become commonplace with people of Stengel's age.

Casey Stengel had always been a major medical miracle, withstanding broken bones throughout his career, showing an energy level uncommon with people his age, moving with rapid, athletic movements at a time when most people his age were either "dead at the present time" or moving as if they expected to be shortly. Stengel, by sheer power of his will, refused to give in to age or this crippling injury. Stengel was medically certified as "out of danger" in twenty-four hours and babbling normally in two days. Ten days after the operation, the press was summoned and Stengel was in fine fettle. He bragged about the value of the metal in his leg, would not consider it impossible if he returned to the dugout soon, complimented his chosen-successor Wes Westrum ("Wes is the man," he said, shortly before going under Dr. LaMotte's knife) about how aggressively the team was playing, and continued to amaze all the laws of nature and age.

In late August, still in some pain, home now in the Essex House, walking with the aid of a strange, crooked, shining, black cane, he acceded to Edna's wishes. "I'll tell them I quit," he said. Board chairman M. Donald Grant had been urging him out, using Weiss as his hatchet man, hoping Casey would go gracefully and they could get on with the youth program under a new manager. They weren't thrilled with Westrum, a low-key, sometimes morose personality after the flamboyance of Stengel, but he was available. He also worked cheap, always a prime consideration in Mets circles. Casey finally made the expected announcement at a press conference in the Essex House. It wasn't age or senility or pressure from above or any Associated Press stories that made him do it. It was that damn black cane.

"If I can't run out there and take a pitcher out," he said, "I'm not capable of managing."

Limping, slowed by the accident, and reluctant to be anything but himself, Stengel decided he would not have a surrogate manager. If he couldn't do the job his way, he would leave, full of grace and still a little fulla shit. "I'll take them out by the neck with this here cane," he told the press with a smirk.

It was over.

Fifty-five years in baseball, a lifetime filled with desperate days and joyous nights, ten Yankee pennants for his on-field rewards, and the love and affection of millions of fans for his off-field heroics.

In some few days he would return to Shea Stadium for a small ceremony. He walked on the field carrying his black cane, saw his uniform number thirty-seven retired to a glass case in the Diamond Club at Shea, accepted the

Casey fights back tears as he says goodbye to the fans after
breaking his hip and retiring in 1965. The agony of giving up the
life he loved is written in the man's face.

Mets board chairman M. Donald Grant bids Casey farewell after his
retirement at Shea. *(Photo courtesy of Louis Requena.)*

Casey's Mets uniform number thirty-seven is officially retired. With him are old pal George Weiss ("He never bounced a check on me so why wouldn't you like him?") and successor Wes Westrum. The Yankees retired Casey's thirty-seven in 1970. *(Photo courtesy of Louis Requena.)*

For the last time, Casey leaves his "writers" at Shea after retirement. He quit because he couldn't lift a pitcher from the game with his crooked cane. *(Photo courtesy of Louis Requena.)*

plaudits of the press and the praise of his players. There were no tears. Casey Stengel would go off the field laughing, the way he had come on it.

The Mets had named him a vice-president in charge of West Coast scouting and he would continue on salary, proud to be a Met and quick to offer advice when it was asked.

"He still didn't walk all that well when he returned home," says Jack Lawson, "but you could see he missed it. Edna tried to keep him busy, but nothing was more important to him than reading the papers about the games and watching them on television."

He sat in a dugout box at the World Series in Los Angeles. He wore a brown felt hat, a yellow shirt, and a blue tie.

"Just in case," he said, "anybody wants me on television."

Walter Alston, the Dodger manager, came over to say hello and Casey said, "If I wuz you I'd open with Koufax and pitch him three or four times."

He rested at home through most of the winter. The mail that had be piling up at Shea for him was shipped to Glendale and Edna set out to answer as many as possible. Surprisingly, so much of the mail came from children. One ten-year-old boy named Nicholas DeBonna wrote, "I love you, Casey. Could you send me your autograph? Do you think the Mets will ever win a pennant?" Edna answered the boy's letter, saying, "Casey thinks the Mets will be in the World Series before you are in high school."

In December, feeling stronger, walking daily up and down the street in front of the house, going out to dinner now, and visiting with friends, Stengel received a call from George Weiss.

"How would you like to come to spring training?" he asked.

"Why wouldn't ya?" he said.

So early in March he flew to St. Petersburg with Edna and sat by the pool on sunny days, talked to the writers, entertained the guests at the Colonial Inn, visited the park for a couple of squad games, sat at the hotel bar at night, and showed no signs of ailing health. A reporter asked him kiddingly if he would take a job managing another ball club. He almost snapped his head off. "I work for the Mets and when they pay me they get me," he said.

It was as certain a sign as possible that Casey was back in tiptop form. He would show it several days later on the green grass at Huggins-Stengel Field in St. Petersburg. The Stengels had been summoned there under a ruse with Casey being told George Weiss was being honored and he was being asked to say a few words about his old pal. There were newsmen and photographers and club officials, including Mrs. Payson, local guests, the Commissioner of Baseball, air force general William D. Eckert ("Who he?" asked Willie Mays when his name first surfaced and he would forever after be known as the Unknown Soldier), and former commissioner Ford Frick. Soon Frick was standing at the microphones. "We have had a special election," he began, "and Charles Dillon Stengel was unanimously elected to the Hall of Fame."

Stengel seemed puzzled at first, knowing the green grass at a spring training field was not the usual scene for such significant baseball announcements, but soon recovered. Edna gave him a soft kiss on the cheek, tears filling her eyes, Casey warmly touching her hand, turning now back to the microphones, thanking all concerned, now walking to the stands and thanking the fans who had turned out for the game.

"I think it's a terrific thing to get in while you're still alive," he said.

He had been allowed to smell the roses as it were, and baseball people were to be applauded editorially for such a gracious act. A baseball rule prevented election for anyone until five years after his playing career ended, and when Stengel failed to gain entrance after his Yankee years, his chances seemed slim.

But with the Mets he had emerged as more than just a manager, crossing that threshold into public personality, spokesman for the game, salesman, figure of such size that his every movement, his every convoluted word would be recorded for posterity.

There was one act left in his official baseball career and it would take place at 10 A.M. on July 25, 1966, on the steps of the Baseball Museum and Library at the Hall of Fame in Cooperstown, New York, a sleepy little village in the northern part of the state. It sits quietly for three hundred sixty-four days a year, sliced out of some other time and some other country, until the installation day when the town is overrun by tourists and the banners line main street and the bands play and the baseball pennants fly and the kids press their noses against the glass-enclosed pictures of Ty Cobb and Honus Wagner and put their hands on Babe Ruth's locker and Lou Gehrig's glove and Christy Mathewson's shoes and all America, young and old, rich and poor, black and white, seem linked by the nostalgia of a hundred years and more of the Great American Pastime.

On that July day in 1966, with the sun drenching the small podium, Casey Stengel sat quietly in a wooden chair, his legs crossed, his eyes fixed on the figure of a fellow new Hall of Famer, Ted Williams, the great slugger of the Red Sox. Williams, a handsome, large man, with an open collar, stood above the crowd and relived his brilliant career with much thanks to all who helped him, even giving a gentle nudge to the press for installing him by their votes, despite so many years of bitter wrangling. Then he said, "I hope that some day Satchel Paige and Josh Gibson will be voted into the Hall of Fame as symbols of the great Negro players who are not here only because they weren't given the chance." And soon a march of great black players would follow with Paige and Gibson and Judy Johnson and Cool Papa Bell getting admitted, even though baseball's racial rules kept them from enjoying the true fruits of their athletic skills.

Now it was time for the Unknown Soldier to introduce the best-known manager, and Casey Stengel moved to the rostrum. He was a handsome figure of an old man, his new summer suit fitting tightly, his dotted tie stuck into his shirt and held on with a Mets tie clip, his hair neatly plastered down, his shoes highly polished, his eyes aglow as he looked out at the crowd. The applause was deafening from a crowd of some ten thousand people, most of them standing against rope barriers, some of them sitting on tree limbs, many of them using binoculars to catch this elegant thespian's "changes of face."

"I want to thank everybody," he began, "I want to thank some of the owners who were amazing to me and those big presidents of the leagues who were kind to me when I was so obnoxious."

He tripped and slid through his career verbally, touching all bases, thanking all peoples, applauding all who had helped, showing nothing but warmth and humor and love and ending with, "And I want to thank the tremendous fans. And keep coming to see the Mets play."

And there was more wild applause and cheering and above all, as there had been for fifty-five years on the field and there would be for a lot more to come off the field, there was laughter, deep, rich, full laughter, smiles bending through the scattered faces, joy being spread by this gnarled old man, optimism and hope and good feeling created by his very presence.

Casey and Edna were taken by car after the installation ceremonies to the gigantic lobby of the Otesaga Hotel and a huge buffet luncheon was held in their honor. While Edna ate with her family and friends, Stengel walked and talked, carrying a single bourbon in a glass, never sitting down for one moment, moving from one group of old players and Hall of Famers to another, marching from one group of reporters to another, pausing to talk to fans and strangers, soaking up the warmth of the afternoon.

Soon it was over and he would journey back to New York for a couple of days and then fly home to Glendale. There were baseball dinners ahead and banquets to attend and details at the bank and long, lovely trips planned by Edna and continued efforts for the Mets and help for the press.

And everywhere he went he was stopped and loved and laughed at and pointed out, a national monument, aging gracefully now, unburdened of his passion for excellence, an astute observer of the scene, from home plate to third base, from right field to left field, from ball park to ball park. He would always be called on for comment everywhere he went and would always have the most astute observation. When the new Busch Memorial Stadium was opened at the All-Star game in St. Louis in 1966, with the blazing sun beating down on the new park and the temperatures crossing the one-hundred-degree mark, Stengel's opinion of the park would be forever quoted. "The new park," he said, "does hold the heat very well."

And with the laughter there would always be the autographs, carefully, personally written, never cheating a single person who asked, writing his signature always from that July 25, 1966, day thusly: "Casey Stengel, Hall of Fame, New York Mets."

16. Greatest Living Manager

CASEY STENGEL was an old sailor. He didn't fade away. He attended baseball banquets in every part of the country, flying from west to east and back as easily as he used to take the midnight train from New York to Boston, sitting with Edna in the first, first-class seat on the right, being fussed over by stewardesses, being rushed by fans, being entertained by pilots and co-pilots who took him into the cockpits for private inspections. He was an honored guest almost every time a new baseball park opened, journeyed to Cooperstown each summer for the Hall of Fame installation, traveled to New York each winter for several weeks to attend the Baseball Writers' Dinner and the Long Island Booster club dinner. He read the sports pages in his home or hotel each morning, discussed the doings of the Mets each day with various friends, including Dutch Zwilling and Babe Herman in Glendale, Mets scout Harry Minor in Los Angeles, and Mets officials who called by phone. In the summers he would visit Dodger Stadium each time the Mets were in town and he would attend Old-Timer's Days regularly in New York and in other cities.

All of the crustiness was gone now, all of the bitterness, only his records, his humor, his burning passion for the game of baseball remained. His tongue remained as quick as ever as he approached eighty years of age.

There had been a serious airplane crash just shortly before Stengel flew to New York for an Old-Timer's Day. It was front page as he stepped on the field at Shea, wearing his Mets uniform number thirty-seven and a specially made cap with the emblems of all the teams he had played for and managed in a circle.

"How was the trip, doctor?" he was asked.

"Don't ask me about the trip," he said. "Ask me about my body." Then in obvious reference to the plane crash he said, "I'm alive."

Former players always came over to pay homage to him, their anger faded with time. Jerry Coleman, who always suggested Casey overmanaged, especially when he pinch-hit for Coleman, was amused by one of Stengel's rapid monologues as Coleman approached. He called Coleman "one of my brightest men" and the handsome ex-marine fighter pilot beamed.

"When I came back from Korea," Coleman told a friend, "Casey showed me a letter he had received and saved from a guy fighting near Seoul. The guy had criticized Casey for using Raschi over Reynolds in a big game the Yankees lost. He called Casey a dumb manager. Casey sent the guy a telegram at his base. The telegram read: IF YOU'RE SO SMART HOW COME YOU'RE STILL IN THE ARMY?

The Mets had finished last again after Wes Westrum completed the 1965 season as manager for Casey. Then they moved up to ninth for the first time in 1966 and fell back to tenth again in 1967. Two young pitchers arrived on the scene that year who would have much bearing on the future of the team. One was a left-hander out of a tiny rural town of Morris in northern Minnesota by the name of Jerry Koosman and the other was a husky right-hander from Fresno, California, by the name of Tom Seaver. Seaver had been signed by the Mets after an impressive college season at the University of Southern California. He turned down an offer from the Dodgers, signed with the Braves, saw the contract voided by a college-rule technicality, and joined the Mets. His coach at USC was Rod Dedeaux, one of the most successful college baseball coaches of all time and a close friend of Casey Stengel.

"I was going to Hollywood High and Casey was managing Toledo in 1930 when I first met him. A bunch of us kids used to go out to Griffith Park in Glendale and work out with Casey after the regular season·was over. We would sit at his feet and he would explain baseball to us," says Dedeaux.

Stengel would talk baseball with the boys at Griffith Park from the early afternoon until dark. Then they would go back the next day and apply what they had been told.

"I went to USC from Hollywood High, made it to the Dodgers in 1935 when Casey was the manager there," says Dedeaux. "He was the brightest brain in baseball I have ever known."

Dedeaux broke his back and soon drifted out of the big leagues. He went into college coaching, won eleven national championships at USC, and always stayed close to Casey.

"Casey was a great USC fan and we used to go to all the USC football games together," says Dedeaux.

"I went to the football games with Casey several times," says Ron Fairly, a twenty-year major leaguer and also a graduate of USC. "Mostly we talked baseball while the football game was on. One time I asked him how the Mets used to pitch to Stretch McCovey who always murdered the Dodgers. He said, 'Glad you asked me that. I had this here Mr. [Roger] Craig pitching for us and when we went over the hitters I asked him how he wanted the fielders to play Mr. Mac Cov . . er . . ey, in the upper deck or the lower deck.' "

In 1968 one of Stengel's former players with the original Mets, Gil Hodges, took over as manager of the ball club. Stengel was as pleased as could be and congratulated Hodges by telegram: "YOU WERE ALWAYS SPLENDID IN YOUR WORK AND WILL BE, TOO."

On January 11, 1969, with the Mets planning for their first year under Hodges, and Edna and Casey planning on another spring training with the Mets in the Florida sun, Casey suddenly complained of severe stomach pain. The pain persisted for several days. A flu epidemic was rushing through the country and Edna told a friend, "Casey can't seem to shake the Hong Kong flu." He didn't eat much, stayed away from the bank, had trouble sitting still long enough to read the sports pages. Edna finally decided to call a doctor. Casey was examined and immediately rushed to Glendale Memorial Hospital. He had a perforated ulcer. Eleven days later, some six months short of his seventy-ninth birthday, he returned home. By early March of 1969 he was feeling chipper again, boarded a plane in Los Angeles with Edna, and flew to Florida.

Gil Hodges had suffered a massive heart attack (he was to recover for a time and then suffer another fatal attack on April 2, 1972, while walking off a golf course) and greeted Casey warmly at the ball park.

"Yes sir, Mr. Hodges," said Casey, "and how ya feelin'?"

"You're in better shape than I am," said Hodges.

Casey pursed his lips and said, "Well, maybe I'll have to buy one of them new clubs [the National League had expanded into Montreal and San Diego] and run it, but if I don't, I'll do it again when they expand and I'm ninety-six."

Some of his writers gathered around and Stengel caught them up on his doings over the winter, the business at the bank, the healing ulcer, the problems with the California drought, and the hippies.

"We got these flower children," he said, "and you don't know whether to water them or plant them."

"Casey, I stopped drinking," one of the writers said.

"Great, great," said Casey. "My doctor said I can start again. The only thing is I'm supposed to be on a diet with baby food and milk and all that and when I started my diet Edna lost ten pounds."

Casey and Edna stayed at the Mets spring camp until shortly before the club went north. He said to Hodges, "You have a splendid team, and if you teach them all your tricks at first base [Hodges was famous for the fast moves around the bag], you'll win the pennant."

Baseball was celebrating its centennial in 1969. The All-Star game was scheduled for Washington, D.C., and President Richard Nixon had agreed to meet with the players, the officials, and the press at a White House ceremony. There was also to be an All-Star team of all-time present. To mark the hundredth anniversary of professional base-

Two Californians talk baseball at 1969 All-Star game in Washington. Casey was named greatest living manager at banquet. President Nixon had some hard years ahead of him.

ball, two special All-Star teams were being selected in a nationwide poll of fans, press, and baseball officials. A huge dinner for the elected players and managers would be held, the ceremony at the White House would follow the next day, and the game would be played the following evening. As many of the living candidates as could be assembled made it to Washington.

New baseball commissioner Bowie Kuhn introduced the honored guests, including astronaut Frank Borman, producer David Merrick, comedian Alan King, and Archbishop Terence Cooke of New York. Each would name several All-Stars.

To guarantee some semblance of response, the teams were divided into "Greatest Living Players" and "Greatest Players Ever" with one manager to be chosen for each team.

The drama built through the evening. Finally, one by one the announcements came, first the living players and then the greatest ever, with acceptances by relatives, friends, or associates. Ted Williams was named to the team as "Greatest Living Left Fielder" and even as the manager of the local club in Washington, he was not on hand. Williams had sent his lovely wife, dressed in a sequined black low-cut gown to accept his award and when she said, "He didn't come because he was afraid he wouldn't win," nobody seemed to care. The "Greatest Players Ever" were Lou Gehrig, Rogers Hornsby, Pie Traynor, Honus Wagner, Ty Cobb, Joe DiMaggio, Babe Ruth, Mickey Cochrane, Walter Johnson, and Lefty Grove, with Ruth as the best of the best. The manager of that team was Casey's manager in New York, John McGraw. Casey led the applause and beamed as his old chief's name was called. Then came the "Greatest Living Players": George Sisler and Stan Musial tied at first base, Charlie Gehringer at second, Pie Traynor at third, Joe Cronin at shortstop, Williams in left, Joe DiMaggio in center, Willie Mays in right, Bill Dickey catching, Bob Feller and Lefty Grove pitching, and Joe DiMaggio as the greatest.

When the announcement for the greatest living manager was due, astronaut Borman, who was to name the winner, picked up the sealed envelope, read it, and broke into a huge grin. The audience began laughing, looking over toward Casey in a front-row seat, and waiting for the expected happy words, "The Greatest Living Manager," said Borman slowly, "Casey Stengel."

The room was drenched in television lights. A spotlight picked up the form of Casey Stengel, rising rapidly from his chair, hopping and jumping forward to the stage, his mouth moving, his eyes darting across the room, his hands pointing in every which direction, his smile tightly held, his pixie face aglow with joy. "Is this thing on," he bellowed into a microphone, "so you can hear me in this room and on the moon?"

Each speaker had been on and off with his award in sixty seconds, and there were fears Stengel might not be able to get off and allow the program to continue.

"Watch," said Bob Fishel. "He has this inner clock. He'll be in the middle of a sentence and he'll stop."

Stengel applauded Kuhn for the idea of the event, complimented all the voters, made some references to the previous winners, congratulated all other nominees, and finally said, "I wanna thank all my ballplayers for making me one of us." Then he sat down. He had spoken fifty-nine seconds.

The next afternoon all hands were in attendance at the White House. President Nixon came into the Blue Room, addressed the group, and said, "If I had to do it all over again I would have been a sportswriter."

Broadcaster Joe Garagiola, baseball's George Jessel, said, "I won't sleep any better tonight knowing Nixon wants to be a sportswriter."

Each of the guests was ushered through a receiving line for a chat with the President. When it was Stengel's turn the President stood with a fixed smile as Stengel said, "Now I could make you one of my writers, but I don't have a team which isn't so bad since they are doing good."

They were doing good, all right. The Amazin' Mets of Gil Hodges had actually jumped into a serious pennant race with the Cubs of Leo Durocher, an old combatant of Stengel's.

"The Babe thought Leo stole his watch," Stengel said of one of the old Durocher legends, "and it wasn't the worst thing he done."

In early September of 1969 the Mets climbed into first place. Gil Hodges had his team playing amazing baseball. They swept past Durocher's Cubs, beat the Atlanta Braves and Hank Aaron in the first divisional play-off, and won the World Series over Baltimore. When the last out was recorded on a fly ball to a kneeling Cleon Jones in left field, Casey Stengel leaped from his seat and let out a loud whoop. He then squeezed through the crowd, walked rapidly to the Mets clubhouse (he was waddling after the hip surgery and not really walking), and pushed into Hodges' office. There, in one of the most touching scenes of the night, the grizzled old manager, just short of his eightieth birthday, leaned his face on his ex-first baseman's chest. Hodges put his huge arms around the old man and they hugged warmly for a long while. Photographers snapped pictures and tears ran down the cheeks of several hard-boiled sportswriters, Casey's "writers," who had never seen this show of affection from either man before.

In some few weeks the Mets would deliver handsome gold World Series rings to all their players, club officials, and several members of the press. A ring would be mailed to Glendale, California, for the Mets West Coast vice-president. He would wear it in pride on his left hand for the rest of his life.

In the spring of 1970 Casey and Edna returned to Florida again. It was Casey's sixtieth year in baseball.

"Why wouldn' ya like the game if you can make a livin' at it," he told waiting reporters at the hotel.

He was now less than five months short of eighty and he showed no signs of slowing down. His step was quick, albeit a little lopsided, but he had always walked sort of odd ever since the cab got him in Boston. His eyes were clear, his voice was full and rich as always, he seemed, to all who saw him, an indestructible human being. He chased around the country from ball park to ball park, from banquet to banquet, like some traveling after-dinner vaudeville act, coming up always with something fresh and new for each dinner, each town, each group he visited. The highlights of the summer always seemed to be the return to Shea for the Old-Timer's Days and the trips to Cooperstown where he could mingle with some of his oldest pals, Rube Marquard, Burleigh Grimes, Al Lopez, Waite Hoyt.

"I was up there one year," says Hoyt, "and I came out of my room in the hotel and Casey is sitting in the lobby. There are about three or four young kids, teen-agers maybe, and I hear names like Ruth and Cobb and Wagner falling off his lips. I waved to him and he waved to me out of the corner of his eye. I went into breakfast and came back and he was still there, except now the group of kids had grown to about twenty. I left the hotel, went into town, went for a long walk, visited with some friends, and came back about two o'clock. Now there were about a hundred kids around Casey, all sitting on the floor Indian fashion, in this huge circle and he's saying, 'Now the Babe

After retirement, he lounges on the beach in St. Petersburg while Edna enjoys the sun. Like any old ball player, he was always ready for a catch.

could hit a ball over a building,' and I just shook my head.
What an amazing man. What a human being. What a
salesman for baseball."

It was August of 1970. The hot summer sun beat down
on the huge crowd at Yankee Stadium. The Yankees, who
had invented Old-Timer's Days, were bringing back some
of their greatest stars, Joe DiMaggio, the recently retired
Mickey Mantle, Whitey Ford, Yogi Berra, so many of the
players who had contributed to the five straight World
Series triumphs under Casey Stengel. For some years
Casey had refused to attend these events at Yankee Stadium, still carrying a memory of an unpleasant ending to
a pleasant career. The men who had hurt him, Dan Topping, and Del Webb, were no longer with the Yankees
and the Columbia Broadcasting System ownership under
Michael Burke wanted Stengel for this special event.
They asked the Mets to ask him to come, and he finally
agreed. He walked on the field to huge applause and
Burke stepped forward to a microphone and said, "We
honor you today for your contributions to the greatness
and the legends of the Yankees." He carried a Yankee
uniform number thirty-seven on his arms, presented it to
Stengel, and said it would be retired forever more with no
Yankee ever allowed to wear the number again. It would
be officially retired with the uniform numbers three of
Babe Ruth, four of Lou Gehrig, five of Joe DiMaggio,
seven of Mickey Mantle, eight of both Yogi Berra and Bill
Dickey.

"Now that I finally got one," said Stengel, as he fondled
the pinstripes of the Yankees, "I'll probably die in it."

"We had invited him every year," says Marty Appel,
former Yankee public relations director now working in
the baseball commissioner's office. "He would get our invitation and scratch, 'Can't come,' in large letters and
send back the invitation. Then we sent out the 1970 invitation and for some reason, still unknown, he sent back the
invitation, 'I'm tickled to attend. Casey.' He came and was
received warmly and had a marvelous time. We gave out
trays and inscribed glassware to all the old-timers."

The next morning the phone rang shortly after 9 A.M.

The greatest player Stengel ever managed, Joe DiMaggio, in warm reunion at Shea in 1970. Casey once said, "DiMaggio could hit a ball off the moon." *(Photo courtesy of Louis Requena.)*

in Appel's office. Without any identification, without a deep breath, a gravelly voice bellowed, "It was splendid, splendid, so glad you asked me. Thank you, three thousand thank yous, Mantle looked like he could still hit a ball over a building and Yogi was handsome and Whitey don't sweat [Ford had an operation that hampered his sweat glands] and why wouldn't ya play run, sheep, run, if you had Kubek and Richardson who could and did." There was another five minutes of nonstop monologue on the Yankees of Stengel's time and the Giants of McGraw and Frankie Frisch and Christy Mathewson and George Kelly and so many other names in a stream of conciousness. Then Stengel paused finally and said, "And thank you for the prize."

"It sounded," says Appel, "like a man who had just opened up a Cracker Jack box."

It was a marvelous homecoming, but, even though he had his Yankee uniform and had returned happily to the stadium, he was still a Met in his heart. He showed no signs of dying and made appearances for the Mets through 1971 and 1972. He followed the same pattern. He attended the Baseball Writers' Dinner in January, talked at some Met promotional affairs, journeyed to spring training, went back to California in April, came east again in July for Old-Timer's Day, traveling to the play-offs and World Series games in West Coast series, closing up the bar in most hotel pressrooms at two or three or four in the morning, opening the coffee shops at seven with a newspaper and a cup of black coffee. Slowly, subtly, his monologues drew smaller audiences, the old friends disappearing from the scene, the younger baseball officials and sportswriters less interested in McGraw and Ruth and DiMaggio and Mantle and more interested in Jackson and Bench and Seaver. Casey talked of them, too, always relevant, always on the hot man in the game, but somehow less believable to most people. He turned more and more inward, spending less and less time with casual acquaintances and more with his trusted friends, people like Rod Dedeaux, Charlie Deal, an old ballplaying friend, Harry Minor, and Dutch Zwilling.

Zwilling, two years older than Stengel, was still actively scouting ballplayers in his eighty-second year. He was driving a car and would often take Casey with him. Stengel's license had been revoked by the Glendale police ("Them brilliant blue-suiters," he called them) and he depended on Zwilling for transportation.

"I would stay up all night waiting for them to get back from a scouting trip," says Fern Zwilling. "Dutch wasn't a good driver by then and I had to let him go anyway. When I heard the key in the door I would shut the bedroom light real quickly and make out like I was sleeping all the time."

One day Stengel was talking with Dutch Zwilling's son.

"Where's Dutch?" Casey asked Robert Zwilling.

"He's at home."

"What's he doing there?"

"Reading his Bible."

"Whatinhell is he doing that for?" asked Stengel.

"Because he thinks he might find a shred of truth in it," said Zwilling.

Three great New York centerfielders, Joe DiMaggio of the Yankees, Willie Mays of the Giants, and Casey Stengel of the Brooklyn Dodgers at Shea reunion in 1971. *(Photo courtesy of Louis Requena.)*

Five old New York Giants at Shea reunion, Casey, Leo Durocher,
Bobby Thomson, Ed Stanky, Wes Westrum.
(Photo courtesy of Louis Requena.)

All Hail Casey at Shea in 1971 reunion as Stengel enters field in chariot. "He was born old," but didn't know Caesar.
(Photo courtesy of Louis Requena.)

Said Casey, in his best gravelly-voiced stage whisper, "I was afraid of that."

Some afternoons he sat in the sun next to his pool with old pal Babe Herman. The talk would ramble and Herman remembers Stengel going on for many minutes without a name ever being mentioned. "He always knew who he meant," says Herman. "Even when he was off baseball you knew who he meant. We had one famous person come from Glendale. Casey called him 'the druggist's boy.' It was John Wayne. His name used to be Morrison and they owned a drugstore in town."

In 1973 Casey and Edna came to New York at the start of the season. They visited with friends before returning to California. Casey returned for the Old-Timer's Day again and in October, when the Mets had won their second pennant, he threw out the first ball at the Shea Stadium opener.

There was still much spring in Casey's step, but Edna suddenly seemed older. She would have lapses of memory and stumble over some words. Late that year she was hit with a stroke and was soon under constant nursing care.

Casey continued to carry on as normally as possible. He cut down on the banquets and dinners and appeared only at some special events. He attended the Old-Timer's Day in Shea, hopped out of an antique car wearing his Mets uniform and many emblemed cap, waved to the crowd, danced to the receiving line, and drew loud applause and much laughter.

On the bench they were telling stories about him and Met coach Joe Pignatano said, "I was in the bullpen at the Polo Grounds in 1962. Casey had this thing with names. He called down and said, 'Get Nelson ready.' We didn't have a Nelson. I said 'Who?' He says, 'Nelson, for criss-akes.' I stand up and yelled to the guys on the bullpen bench, 'If there's a Nelson in here, Casey wants you to get ready.' Then Bob Miller got up, started peeling his jacket off, and says, 'I'm Nelson.' "

Casey also had trouble with Pignatano's name. When Pignatano joined the club in 1962 he sat on the bench with Casey for an hour discussing the opposition hitters. A

The Original Mets at
Shea reunion, front row,
Jay Hook, skipper
Stengel, Al Jackson, back
row, Wes Westrum,
Frank Thomas, and Carl
Willey.

Stengel spruces up
before final on-field
appearance at Shea in
1974 reunion. A
chipper-looking
eighty-four-year-old man
before cancer began to
attack him.
*(Photo courtesy of
Louis Requena.)*

sportswriter came over and asked, "Who's catching today?" Said Casey, "That Pignatelli fella, if he ever gets here."

In July of 1974, with Edna weakening and now living in the Glen Oaks Convalescent home in Glendale, Casey flew to Dallas to honor his two former pals, Mickey Mantle and Billy Martin. On May 18, 1974, Dan Topping had died and on July 4, 1974, Del Webb passed away. When he arrived in Dallas a sportswriter asked him about the death of the two Yankee owners.

"They set up an annuity for me worth $160,000 and it ain't hay if you can find the money," said Stengel. "And it's a shame I waited until they passed away until I mentioned it."

Then he was asked about Edna and said, "I've gotta tell you one thing, I ain't goin' dancin' with her when she ain't dancin'."

The Oakland A's played the Los Angeles Dodgers in the 1974 World Series; Casey attended every game.

He would sit with Mets officials, watch the game carefully, talk continuously, sign autographs, talk with players who came by near his box seat. At night he stood at the bar at the pressroom and soon people would smile and filter away, excusing themselves with some gesture or simply walking away as he talked. A few faithful old sportswriters or old baseball friends hung onto his every word. He was nearly eighty-five years old now and almost overnight the wear and tear of time, the long nights and long games, the train trips and the bus rides and the jet trips, began weighing heavily on him. His mind was still crisp, but his energies were faltering.

On the final night of the Series he sat alone in the pressroom at a long table. The bar was crowded and baseball talk filled the huge room. People walked aimlessly around the room looking for a friend to talk to, someone to go over the game with, somebody to share a drink or a laugh with. There were so many young men in the room and so many of them slid by this lonely old man as he sat with a half-touched bourbon and soda.

Then one of his New York writers showed up, spotted

him alone across the room, and walked over. "Doctor, how are you?" he said. "Splendid, splendid, but I can't get my body goin'."

The lines in his face were crevices now, the flesh hanging wearily from his neck, his floppy ears sagging, his eyes a pale blue, his hands bony and rough, like a piece of sandpaper had been rubbed on them until they bled, his skin dry and parched from too many days in the sun, color almost gone from his cheeks, a terrible look of doom about him.

The writer and the old man talked for an hour, the words coming slowly for both, the crush of the years on the man suddenly wearing him down, weakening him, slowing his step and chopping away at his flesh. It was barely past midnight when we walked to his room. He opened the door with a shaky hand and said, "See ya."

Then I took the elevator up to my room, called my wife on the phone back in New York, and burst into tears.

17. There Comes a Time in Every Man's Life and I've Had Plenty of Them

IN THE CHILL of an Oakland night, Casey Stengel had picked up a bad cold. He sat alone in the Oakland airport after the last game of the 1974 World Series. He dozed on a bench. People walked by him and pointed at him.

"I got there with some American League officials," says Bob Fishel, "and I was amazed that he could be alone late at night at an airport at his age. I thought somebody should have been with him."

Fishel helped Casey find his plane. He boarded the flight to Los Angeles, got a cab at the airport, and dragged himself inside the empty house in Glendale.

"I was worried about him," says Fishel. "A couple of weeks later I had occasion to be in Los Angeles. I called him from the airport. First, he didn't know who I was. I kept saying, 'Fishel, from the Yankees, Bob Fishel,' and he didn't seem to know. Then something clicked and he said, 'For crissakes, why didn't you say so,' and he was off and running, rambling on about the Yankees and naming so many of the players. While he talked my time ran out on the phone and before I could find another coin I was cut off. I rushed over to a newsstand, changed a dollar bill, and dialed his number back. He picked up the phone and was still in the same conversation . . . 'Why wouldn't you use Woodling if you had Bauer. . . .' He never had stopped. He never answered the phone with a hello."

Harry Minor, the Mets scout on the coast, told club officials Casey wasn't well. The information was passed on to the press casually and a couple of days later I called him at home from New York. The phone rang five times and when it was picked up a raspy voice shouted, "I ain't dead, I just lost my voice."

Then I identified myself, and he asked about the weather and the writers back east, said he was feeling better, and apologized for not being able to make it to spring training for the first time since 1910.

While the Mets opened their 1975 spring training camp in St. Petersburg, Casey sat alone in the big house in Glendale. The Lawsons dropped by to check on him and Babe Herman came over once in a while and Rod Dedeaux looked in on him and Harry Minor called, but mostly, he was alone. Edna had always taken care of everything in the house, the routine functions of buying food and preparing it, of having the house cleaned and the bills paid and the grass cut and the mail pulled from the mailbox. Soon he began eating only canned foods, sometimes without even heating it, sleeping every night in the same unmade bed, letting mail and bills accumulate in the mailbox, taking the phone off the hook, leaving the radio and television on through the night, falling asleep with his clothes on in a living room chair. The Lawsons realized he needed help and urged him to bring someone in. He wouldn't hear of it. "Goddammit, I can take care of myself," he said.

"Casey was not an easy man to move," says young John Lawson, Edna's nephew. "He couldn't be told to do anything. You had to make him think it was his idea."

A couple of years earlier he had met a middle-aged divorcée at a Hall of Fame gathering at Cooperstown. Her name was June Bowlin, she lived in Ohio, she had three grown daughters and a fourteen-year-old son named Greg. Mrs. Bowlin was friendly with the daughter of Hall of Famer Jesse (Pop) Haines and had become a driver, companion, and friend for Pop. She was introduced to Casey and soon he was calling her on the phone in Ohio to do favors for him.

"He called me his foreign secretary," says Mrs. Bowlin. "He wasn't too skilled on the time difference between Ohio and California and I got a lot of calls from him at two and three o'clock in the morning."

The marvelous, warm, comfortable home of Edna and Casey and their memories at 1663 Grandview Avenue in Glendale, California. It was built in 1924, was their home for the rest of their lives, and was sold in 1978.

In early April, with the house falling apart, his clothes unclean, empty cans sitting on the kitchen table, and cash being squashed into every cubbyhole, urged on by the Lawsons, Casey called Mrs. Bowlin.

"Could you come out here and help me clean up?" he asked.

Haines had family to look after him. Casey was alone. So Mrs. Bowlin gave up her Ohio home, packed her belongings, put her son in her car, and drove to California. "He was too great a man to turn down," she says.

Mrs. Bowlin, a tremendous baseball fan, set about to organize Casey and organize the house.

"Things were a mess when I got there," says Mrs. Bowlin. "It took me several days to get that house together again."

She cleaned the house and repaired the damage. She paid the bills. She took in the mail. She organized his life. She gave him incentive and hope.

"His eyes were going bad and he didn't have the energy to read the paper anymore," she says. "I would bring a bowl of strawberries up to his bedroom each morning and read the paper to him. Then I would urge him to get dressed and come on down. There would be only one thing on his mind. 'When are we going to see Edna?' That was how he planned his day, around the visit to Edna."

After the police had taken away his driver's license, Casey had been forced to walk everywhere he wanted to go. The only place he wanted to go was to the Glen Oaks Convalescent home some twenty blocks away, mostly uphill. He would walk it most every day, sit with Edna, hold her hand, ask the nurses if she was improving (she was not), and leave.

"When I arrived we could drive in Casey's old car," says Mrs. Bowlin. "It was all banged up from his accidents, but it still ran."

The days passed slowly. Casey was in some pain now, weak, tired most of the time, pushing himself to get into the car and visit Edna each day.

"One morning he came down for breakfast and he was eating his strawberries. He suddenly looked up at me and said, 'When I'm gone, don't forget to hold her hand.' "

The nights were long and lonely. His beloved Edna could no longer recognize him. The world of baseball seemed no longer to need him or care about him. Except for some close friends, no one called. He stayed in his room most of the time, listening to the radio, watching the games on television.

"The radio became very important to him. He had trouble sleeping and he would keep the radio on all night. He loved the talk shows. Once in a while we would be downstairs, Greg and I, and we would hear him bellowing upstairs," Mrs. Bowlin says.

It was the hidden voice on a radio that was feeling the full fury of the incorrigible arguer, a loud "Yer fulla shit and I'll tell you why" being blasted into the speaker.

He would spend less and less time outside the house now, ducking most phone calls, trying to escape the embarrassment of his declining health, an insidious cancer of the lymph glands eating away at his body, his inability to ask for medical help so typical of the man. The pain became more severe each day. He would walk in the back of the house to escape it. Sometimes he would come downstairs from his bedroom, walking slowly, bent and tired, wearing an old, threadbare, woolen New York Giants sweater, with the huge NY on the side, moving past June without a word, stepping out into the garden, walking to the tennis court, moving slowly on the concrete, and June could hear the raspy voice saying, "Yes sir, Mr. McGraw, that's just the way I was gonna do it."

June suggested gently that he visit a doctor as the pain increased. He refused. He simply said, "I ain't gonna be cut again."

On July 20, Billy Martin was fired as manager of the Texas Rangers.

"I got the paper and read the story," says June. "As I read it tears filled up his eyes. He loved that boy so."

On July 30, 1975, June made a birthday cake for Casey, had the Lawsons and the Hermans over, spent a pleasant evening, and opened up more than two hundred birthday cards that arrived in the mail.

"He was always in pain," says Mrs. Bowlin, "but when there was some special event, some baseball happening, it seemed to be lessened."

On August 1, Billy Martin replaced Bill Virdon as manager of the New York Yankees. Martin was back home. Stengel was a happy man. On August 5, Yogi Berra was fired as the manager of the Mets. When June read that news to Casey he said, "Don't worry none about Yogi. They ain't throwin' no benefits for him."

The pain persisted. It became evident that Casey would need medical help to relieve it. He finally agreed to an examination. "I ain't lettin' them cut me." The examination revealed the cancer and surgery was scheduled. Casey insisted it had to be postponed. He had an important date.

The Dodgers were playing their old-timers game at Dodger Stadium. One of the honored guests was Casey Stengel. Mrs. Bowlin asked if he wanted to go, thinking he might agree to an apologetic telegram to the Dodgers in place of the difficult trip to Chavez Ravine.

"For crissakes," he said, "why wouldn't I wanna go? It's baseball, ain't it?"

She gave him a bath and shampooed his hair and blew it dry and put lotion on his craggy face. His suit was neatly pressed and she looked at the baseball uniform he had hung in his closet and the cap with all the emblems.

"Maybe we don't have to put the uniform on," she said. "Maybe the cap will be enough."

"I want the uniform," he insisted.

He finished washing and drying and dressed for the game. He looked neat.

"You look just like Spencer Tracy," Mrs. Bowlin said.

"By God," said Casey, "I do."

They drove to Dodger Stadium, where he laboriously changed into his uniform, stood for applause, walked off the field with a wave, and sat down exhausted in the clubhouse. The clubhouse man, Nobe Kawano, and Greg Bowlin helped him dress. Mrs. Bowlin waited outside and she was shocked when she saw how tired he looked. They drove home in silence, Casey falling asleep almost as soon as the car turned on Sunset Boulevard.

On Monday, September 15, he went into Glendale Memorial Hospital. Surgery was scheduled for the following Wednesday.

"He was crying as we drove to the hospital," says Mrs. Bowlin. "Greg and I were helping him out of the car and he said, 'You don't have to hold me up, what am I, a goddamn cripple?' Then he looked at Greg and tears filled his eyes. 'I wish Mrs. Stengel and I had a dozen kids, and we'd put them all in the pension plan.' "

The surgery was performed. The cancer was inoperable, large metastasized masses found throughout his body.

"Six months at the outside," said Dr. Don Heckle. "At his age maybe a lot less."

He woke up after the surgery and asked June Bowlin, "What hotel am I in?"

"No hotel, Case," she said. "This is Glendale Memorial Hospital. They're gonna fix you up here, make you well, take away the pain."

"I gotta go to the bathroom."

"I'll help."

"I don't need no help. If you get out of the way I'll go myself."

He got up and walked slowly to the bathroom. June left the room. She turned to her son who waited outside and said, "He's in full voice."

Each day he grew weaker. On the night of September 28, 1975, the television set was tuned to the Dodger game. The recording of the National Anthem was being played. Suddenly, Casey Stengel, wretched with pain, swung his legs over the edge of the bed, pushed his body to the floor, and stood up. He placed his right hand over his heart and looked at the set.

"I might as well do this for the last time," he said.

At 10:30 on the following night, September 29, 1975, June Bowlin, tired and drawn from these long days and nights with Casey in the hospital, left his room. Edna's niece, Lynn, said she would stay with Uncle Casey until he fell asleep. She sat on the edge of his bed saying a rosary. There was a gasp, his eyes blinked or winked, his mouth moved in a final attempt to say something, and at 10:58 Casey Stengel was gone.

The news was phoned to Rod Dedeaux. He called Joe McDonald, the general manager of the Mets in New York who notified the publicity director, Harold Weissman. He informed the press, and soon the wire services, all of the New York newspapers, and most of the out-of-town papers were setting prepared obituaries on Casey Stengel.

The call came to my house from Weissman shortly after 2 o'clock in the morning. Weissman had called earlier in the evening with the first word that Casey was slipping. It was not a surprise. Casey Stengel was dead at the present time and I moved to my typewriter.

"He is gone and I am supposed to cry, but I laugh.

"Every time I saw the man, every time I heard his voice, every time his name was mentioned, the creases of my mouth would give way and a smile would come to my face.

"On this day I mark the passing of Casey Stengel as I have measured every other day of my life I came into contact with him. I smile.

" 'Now wait a minute for crissakes,' he would bellow and his floppy ears would wiggle, his face of a thousand lines would ebb and flow, his bent legs would twist and his strong finger would dig sharply into his upper chest cavity.

"Casey Stengel was not a man. He was a presence. He was a force of energy, a happening, a steamroller of excitement and vigor.

"He loved life. He loved it with a passion that consumed him. He loved laughter. He loved people. Above all, in his deepest recesses, he loved the game of baseball."

The *New York Post* ran the column on its front page with a picture of Casey Stengel wearing a tuxedo. He had purchased a new tuxedo when he was seventy-five, not to be buried in, but to be praised in.

The tributes poured out from writers across the country, each with his favorite Casey Stengel story, each identifying with this grand old man of the game, each repeating his favorite Stengelism. Perhaps, columnist Jim Murray of the *Los Angeles Times* said it best when he wrote, "Well, God is certainly getting an earful tonight."

At the Stengel home, the Lawson family members went through the house, discovering dollar bills squashed into suitcases and drawers, found ticket stubs and old letters, came up with hotel bills from trips to Japan, and saw scribbled autographs on old letters that had never been mailed out. June Bowlin went into his closet and pulled out a new striped blue suit. She also took out his neatly folded Mets uniform and a neatly folded Yankee uniform. They would be buried with him.

It is a soft summer afternoon in 1978. The rains had finally come heavily and the grass was thick and lush and green along the gentle, slopping hills of Glendale, California. It was a Saturday and the roads were not choked with traffic and the air was free of the remnants of a heavy day on the freeways. Soon the road edged toward the left and

Stengel dining room with silver cups and trophies and photo of the old professor at the height of his Yankee managerial fame.

Sitting room where the bats and the balls and the plaques of sixty years in the game were collected.

the huge sign appeared, "Forest Lawn Memorial Park."

"See that duck pond," June Bowlin told this writer, "I took Casey up here once. We drove around and parked along the pond. The ducks wobbled over toward the car and Casey looked at them and began quacking at them, 'Quack, quack, quack,' and they all stopped and looked up at him."

We soon drove past the duck pond, winding and turning to the heights of the park, passing through an area with a road sign reading, "Court of Freedom" and stopping under the trees at the peak of the cemetery grounds. Below lay Glendale and Hollywood and Burbank and dozens of other small Los Angeles bedroom communities.

There was a wall of Vermont marble. It shaded the plot where Casey Stengel and Edna Stengel (she had died on February 3, 1978) lay in a single grave. There was a huge plaque on the wall with crossed bats (one of them a Yogi Berra model and why not?) and the face of Casey Stengel in bronze, a strong likeness, the eyes turned outward, the lips pursed with a half smile, a baseball cap at a rakish angle, and twenty-five words, written beautifully by June Bowlin, capturing much of the man and his times.

FOR OVER SIXTY YEARS ONE OF AMERICA'S FOLK HEROES WHO CONTRIBUTED IMMENSELY TO THE LORE AND THE LANGUAGE OF OUR COUNTRY'S NATIONAL PASTIME, BASEBALL.

The simple facts of this complex life were spelled out in bronze beneath his likeness.

SON OF LOUIS E. AND JENNIE STENGEL
BORN KANSAS CITY, MISSOURI JULY 30, 1890
MARRIED EDNA LAWSON AUGUST 18, 1924
INDUCTED NATIONAL BASEBALL HALL OF FAME JULY 25, 1966
DIED GLENDALE, CALIFORNIA SEPTEMBER 29, 1975

He was a wordsmith, this Charles Dillon "Casey" Stengel and no one could write his epitaph better than he alone could. So when it came time to sum up his existence in a few short words, of all the uncounted torrents of verbiage that had spilled from his lips, this had been chosen by June Bowlin and the Lawson family and inscribed at the base of his plaque:

"THERE COMES A TIME IN EVERY MAN'S LIFE AND I'VE HAD PLENTY OF THEM."

CASEY STENGEL

18. Alive at the Present Time

ON MONDAY, October 6, 1975, an off day in baseball, Casey Stengel's funeral was held at the Church of the Recessional in Forest Lawn. The day dawned bright and clear and soon turned cloudy, with a threat of rain hanging heavy overhead.

Among the early arrivals at the church was Billy Martin. He had flown out from New York, arrived at the Stengel home the night before after some heavy drinking, told June Bowlin he was staying for the night, and went to sleep in Casey's bed under the red covers. He was still in a deeply emotional state as he pulled into the parking lot of the cemetery.

"I got there early," says Rod Kanehl, the only former Mets player to show up, "and I was disappointed there weren't more baseball people there. My God, this was Casey Stengel they were saying good-bye to."

Neither Mickey Mantle nor Yogi Berra attended the funeral. The Yankee players included Charlie Silvera, Irv Noren, Tom Morgan, and Jerry Coleman with Babe Herman, Dutch Zwilling, Fred Haney, and Buzzie Bavasi, the former Brooklyn Dodger general manager when Casey's Yankees were beating them regularly, representing the past associates.

General manager Joe McDonald represented the Mets and other baseball people included Maury Wills, Emmett Ashford, Monte Irvin, old teammate George Kelly, Red Patterson, Tommy Lasorda, Jocko Conlan, and, of course, Rod Dedeaux.

Commissioner Bowie Kuhn, a tall, distinguished figure,

was called on to deliver a eulogy and said, "No one has a greater debt to Casey Stengel than baseball. When you think of all the things he could have been, and had been outstanding at, to have him one hundred percent in baseball was a wonderful thing for us. He helped us not to take ourselves too seriously. He made more fans for baseball than any man who ever lived."

Rod Dedeaux said, "He was kind, loving, and a wonderful friend."

There were more than two hundred people there, not nearly enough, and when it was over the casket was carried past an honor troop of Boy Scouts and Little Leaguers, all dressed in uniforms, seeing the old manager off.

The clouds had darkened and it began to rain shortly after Dr. Kenneth A. Carlson of the First United Methodist Church of Glendale closed the services. People stood in the alcove of the church and soon the baseball people and the friends and the family were telling stories, remembering happier days, laughing at the broken syntax of the Old Professor.

"It was gray and gloomy and the rain was falling as we stood there," says Rod Kanehl, "and all of a sudden it stopped and from above the hill I could see this gorgeous rainbow forming, the sky brightening, and everybody started smiling."

The baseball people adjourned to Stengel's home with the Lawson family and June Bowlin opening the doors wide. The scene was warm and joyous now, the memories only rich and present, the eating and drinking and talking all part of the ritual. Billy Martin, looking as if he might collapse at any moment, was almost inconsolable.

A month later, on November 4, 1975, Casey Stengel was eulogized again at an Ecumenical Service at St. Patrick's Cathedral in New York. Robert Merrill of the Metropolitan Opera sang the Lord's Prayer, Bowie Kuhn read from the Book of Wisdom, and Yogi Berra attended with his wife, Carmen. Mets chairman of the board M. Donald Grant delivered the eulogy. It was warm, touching, and uncharacteristic of the man. Stengel, even in death, seemed to bring out the best in people.

"For me to try to eulogize Casey would be redundant after all that has been written about him," Grant began. "He spent his last few years in baseball in the fold of the Mets and he did so much for them. This city adopted him.

"Casey was a good man who knew where he wanted to go and, in spite of the different way that he said it, he knew exactly what he was saying."

Then Grant told a story about Casey Stengel.

"I remember in our first years I would make a point to wait until after the game to drive Casey to his hotel for the wisdom of his words.

"When we would get into the car, I would ask him, 'How about that young man at first base?' And Casey would say, 'Let me tell you about him.' As we passed the LaGuardia airport and he would mention something I would ask him, 'Are you talking about the first baseman?' and he would say, 'No, the second baseman.'

"At the Triborough Bridge I would ask him, 'Are you talking about the first baseman?' and he'd say, 'No, the shortstop.'

"At about Ninety-sixth Street I'd ask him if he was talking about the first baseman yet and Casey would say, 'No, the third baseman.' At about the time we got to the hotel and he was leaving my car he would just be at the end of the sentence and I would ask him, 'Are you talking about the first baseman?' And he'd answer, 'Yes, that's what you asked me about, isn't it?'

"People asked me when they heard the service was going to be here, if Casey was a Catholic. I would say no, Casey came close to any religion you wanted.

"He was a good man and he was a religious man. Casey is up there now managing a good team."

Grant then paused, looked at the ceiling of the magnificent church, and said, "Casey, pray for us, we miss you."

"You know," Al Lopez said, after his death, "people really had to know Casey to really understand him. He had a sharp tongue, all right, but he never deliberately hurt anybody. This is not something you can say about a lot of people."

"I remember this one time he had a shouting match with Andy Carey on the bench," said Jerry Coleman. "He pulled Carey from the game, they started yelling and Carey said, 'Fuck you, Casey' and Casey turned to him and said, 'And fuck you, too, Carey' and then they both sat down. The next day Casey played Carey like nothing happened.

Edna and Casey had once traveled to Rome and while Edna went to the Vatican to pray and to look at the Sistine Chapel, Casey stayed back at the hotel.

"All he wanted to do," Edna said, "was talk baseball with the bellboys. They couldn't speak a word of English, but he talked baseball. Somehow they understood."

"Let me tell you something about Casey," says Ernie Mehl, the Kansas City sports columnist who knew Stengel for a lifetime. "He never said anything, never, that didn't make sense. If you listened and you thought about it and you rolled it around your head for a while it made sense."

In 1976 Billy Martin filled his Yankee Stadium managerial office with Casey Stengel pictures and took the field for opening day wearing a uniform with a black stripe around the left arm. He would wear it all year and dedicated the season—the first Yankee pennant since 1964—to Casey Stengel.

At last count there were twenty-three former players of Casey Stengel who were now or had been managing in the major leagues, more than one hundred coaches, more than two hundred scouts and other baseball officials.

"When you think about it," says Rod Kanehl, "the man had an incredible influence not only on baseball for sixty-five years but on all America. Baseball is the National Pastime and Stengel was baseball. Just think of the millions of people motivated by baseball and directly, or indirectly, motivated by Casey Stengel."

Late in 1978 the Stengel home was sold. Billy Martin wanted baseball to buy it and convert it into a home for aged, destitute ballplayers, but the family decided against it. They had saved some of his things and promised to build a museum in his honor in Glendale. Other remembrances were turned over to the Baseball Hall of Fame in

Cooperstown for the establishment of a Casey Stengel room, along with the sections reserved for the Babe and Lou Gehrig and Ty Cobb and other greats.

Some four years after his death, as the ninetieth anniversary of his birth approached, he was still being talked about, still being quoted, still as relevant to the game and to the fans as he had ever been. Billy Martin and Yogi Berra and Mickey Mantle and Whitey Ford and Richie Ashburn and Rod Kanehl and Marvelous Marv Throneberry and all of his aged friends, alive at the present time, would talk of him and laugh and reminisce about the master of elocution.

"The thing is," said Burleigh Grimes, as he sat on the back porch of the Otesaga Hotel in Cooperstown at a Hall of Fame reunion, as his own eighty-eighth birthday approached, "Casey Stengel and baseball are linked forever. As long as you've got baseball in this country, you'll have Casey Stengel."

On almost every baseball team as the 1970s drew to a close, there was somebody who knew Casey Stengel. It was a sure thing that on some night in this season or the next, usually in some hotel bar, as the drunks fell away one by one, his name would come up, a story would be told, and somebody would laugh.

He was alive at the present time. He always would be.

Index